RACING POST
ANNUAL 2023

Racing Post Floor 7, The Podium, South Bank Tower Estate, 30 Stamford Street, London, SE1 9LS. 0203 034 8900

Editor Nick Pulford
Art editor David Dew
Cover design Duncan Olner
Chief photographers Edward Whitaker, Patrick McCann
Other photography Mark Cranham, Getty, John Grossick, Caroline Norris
Picture artworking Stefan Searle
Feature writers Mark Boylan, Scott Burton, David Carr, Richard Forristal, Jonathan Harding, David Jennings, Lee Mottershead, Tom Peacock, Lewis Porteous, Nick Pulford, John Randall, Alan Sweetman, Peter Thomas

Dialogue Content Marketing Ltd
Advertising Sales
Gary Millone, 07843 369124,
gary.millone@dialogue.agency
Advertising Production Manager
Kay Brown 01603 972347
kay.brown@dialogue.agency
6th floor, Fuel studios, Kiln House Pottergate, Norwich NR2 1DX
dialogue.agency

Distribution/availability
01933 304858 help@racingpost.com

Published by Pitch Publishing on behalf of Racing Post, A2 Yeoman Gate, Yeoman Way, Worthing, Sussex, BN13 3QZ

A CIP catalogue record is available for this book from the British Library.
ISBN 978-1-83950-112-8 [UK]
ISBN 978-1-83950-113-5 [Ireland]
Printed in Great Britain by Buxton Press.

racingpost.com/shop

WELCOME to the Racing Post Annual 2023 and our five cover stars: Baaeed, Honeysuckle, Desert Crown, A Plus Tard and Alpinista. From Flat to jumps, summer to winter, they proved themselves a special bunch.

Going unbeaten through a campaign – whether it is in Britain and Ireland over jumps or across Europe on the Flat – is a colossal feat and collectively our famous five nearly did it, with a mere handful of narrow reverses amid an abundance of wins.

But what characterised them above all was an unflinching appetite for the toughest competition. Together they ran in and won the Cheltenham Gold Cup, the Derby, the Arc, the Champion Hurdles of Britain and Ireland, the Queen Anne and International Stakes, and other top contests besides.

It was a year of tremendous strength in depth. Among the others who would not have looked out of place in our pictured group were Allaho, Energumene, Kyprios, Shishkin, Highfield Princess and Nature Strip, as well as rising stars Galopin Des Champs and Constitution Hill.

All feature prominently in this publication and it has been a pleasure to look back on their incredible stories and bring them to life in these pages.

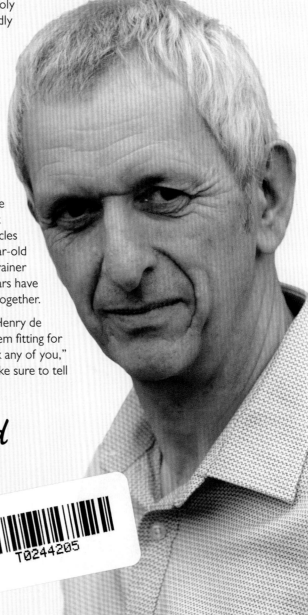

There have been more melancholy events too. Racing was profoundly grieved by the death of its greatest supporter, Queen Elizabeth II, and the sport also lost one of its titans in Lester Piggott. And nor was racing immune from the cost of living crisis and the shockwaves from the war in Ukraine.

Jonathan Harding's superb yet harrowing account of his trip to the Poland-Ukraine border is the closing article in this book and it is a difficult read. So are the articles about the tragic death of 13-year-old Jack de Bromhead, the son of trainer Henry and his wife Heather. Tears have been shed putting those pages together.

In his eulogy to his young son, Henry de Bromhead found words that seem fitting for all of us in dark times. "I just ask any of you," he said, "whoever you love, make sure to tell them."

Nick Pulford

Nick Pulford
Editor

CONTENTS

BIG STORIES

Baaeed joined the pantheon of Flat racing superstars with an astounding victory at York but lost his unbeaten record at the very end

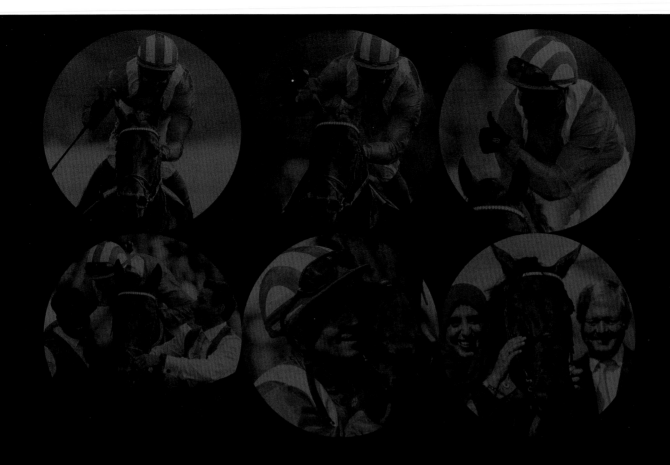

ALL-TIME GREAT

By Lee Mottershead

I TWAS a race whose result appears in no form books but, like the horse who won, it almost immediately attained fabled status. Aside from those connected to the three runners, nobody was there to spectate, except for a few fortunate employees going about their daily business on

a typically windy morning at Chelmsford.

What happened in the race was anything but typical, for on that first Tuesday in May, Baaeed made it obvious to those present that he was even better than they had dared to dream. He would prove this again and again over the course of the year, but Chelmsford came first, just as Baaeed would do until an

unbeaten record cherished by connections was lost in a farewell appearance that left Ascot deflated.

Much lay ahead for him that May morning but plenty had already been achieved. It had been only the previous June when the Shadwell homebred made his belated racecourse debut. He won as a raw three-year-old that afternoon at Leicester and then

continually enhanced his reputation through five further races, ending his opening campaign with two workmanlike Group 1 victories in the Prix du Moulin and Queen Elizabeth II Stakes.

Among the class of 2021 he was officially bracketed as one of four horses sharing sixth position, his excellent 125 rating leaving him
▸ *Continues page 6*

BAAEED

4lb shy of America's world champion Knicks Go. The son of Sea The Stars entered the spring as one of the sport's most exciting and yet in some ways unexposed talents. We knew he was good, but just how good could he become? The first answer to that question came at Chelmsford.

Trainer William Haggas had managed to keep it all quiet, which meant the exercise was a partial success even before the three stable companions began galloping at the seven-furlong pole. Cieren Fallon set a proper gallop on Montatham, closely followed by the Michael Hills-ridden Aldaary, a decisive winner of the Balmoral Handicap on his final run the previous year. In third was Baaeed, with Jim Crowley on his back for the first time since Champions Day. Crowley watched and waited. From the Chelmsford clock tower so did Haggas, wife Maureen and Shadwell duo Angus Gold and Richard Hills.

Not long after turning for home, Baaeed was steered wide, shown daylight and asked a question. The answer was incredible. He moved through the gears in a way his jockey had never previously experienced. It was only when crossing the line that Baaeed truly hit top gear, yet when his rider looked over his shoulder he saw a margin of at least ten lengths had been created over runner-up Aldaary. Crowley could hardly believe it.

It took him an age to pull up Baaeed. When groom Ricky Hall was reunited with the horse, he and Crowley looked at each other. Neither could stop smiling. They knew the importance of what had just happened. They knew what it meant. They knew that for this fabulous four-year-old, anything was now possible.

★★★★

THEY were happy that Tuesday and even happier the following Saturday.

Aldaary had not been given a hard time on his excursion to Chelmsford but nor could he have got much closer to Baaeed had he received a smack. It was therefore more than a little encouraging to see him win Haydock's Listed Spring Trophy by three and a half lengths, earning a Racing Post Rating of 119. It suggested he was almost certainly good enough to win

▸ *Continues page 8*

'I was really proud of him and the horse loved it too'

Ricky Hall, Baaeed's groom, on life with a superstar

"Horses like him are what make you want to get up in the mornings. It's been a pleasure to ride him. He likes his work; he likes to gallop. I don't think I will ever look after a more straightforward horse.

"It's funny how things turn out: Baaeed wouldn't have come my way if I hadn't stopped travelling with the horses, which I used to do. Then my partner got pregnant, so I thought I'd better spend a bit more time at home.

"Taking him to York was fantastic. There were so many people cheering when he came into the winner's enclosure. I was really proud of him and the horse loved it too."

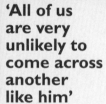

▲ Special times: Baaeed canters under Ricky Hall; below, trainer William Haggas and wife Maureen with their stable star

'All of us are very unlikely to come across another like him'

William Haggas on Baaeed

"We'll look back and say how bloody lucky we were to have him. It's been a great experience for all of us and I know I'll get letters in ten years' time from people who were here, saying they didn't really appreciate what they were experiencing at the time, because very few horses are like him and all of us are very unlikely to come across another.

"It's his mind as much as anything – he's amazing, he just doesn't care, he's not fazed by anything. A horse has to have ability, but his mind and his heart are big pieces of the jigsaw. A lot of them don't have the mind and they don't have the guts, which means the ability is no good to them.

"The exceptional ones are hard to find."

Best bar Frankel

Baaeed took his form to a new level with his sensational victory in the Juddmonte International, the step up in trip proving the key to unlocking the sort of performance he had hinted at over a mile, *writes Paul Curtis*.

A mighty Racing Post Rating of 138 ranks him alongside the best behind Frankel (143) on the list of the top turf horses in RPR history. His sire Sea The Stars and Daylami are also on 138.

In the context of the Juddmonte International, his figure also rates as the best bar Frankel (143), ahead of previous top winners Sakhee (135, 2001) and Royal Anthem (134, 1999).

TOP TURF HORSES BY RPR

143 Frankel
138 Baaeed
138 Daylami
138 Sea The Stars
137 Generous
137 Peintre Celebre
137 Zilzal
136 Dayjur
136 Mark Of Esteem
136 Montjeu

Since Racing Post Ratings were introduced in 1988

▼ Brilliant best: Baaeed and Jim Crowley land York's International in stunning style

or go close in a Group 1. Baaeed had made him look ordinary.

One Saturday later, it was Baaeed's turn to go public. The Lockinge Stakes was the obvious spot for his return. It was also the contest used by Sir Henry Cecil to launch Frankel's final campaign. Baaeed, who had also emulated Frankel when claiming the Queen Elizabeth II as a three-year-old, had been handed a provisional map that would see him trace the steps taken a decade earlier by a legend.

That meant starting out at Newbury, where anything but a win would have been a shock.

Baaeed duly delivered, leading over a furlong out before quickening clear. The winning distance was not as large as it had been at Chelmsford but, in all other regards, it was more of the same, a straightforward stroll, albeit this time with an audience.

Haggas confirmed his pleasure but he was otherwise keen not to dish out superlatives. He refused to hail Baaeed as the world's number one. He even declined to name him the finest to have run in his name, bringing his 2018 Arc runner-up into the equation.

"I don't know if he's the best I've trained," he said. "Sea Of Class

was a star and I loved her dearly. Most horses with a good turn of foot are good and he's got a nice turn of foot, which she had too. I was impressed, though."

He was similarly pleased at Royal Ascot, although he admitted to having endured more nerves prior to a Queen Anne Stakes that was watched on course by Sheikha Hissa, the daughter of Baaeed's late breeder Sheikh Hamdan.

Godolphin's Real Class, who had finished second in the Lockinge, once again filled the same spot. In stretching his winning spree to eight, the 1-6 favourite was

brilliant and ruthlessly efficient. The flamboyance and fireworks of Frankel's Queen Anne were missing but Baaeed nonetheless appeared untouchable at a mile. This made it all the more exciting to hear Haggas and Sheikha Hissa make clear York's Juddmonte International was the big aim.

"I was always in control," Crowley reflected. "It's a long season and there was no need to go and do it by ten lengths. Sterner tests await and we'll keep testing him, but I'm sure he'll be fine."

Willie Carson, for so long Sheikh Hamdan's man in the blue and white, was equally certain

'A spectacular performance'

Reflections on Baaeed's six-and-a-half-length win in the International at York

William Haggas, trainer "It's rarely you see in a high-class race a horse appear on the bridle with two to run looking like he could go at any time. He's just good, isn't he? It was a spectacular performance and I'm glad now that everyone will believe in him.

"We think he's fantastic and we have thought so for some time. Sure, I've been slow to get him up in trip but he's been so dominant at a mile. This was the perfect opportunity and he clearly stays it well. He's just got a fabulous engine and a fabulous temperament."

Jim Crowley, jockey "It was unbelievable, everything went perfectly. I suppose you could say there was a lot of pressure coming here to get the job done but I never really felt it. I knew how good he was. I was never worried about the trip.

"He's special and I've known from day one. The first time I rode him William said, 'How good do you think he is?' and I said, 'He's the best you've got, he might be the best you've ever had'. He's the perfect racehorse."

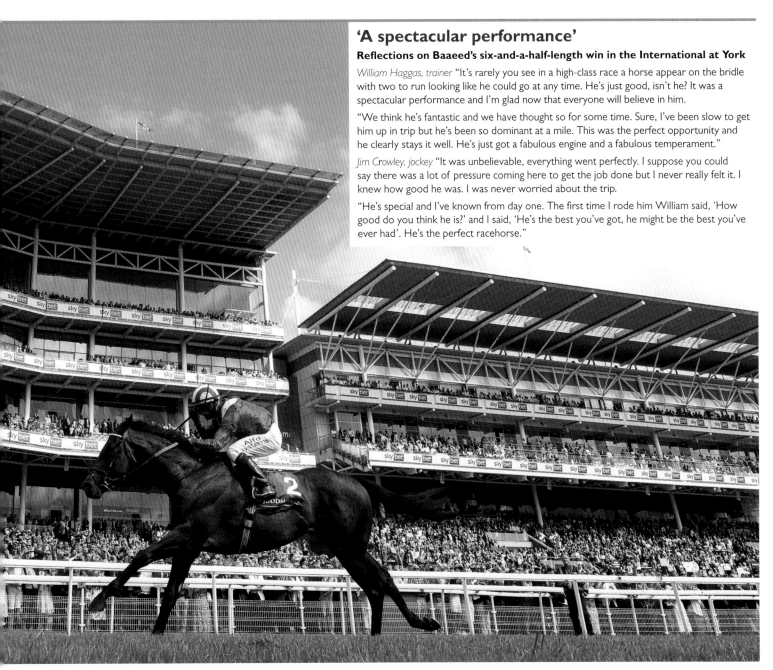

Gold was wrong to suggest his own greatest Shadwell star, Nashwan, might not have possessed the same electric speed as Baaeed.

"Oh, f*** off! Nashwan could have won over six furlongs," replied Nashwan's jockey, before releasing one of his famous cackles. He would have more to say on the subject after York, but first there was Goodwood, where Baaeed made it nine out of nine in the Sussex Stakes. By now he had become the highest-rated horse on the planet. There was nothing in his latest tour de force to suggest that was unwarranted.

"This horse has got gears that other horses do not possess," declared racecourse commentator Simon Holt, who was smitten. So was Crowley.

"It does feel a little unfair sometimes, but I'm not complaining," said the beaming rider. He stressed that the winner had been "much better" than the bare result and responded with a hopeful affirmative when asked if his magnificent mount could be even better once he was upped in distance on the Knavesmire.

"Quite possibly, if he can show that turn of foot over ten furlongs," Crowley said. "Mile-and-a-quarter horses can't quicken like that. He

quickens like a sprinter."

Remarkably, given the pressure of partnering such a valuable thoroughbred, Crowley appeared to be taking the journey without a worry. You sensed it was rather more stressful for Haggas.

"William and I keep reminding ourselves to just enjoy it but we're both very nervous," said Sheikha Hissa at Goodwood. Yet when asked if her anxiety might be so strong that she would hide away during Baaeed's races, the answer was unequivocal.

"Never," she said. "I don't want to miss a thing."

Racing fans felt the same.

★★★★

WHAT they saw at Chelmsford, we saw at York.

In winning the International, Baaeed elevated himself from being a great horse to one of the sport's all-time greats. In God's own county here was God's own horse, not the very first to be worthy of such billing but undoubtedly one whose fledgling mile-and-a-quarter mission yielded an exhibition of such outrageous brilliance that it immediately defined him for us and future generations.

It might not quite have earned the stratospheric figure given to

▶ *Continues page 10*

Frankel at York, but it easily surpassed what Baaeed's own sire had accomplished on the Knavesmire. It came in the showpiece connections had been fixated on all year, the one that had seemingly mattered more to them than any other. That much was obvious in the way they reacted to Baaeed thrashing the 2021 winner Mishriff by six and a half lengths having cruised alongside him like a thoroughbred powered by the engine of a sports car.

Haggas made a point of telling members of his team to savour every second of the occasion. "A lot of people put a lot of work into this horse," he explained. "They need to get the enjoyment out of this moment." There was also a new contribution from Carson, who was asked if he might now be prepared to revise his Ascot opinion.

"Unfortunately, yes," Carson said. "He's better than Nashwan. I don't think Nashwan could have beaten Mishriff by six and a half lengths. Nashwan was a very good horse, a great horse, but I think I've just seen one of the greatest. He's in the Frankel class. He might even be better."

But not judged on ratings. Baaeed's 138 York RPR was 5lb shy of Frankel's peak. It was not long until we learned that this British champion was not even officially the world's best racehorse.

In California on September 4, Flightline caused jaws to drop. On his fifth racecourse outing he won Del Mar's Pacific Classic in a manner that evoked memories of Secretariat's Belmont. From the five pole to the wire, he powered ever further away from toiling opponents, thrashing Dubai World Cup winner Country Grammer by what should have been an impossible 19 and a half lengths. The RPR was 140.

In a Racing Post feature in September, Haggas mused on the fact both Baaeed and Flightline had been unraced at two and asked rhetorically would Baaeed have run in the Dewhurst had he been trained by Aidan O'Brien? At the same time, racing fans were asking if Haggas would run Baaeed in the Prix de l'Arc de Triomphe.

From that possibility sounding barely worth talking about at York,

Bay Bridge comes good with dramatic upset

Baaeed was below his best in the Qipco Champion Stakes. Bay Bridge was the perfect example of Sir Michael Stoute at his best.

As a juvenile he raced twice, never threatening to lose his maiden tag. At three he was unbeaten, going from a novice event into two handicaps and then a Newmarket Listed event. The son of New Bay was the typical late-developing Stoute project. As a four-year-old he developed into one of the best around.

A stunning five-length success in the Brigadier Gerard Stakes marked him out as special, a Group 1 winner waiting to happen. The wait, however, took longer than expected. In both the Prince of Wales's Stakes and Eclipse he started favourite under Ryan Moore, only to finish second and fifth. On both occasions he had excuses. At Ascot in October, none were needed.

"He was in very good shape, very good shape," said Stoute after his winner's half-length defeat of Adayar. It was the way he said it, not just what he said, that made you certain he meant it.

For Stoute and his 2022 Derby-winning jockey Richard Kingscote, it was a super end to a super season. Helped by his trainer's patience and skill, Bay Bridge confirmed himself to be a super horse.

hopes were raised the following day and then elevated again, to the point that the Arc was named the horse's preferred target. One week before the Arc it was revealed Sheikha Hissa had changed her mind. Baaeed would bow out in the Champion Stakes, just as Haggas made clear he had always wanted.

★★★★

WHAT Haggas wanted more than anything – what they all wanted – was for Baaeed to head into his next life as a stallion with his unbeaten record intact. That must have influenced the decision to swerve the Arc. There had been understandable fears that if Longchamp succumbed to gruelling ground, a mile and a half might prove a test too severe. The rain did indeed fall in Paris, so much so that it would never have been deemed suitable for a colt with uncertain stamina. The irony is that underfoot conditions were also cited as the reason why Baaeed could manage only fourth in the Champion Stakes.

▲ Beaten at last: Baaeed (right) toils in fourth as Bay Bridge (left) takes the Champion Stakes; below, a dejected Jim Crowley after the unblemished record had been lost

"It was just the ground – as simple as that," said Crowley after seeing Bay Bridge, Adayar and Baaeed's stable companion My Prospero all get to Ascot's winning post before the 1-4 favourite. If it was the ground, it should be noted that the racing surface was nowhere near as arduous as it has been on some Champions Days. Perhaps for Baaeed, it was simply an off day, for even Frankel was not at his best when signing off in glory ten years earlier.

"It's sad that he's got beaten, obviously, but it's a horserace, not a world war or anything like that," noted Haggas as he headed off to saddle his runners in the Balmoral. One of them was the Chelmsford gallop pacesetter Montatham.

"We've enjoyed the ride," said Haggas, magnanimous in a defeat he had so hoped to avoid.

It was a somewhat unfortunate ending to Baaeed's glorious career as a racehorse. Everything that came before was marvellous. That's what we should remember.

EVERY RACING MOMENT

HORSE RACING IRELAND

2023 MAJOR FESTIVALS

LEOPARDSTOWN
Dublin Racing Festival
4th – 5th February

CORK
Easter Festival
8th – 10th April

FAIRYHOUSE
Easter Festival
8th – 10th April

PUNCHESTOWN
Festival of Racing
25th – 29th April

KILLARNEY
Spring Festival
14th – 16th May

CURRAGH
Irish Guineas Festival
26th – 28th May

DOWN ROYAL
Ulster Derby
23rd – 24th June

CURRAGH
Irish Derby Festival
30th June – 2nd July

BELLEWSTOWN
Summer Festival
6th – 8th July

KILLARNEY
July Festival
17th – 21st July

CURRAGH
Irish Oaks Weekend
22nd – 23rd July

GALWAY
Summer Festival
31st July – 6th August

TRAMORE
August Festival
17th – 20th August

KILLARNEY
August Festival
24th – 26th August

LEOPARDSTOWN & **CURRAGH**
Irish Champions Weekend
9th – 10th September

LISTOWEL
Harvest Festival
17th – 23rd September

DOWN ROYAL
National Hunt Festival
3rd – 4th November

NAVAN
Festival of Racing
18th – 19th November

PUNCHESTOWN
Winter Festival
25th – 26th November

FAIRYHOUSE
Winter Festival
2nd – 3rd December

LEOPARDSTOWN
Christmas Festival
26th – 29th December

LIMERICK
Christmas Festival
26th – 29th December

HRI.ie

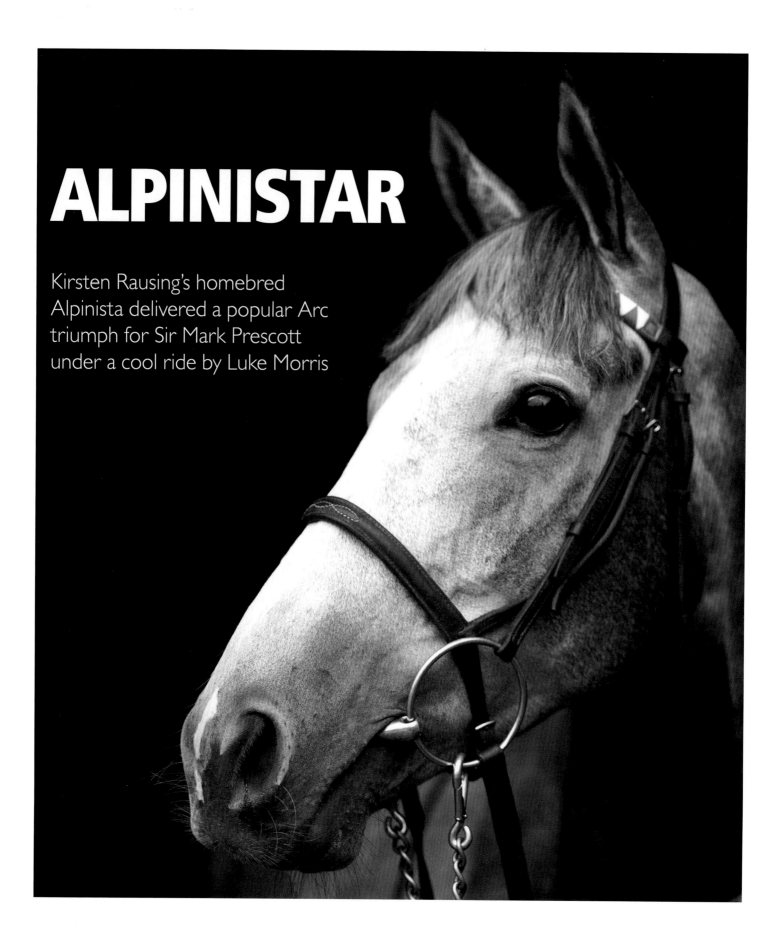

ALPINISTAR

Kirsten Rausing's homebred
Alpinista delivered a popular Arc
triumph for Sir Mark Prescott
under a cool ride by Luke Morris

By Nick Pulford

WALKING the track before the biggest ride of his life, Luke Morris made a vow. Whatever happens in the race, he told himself, try not to get too excited in the moment. The way the Prix de l'Arc de Triomphe unfolded, it was a hard promise to keep. Morris was going so well on Alpinista from a long way out that he had to remind himself to keep a lid on it.

"When we reached the top of the hill seven out, and began to swing around and run downhill, it felt like I had a huge amount of horse underneath me and I was thinking 'Don't get too excited'," he recalled.

Across the expanse of the Longchamp infield lay the finishing post. Morris and Alpinista would be there in about a minute and a half. Already there, down by the rail, was the mare's devoted and exuberant groom, Annabel Willis. She had become a YouTube hit for her wild cheering and celebrations with Alpinista and there was going to be no stopping her excitement.

Even Sir Mark Prescott, who has seen it all in his 53-year training career and done most of it himself, shared the mounting sense that he was about to reach the pinnacle, although it was tempered by a dose of wariness. "If I hadn't trained her myself and worried about the race,

then you'd say she always looked like winning," he said. If he could have given a message to his jockey at that stage, he said, it would have been: "Wait, wait, wait."

The final reckoning was getting closer now. "From five out I knew it'd take a real good one to beat me and I just had to stay cool and deliver her at the right stage," Morris said. "When you've got plenty of horse the race opens up for you." From his prominent berth on the rail behind the leaders, cool hand Luke waited for his moment. Finally, he let his mount slide to the front two furlongs out and she responded magnificently. A decisive gap was opened.

"Go on! Go on! Go on!" Willis shouted over and over as Alpinista and Morris galloped past her with the line in sight and Vadeni, Torquator Tasso and Al Hakeem in vain pursuit. Moments later, the victory that had looked there for the taking for almost the entire race was in their possession.

The winning jockey, having bottled up his fizzing excitement, could now enjoy the moment. After passing the post with half a length to spare, he stood up in the irons and punched the air. Then he put his hand to his face in disbelief. "I can't describe it," he said as he turned back towards the stands. "I'm very emotional."

He wasn't alone. Willis collapsed into the arms of Molly Nash-Steer,

Morris's partner, and then to her knees. Her repeated refrain had changed now to "Oh my God! Oh my God! Oh my God!" A tearful Nash-Steer put her hand to her chest: "Oh, my heart . . ."

There was a more measured response from Prescott and Kirsten Rausing, Alpinista's owner-breeder, but a deep well of satisfaction and achievement. "Marvellous," the 74-year-old trainer said. "I've trained for Miss Rausing for 35 years and I trained Alpinista's grandmother and the mother, and Luke has been with me 11 years. It's hard to imagine a better day training."

Greeting her Arc winner, after more than half a century as a breeder and owner, Rausing said: "She's my sixth-generation homebred. I'm delighted, thrilled and extremely grateful to Sir Mark for producing this marvellous mare, and to Luke Morris. He produced a fantastic riding performance."

★★★★

ALPINISTA had possessed the form of a potential Arc winner since the summer of 2021. In her breakthrough campaign as a four-year-old, she recorded a first Group 1 win in the Grosser Preis von Berlin at Hoppegarten in early August, beating Torquator Tasso by two and three-quarter lengths. The performance did not make waves at the time but two months later it looked a whole lot better when

Torquator Tasso caused a 72-1 shock in the Arc. Suddenly there was a harder edge to what many had been inclined to dismiss as a 'soft' German Group 1.

In the meantime Alpinista had landed a second top-level prize there in the Preis von Europa and a third followed in November when she rounded off her season in the Grosser Preis von Bayern. That completed a perfect record in five races in 2021, taking her from a Goodwood Listed race to the Group 2 Lancashire Oaks and then the three German Group 1s.

After Torquator Tasso's victory at Longchamp, Prescott revealed there had been detailed discussion involving Rausing and assistant trainer William Butler about supplementing Alpinista for the Arc. "William did a very interesting paper on thinking about it and why we should and why we shouldn't supplement her," he said. "But in the end we thought we'd stick to the original plan and go to Germany, and please God try and win that [the Arc] next year."

Patience has always been a byword for Prescott and Rausing. Knowing Alpinista's heritage so well, they were prepared to play the long game. It is an approach that has brought the best out of the celebrated family. Alpinista's grandmother Albanova was also a three-time Group 1 winner in Germany and her great aunt

▸ Continues page 14

Alborada landed back-to-back triumphs in the Champion Stakes, earning themselves bronze statues at Prescott's Heath House Stables.

Alwilda, dam of Alpinista, was not such a high performer but importantly she earned winning black type, again in Germany. That was the first aim for her daughter too, but once that had been achieved the ambitions grew. By the start of 2022, the Arc was chief among them.

★★★★

THE intended starting point on the road to Longchamp was the Coronation Cup at Epsom, but Alpinista wasn't ready in time and instead went off on her travels again to contest the Grand Prix de Saint-Cloud in early July. The five-year-old returned home with a fourth Group 1 prize after stamping her authority on a race in which odds-on favourite Hurricane Lane, who had finished third in Torquator Tasso's Arc, was a disappointing eighth.

With the strength of her overseas form still being questioned, Alpinista had the chance to impress a home audience on her next run in the Yorkshire Oaks. Two years earlier she had made her first Group 1 appearance in the same race, just seven days after her black-type breakthrough in a Listed contest at Salisbury, and had run creditably as a 33-1 shot, albeit beaten five lengths into second by Love.

This time she was 7-4 favourite but faced a strong collection of younger fillies. Second favourite at 7-2 was Tuesday, who like Love was an Aidan O'Brien-trained Oaks winner. Irish Oaks scorer Magical Lagoon was also there, along with Group 1 Pretty Polly winner La Petite Coco and Andre Fabre's progressive Raclette.

Alpinista had their measure. Sent on two furlongs out by Morris, she kept finding extra under pressure and was

▶ *Continues page 16*

▶ Number one: Luke Morris savours the Arc winning moments on Alpinista; below, trainer Sir Mark Prescott

▲ Driving home: Luke Morris urges Alpinista to victory at Longchamp; inset, the front page of the next day's Racing Post

always doing enough to hold off Tuesday by a length. "I could feel Tuesday coming and I felt that when Alpinista sensed her coming she dug deep," the jockey said. "She's very tough and honest. Since she's been on better ground this year she's looked like a filly with more class."

One with enough class to win the Arc? Prescott hoped so. "This was as good as Saint-Cloud," he said. "Whether it will be good enough for Paris is another thing. She's just good enough to go close. You've got a chance, therefore you must go."

While Alpinista was a Group 1 star on the home stage at last, the best performer in a supporting role was Willis. As her pride and joy battled to victory, the 23-year-old groom was a bouncing, shouting, urging ball of excitement in the middle of the York parade ring. A 30-second YouTube clip of her wildly energetic performance had more than half a million views.

It showed just how much Alpinista means to Willis, who has looked after and ridden the diminutive grey since her arrival at Heath House as a

yearling in November 2018. "I was put down to ride her on the first day," she recalled. "I liked the look of her and I was interested by the pedigree, and when I started riding her I very quickly realised this was a horse I wanted to look after. It's such an intimate relationship looking after a racehorse, especially one you've been with for so long. They mean the absolute world to you. She's incredibly special to me."

Morris, 33, known for so long as Britain's hardest-working jockey, also treasured his association with Alpinista. He was no stranger to Group 1 success, with his CV including the Prix de l'Abbaye and Nunthorpe on Marsha for Prescott during their 11-year relationship, but nor was he a regular at the top table. "When Alpinista came along it was a godsend," he said. "It's very difficult to find these types of horses and when you do find them it's tricky to either keep them in the yard or keep the ride on them."

With the steadfast backing of Prescott and Rausing, there was never
▸ Continues page 18

Happy together

A faithful friend shared the winning moment with Alpinista after the Arc. Pilgrim Dancer, assistant trainer William Butler's hack, has been a travelling buddy on the grey's remarkable journey and his soothing presence was crucial again at Longchamp.

Explaining how the 15-year-old's part came about, groom Annabel Willis said: "When Alpinista first went racing to Epsom, she got on the box and seemed unsettled, so we quickly put Pilgrim on board and it worked. It's evident she's happy as long as she's got a friend. She doesn't like being alone. She's very happy as long as she sees him and she'd never worry then."

▲ Best of friends: Alpinista and Pilgrim Dancer at Longchamp with Annabel Willis and Shannon Moore (right)

Hamish Mackie

HAMISH MACKIE SCULPTURE

LIFE IN BRONZE

any danger that Morris would lose this opportunity. "You're always dreaming that one day you'll ride in the Arc and you'll ride a horse with a realistic chance," he added. That time had come.

★★★★

WILLIS had been with Alpinista almost every step of the way along her remarkable journey, and so had Morris, but not so the trainer and owner. Prescott, famously averse to going racing abroad, had missed all the Group 1s in Germany and France, while York was the first time Rausing had seen her mare at the races.

They were all at Longchamp on October 2, however. "Miss Rausing has insisted I go to Paris and she's taking it very seriously. I think we're going on a flying carpet," Prescott said in the week before the big day. "They tell me the Arc is the best race in the world, so I'll be there, over in the morning and back in the evening."

The flying visit was well worth the effort. Alpinista's Arc was the crowning glory for Prescott, the doyen of the Newmarket training fraternity and a universally popular figure. Among the first to greet him in the winner's enclosure was Jean-Claude Rouget, trainer of runner-up Vadeni. "My friend Mark has won," he said. "I adore Mark Prescott. What a beautiful day."

Prescott was touched by the warmth of the reaction. "It was a wonderful day and everybody was unbelievably kind," he said. "I was just so surprised by the reception she got in France from the likes of Andre Fabre, Jean-Claude Rouget and a few of my former assistants including Pascal Bary, Francois Rohaut and Christophe Ferland. It was quite humbling really."

Arriving home late that night, the master of Heath House found 295 emails in his inbox. "I think my poor secretary must have been secretly hoping the thing would get beat so she didn't have to reply to them all!" he quipped. The next morning on the gallops at Warren Hill, and later at Tattersalls sales, the great and the good of Newmarket flocked to offer their congratulations.

William Haggas, a former pupil assistant to Prescott, summed up the thoughts of so many. "The win of

▲ Heath House legend: Sir Mark Prescott and Annabel Willis with Alpinista at home

Alpinista was the most universally enjoyed success bar none. A fantastic achievement by all," he said.

It was a triumph for the old-fashioned virtues of loyalty, patience and fellowship. From stud to stable, the Rausing and Prescott teams had worked together to craft and polish a wonderful mare.

Alpinista's place in Heath House folklore was assured before the Arc, with a statue already commissioned to put her alongside illustrious relatives. She returned from Paris with a new inscription for the plaque: 2022 Prix de l'Arc de Triomphe winner. It had a special ring to it.

Older and better

Alpinista was the eighth female winner in the last 12 runnings of the Arc but only the second five-year-old mare to take the prize. The other was Corrida in 1937 when she completed back-to-back wins. Just five other five-year-olds have won the Arc since the second world war.

Alpinista's Longchamp victory was a career-best performance with a Racing Post Rating of 124, up from 121 on her previous start in the Yorkshire Oaks, but ranked her only joint-seventh among the last ten Arc winners.

She was on a par with Found, the 2016 winner at Chantilly, but did not get near the heights of Treve (131) in 2013 or Enable (129) in 2017.

LAST TEN ARC WINNERS

Year	Horse	RPR
2022	Alpinista	124
2021	Torquator Tasso *(right)*	126
2020	Sottsass	123
2019	Waldgeist	128
2018	Enable	122
2017	Enable	129
2016	Found	124
2015	Golden Horn	127
2014	Treve *(right)*	126
2013	Treve	131

Another Arc winner sold at BBAG sales

BBAG

www.bbag-sales.de

Torquator Tasso

Winner Qatar Prix de l'Arc de Triomphe, Gr.1
Gr.1 winner as 3 and 4yo

Spring Breeze Up Sale: 19th May 2023
Premier Yearling Sale: 1st September 2023
October Mixed Sales: 13th and 14th October 2023

CROWN JEWEL

Desert Crown shone bright with an authoritative win in the Derby for Sir Michael Stoute and Richard Kingscote but then was not seen again

By Peter Thomas

IT HAS been the fate of Sir Michael Stoute's last five Derby winners to have followed in the footsteps of the first. Shahrastani, Kris Kin, North Light and Workforce all endured added scrutiny as a result and even now, 41 years down the line, when the trainer wins the Epsom Classic, the first question he's asked – even before "What does this mean for you?" and "Has it sunk in yet?"– is: "Do you think he's as good as Shergar?"

Now, Stoute isn't small, but he has a neat sidestep for a big man and he can evade a pesky racing journalist with ease when he needs to, so it was interesting to hear him field that familiar question after Desert Crown's success in the historic race, without so much as a drop of the shoulder or a roll of the eyeballs. He allowed himself to be cornered and then came straight out with it: "Shergar was very special and he hasn't quite reached that stage, but he has potential." It's not exactly an unfettered accolade for a champion thoroughbred, but in 'Stoutespeak' it means a lot.

The margin of victory had been a respectful yet comfortable two and a half lengths, rather than the ten by which his illustrious forebear had dismissed the 1981 Derby field, but here was Desert Crown being mentioned in the same breath as quite possibly the most famous Flat racehorse of all time – and certainly one of the great Derby winners – and it didn't sound out of place at all.

Such was the authority with which the son of Nathaniel sauntered away from his 16 rivals, it was hard to imagine him ending the season as anything other than a proven champion, with quite likely a King George, maybe even an Arc, under his girth strap and a heap of accolades building up around his stable door.

True, he had only beaten Hoo Ya Mal (150-1) into second place and the luckless Westover (25-1) into third, with 66-1 shot Masekela fourth, but he had looked in a different realm to the entire field when, early in the straight, he unleashed a burst of speed that carried him past the five horses who had preceded him on sufferance down the hill – with second favourite Stone Age left behind like a forgotten relic on the Epsom turf.

Shortly after the two-furlong pole, commentator Simon Holt summed it up, perhaps prematurely, maybe unwisely, but very presciently: "It's Desert Crown that comes sweeping through to take it up. Oh, and it's all over, surely!" Good horses had been left floundering and there was no coming back.

How were we to know that this was to be the last we would see of him for the season? How could we have predicted that our next sight of this impressive creature would come next spring, if at all? It was a cruel second half to the season, but hope springs eternal.

★★★★

IF THE Dante winner's victory as 5-2 favourite in the Derby could hardly be counted as a surprise, his very existence was long odds-against on the morning his mother, a moderate, thrice-raced daughter of Green Desert, decided now might be a good time to make a dramatic mark on her home town of Newmarket.

As a racehorse in the care of Chris Wall, Desert Berry managed one placed effort at Nottingham before landing a Class 5 Lingfield maiden in December 2012 at odds of 4-1. To get herself noticed, however, she managed to get loose one morning and trot off down the High Street, where she decided only at the last minute that hurtling through the front window of a Turkish restaurant would be unwise in the extreme.

Distracted by her own reflection in the glass, she dropped anchor in the nick of time and bounced off the offending pane rather than crashing through it in a catastrophic mess. It was a lucky escape for the wayward filly but a moment of enormous good fortune for the breed.

After her Lingfield success,
▶▶ *Continues page 22*

◀ Master at work: Desert Crown's success made Sir Michael Stoute the oldest trainer to land the Derby, 41 years after Shergar became the first of his six winners

Desert Berry was retired to Strawberry Fields Stud, an unfashionable residence on the outskirts of Cambridge, owned by successful technical engineer and breeding 'hobbyist' Gary Robinson, whose recent career highlights have been producing a Derby winner and inventing a breeze block that can withstand both gunfire and bomb blast. There's nothing like diversification to keep a business healthy.

Following four fruitful visits to Archipenko, Desert Berry produced four foals who at last count had registered 15 wins between them. The pick was Hong Kong Group 3 handicap winner Flying Thunder, who retained pride of place until March 2, 2019, when the mare's liaison with Nathaniel produced something from a different stratosphere entirely.

All of a sudden, Robinson – who confesses to having "looked like an idiot" for the first five years of his breeding venture – found himself moving into the big league, as the Nathaniel colt was knocked down to Blandford Bloodstock for 280,000gns at the Tattersalls October Book 2 Sale, before being dispatched to Freemason Lodge to run in the colours of the Dubai businessman Saeed Suhail.

For the new owner, in whose silks Kris Kin won the Derby in 2003, it was another chance to find 'the new Shergar', although even the most optimistic of souls could hardly have expected what happened next.

★★★★

IF THE trainer was endowed with a gilt-edged pedigree for Derby success, the jockey most certainly was not. Richard Kingscote was one of those riders: talented and admired by those who know the time of day; unknown outside of racing circles yet successful to a point and unflustered by the pressures of the big occasion. But this was the Derby and nobody quite knew.

For the 35-year-old, the headaches in the build-up to the main event had centred not upon his ability to get the job done but on the likelihood of his being in the saddle at the mile-and-a-half start at Epsom on Saturday, June 4.

He had been entrusted with the ride

▲ Comfort and joy: Desert Crown eases to Derby victory; below, winning jockey Richard Kingscote

on November 3, 2021, but that was at Nottingham, not Epsom, in a one-mile, soft-ground, Class 4 maiden, not in the most prestigious race in the world. Of course, he got the job done – Desert Crown won by five and a half lengths, looking like a colt of some promise – but where it would all lead was anybody's guess.

For Desert Crown, now that the niggling conditions of his youth were dealt with, the next step was a long winter's break, to mature and develop, and then a massive step up to confront the demands of the Dante Stakes at York. Kingscote would again be on board, and why not? This may have been a Group 2, but it was an eight-runner Group 2 with no cambers and related complications to worry about, so for an experienced jockey it was surely just another day at the office.

The partnership got the job done again, this time by three and a quarter lengths, but as much as being the end of the preparation, this was where the nervous wait began for Kingscote. Senior trainers with demanding owners had been known to bow to

▶ *Continues page 24*

'A tingle down my spine'

Richard Kingscote on winning the Derby at only his second attempt

"It's a huge achievement. During the day you forget it's a Classic and just how big it is, but it's a big deal. When I crossed the line, the public to my left were shouting "well done" and it gave me a tingle down my spine.

"You always hope there may be another time, but it could be a once in a lifetime and I'll enjoy it. I never really expected I'd be winning a Derby until the last few weeks. I've been confident in the horse for the last few weeks, without wanting to get my hopes up.

"I've been fortunate that I've landed in a good position and things have gone well. Riding any winner for Sir Michael gives me a huge confidence boost, so to be able to win one of the biggest races in the world for him is pretty special."

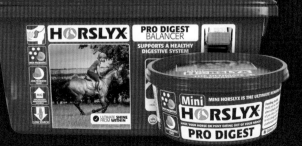

pressure to replace a relative unknown with an established Classic-winning rider, and Kingscote had never even won a British Group 1.

Imagine if the late Lester Piggott had still been around – as a jockey in his pomp rather than as an appendage in the title of the Cazoo Derby (in memory of Lester Piggott). He would have been on the prowl, hunting down what might eventually become a 'spare ride' if he hunted hard enough. Kingscote had developed a strong bond with the yard, but the Derby is the Derby.

In Stoute and Suhail, however, Kingscote had staunch allies. "It took a lot for Sir Michael and the owner to stick with me, in a Derby," he said after delivering a polished Derby-winning display. "I'm not a champion jockey. I'm not Ryan Moore. I've had a good career but I've not had a starlit career. I think it takes a lot for them not to look elsewhere."

In Stoute's mind, there seems to have been no doubt at any stage. He knew his chances of following up Workforce's win 12 years earlier were dissipating with age, but he seemed to regard Kingscote as a definite asset in the quest rather than a wrong piece in the jigsaw.

Seasoned Stoute watchers interpreted the great man's positivity in the wake of the Dante as a sign of enormous, if understated, confidence. Stoute, meanwhile, kept faith in his jockey as much as in his horse. After the Derby, he said calmly that Kingscote was "very cool and rode a beautiful race", as if he'd expected nothing less.

For the heavily tattooed, motorbiking son of Weston-super-Mare, it was a Derby win on only his second ride in the race; a distinction he shares with Walter Swinburn, Kieren Fallon and Moore, the riders of Stoute's previous five winners of the race.

★★★★

THERE was no Queen Elizabeth II at Epsom to see Stoute become the oldest winning trainer in the history of the Derby. We didn't know it at the time, but we'd never see her here again. Stoute, on the other hand, may yet have shots at a seventh success.

In the meantime, rather than

▲ Proud moment: owner Saeed Suhail (right) leads in Desert Crown and Richard Kingscote

spending the winter reflecting on a high summer of achievement from Desert Crown, we await progress reports on his condition.

After the Derby, we expected him to follow the once-traditional route to the King George, but this became less and less likely as the weeks passed and bulletins worsened. The setback he had was only minor and was healing well, we were told, but not well enough to be ready for Ascot, or for Longchamp.

Bruce Raymond, racing manager to the owner, signed off by saying he was "100 per cent confident he will definitely be back next year", possibly starting in the Sheema Classic in Dubai. The final decision, though, will be left with the trainer. Obviously. For the rest of us, it will be a winter spent waiting for good news.

High mark

Desert Crown rated as a superior Derby winner after his comfortable success at Epsom, improving to a Racing Post Rating of 125 that was the best in the race since Golden Horn (127) in 2015.

LAST TEN DERBY WINNERS

Year	Horse	RPR
2022	Desert Crown	125
2021	Adayar (right)	124
2020	Serpentine	121
2019	Anthony Van Dyck	119
2018	Masar	122
2017	Wings Of Eagles	121
2016	Harzand (right)	124
2015	Golden Horn	127
2014	Australia	125
2013	Ruler Of The World	121

At the age of 76 Sir Michael Stoute became the oldest trainer to win the Derby. He also set a record for the longest gap (41 years) between his first and last Derby successes.

STOUTE'S DERBY WINNERS

1981 Shergar	2004 North Light
1986 Shahrastani	2010 Workforce
2003 Kris Kin	2022 Desert Crown

THE
BIGGER
PICTURE

Ten years on from the final season of his 14-race unbeaten career, Juddmonte supersire Frankel gallops in his paddock at Banstead Manor Stud near Newmarket in June
EDWARD WHITAKER (RACINGPOST.COM/PHOTOS)

MASTERCLASS

Rachael Blackmore produced a brilliant ride on A Plus Tard to lift the Cheltenham Gold Cup and erase the pain of the previous year

By Richard Forristal

REGARDLESS of what went before, the 2022 Cheltenham Gold Cup result was one that would reverberate around the world and its impact endure for time immemorial.

Rachael Blackmore had already conquered the Cotswolds. Before March 18, 2022, she had been crowned leading rider at the marquee festival once and won back-to-back Champion Hurdles. She had cemented her sporting immortality by seizing that epic slice of Aintree history on Minella Times in the 2021 Grand National. Her legacy was secure.

Still, the Gold Cup is the purist's pinnacle. It always has been and always will be. Taken at face value, A Plus Tard's 15-length demolition

of the previous year's winner Minella Indo was unequivocal and Blackmore was deserving of such a signature victory. It was a triumph that embellished her haul of unconquered outposts, but in isolation it also constituted a career-defining moment for the sport's most bankable star.

The winning margin was the most emphatic since Master Oats' gruelling demolition in 1995, and it meant Henry de Bromhead became the first trainer to emulate Vincent O'Brien's feat of back-to-back Champion Hurdle and Gold Cup doubles with Hatton's Grace and Cottage Rake in 1949 and 1950.

All of that is remarkable, but the bare facts don't nearly convey the majesty of Blackmore's ride and the context that went with it. It would be remiss to diminish what De Bromhead achieved – including saddling the first two in the race for a second year in succession – or the sheer splendour of A Plus Tard's performance, but Blackmore produced something utterly exceptional to seal the deal.

★★★★

TO FULLY grasp that, you have to first consider the previous 12 months. A year earlier, Blackmore dropped

▶ *Continues page 30*

A PLUS TARD

in A Plus Tard, but she followed the principals throughout and engaged her mount before they crested the summit of the hill, snapping at the leaders' heels as they began the descent. She had to jockey to hold position and A Plus Tard was racing to the point that he loomed upsides Minella Indo at the bottom of the hill before they swung for home. Minella Indo was the slogger, A Plus Tard the classier individual who had Grade 1-winning form over two miles. Locking horns with Jack Kennedy's mount worked to his advantage, not hers.

When A Plus Tard reappeared last season in the Betfair Chase at Haydock, he won at his leisure, filleting the opposition by 22 lengths. However, the race fell apart, and it's hardly unusual for that early Grade 1 to throw up the sort of visually arresting display that busts the ratings meter but ultimately proves an outlier.

It's possible Blackmore and De Bromhead came away from Haydock convinced that stamina was now A Plus Tard's strong suit, because he was again sent about his business early in the Savills Chase at Leopardstown's Christmas meeting. On that occasion, Blackmore moved to lock up Davy Russell on Galvin after they jumped the second last, a manoeuvre that required her to commit before they straightened for home.

It's a long way to the line from there at Leopardstown and Russell had ample time to come back around on Galvin. He collared A Plus Tard in the shadow of the post. It was a display that posed more questions than answers, with De Bromhead's mixed form adding to the uncertainty, but it was probably the moment Blackmore recognised she would have to change tack if she wanted a different outcome at Cheltenham.

"I was happy if I was going to get beaten for doing something different as opposed to being in the position I was in last year, as that definitely didn't work," she mused after A Plus Tard surged to Gold Cup glory. That was an insight into her mindset, but it doesn't remotely reflect the unadulterated nerve she brought to bear in executing the plan.

Speaking in the aftermath of Blackmore's halcyon 2021

◀ Back with a bang: Rachael Blackmore sets the record straight in the Gold Cup with a 15-length victory on A Plus Tard

Cheltenham, Eddie O'Leary of Gigginstown House Stud, who have long been staunch advocates, tried to put his finger on what it was that makes her so good. His take on it might have been crude but it was on the money. "Never mind her tactical awareness or strength, she has bigger balls than any of the boys," O'Leary said.

Now look back at the ride she gave A Plus Tard in the 2022 Gold Cup. Some have wondered whether she did much different to 2021, as she ultimately dropped in and bided her time. However, this time she resisted the temptation to put him into the race until the latest possible moment. As they swung for home, Blackmore still had five horses in front of her, all locked up with nowhere to go. It was exactly where she wanted to be.

Robbie Power had committed on Minella Indo in an effort to stretch the opposition, and Blackmore did only what she had to do to keep A Plus Tard within striking distance, squeezing him through a gap between Protektorat and Al Boum Photo as they approached the wings of the second-last. They touched down in second there, and it was then that she finally sent her mount in pursuit of their 2021 conqueror.

Both horses left the ground at the same time for the final fence, but A Plus Tard lengthened over it to lead on landing before Blackmore chased him up the hill to immortality. The margin of victory screams an utterly dominant performance, but the subtle variation in tactics was at the root of the turnaround.

★★★★

TO THESE eyes, it was the single most exquisite Gold Cup ride in recent times because of the sheer audacity of it and the level of expectation that preceded it. A Plus Tard was sent off the 3-1 favourite, yet Blackmore executed a nerveless strategy that few would dare to even countenance. We're inclined to think of a ride like it as high-risk but, to paraphrase Ruby Walsh, she had the gumption to ride to win rather than ride not to lose.

Power was similarly cool in guiding Sizing John to glory in 2017, but

▸ *Continues page 32*

Record feat

A Plus Tard entered the realms of the greatest chasers of the Racing Post Ratings era in winning the Cheltenham Gold Cup by a record 15-length margin.

The biggest winning distance in a Gold Cup had been set by Kauto Star, who recorded an RPR of 185 when regaining the title by 13 lengths in 2009. That is the highest RPR for a Gold Cup winner since our ratings were introduced in the late 1980s but A Plus Tard is just behind on 184 alongside Denman.

TOP-RATED GOLD CUP WINNERS

RPR	Horse	Year
185	Kauto Star	2009
184	Denman *(right)*	2008
	A Plus Tard	2022
182	Imperial Commander	2010
	Don Cossack	2016
181	Long Run	2011
179	Bobs Worth	2013
	Minella Indo	2021
178	Best Mate	2003
	Coneygree *(right)*	2015
	Al Boum Photo	2019

In terms of Racing Post Ratings, the 2021-22 season will go down as a vintage one. You have to go back to Kauto Star, Denman and Imperial Commander in 2009-10 to find the previous time when three horses were credited with RPRs upwards of 180 in the same campaign, but A Plus Tard (184), Allaho (181) and Shishkin (181) formed a triumvirate of elite performers to break that notable barrier last season.

TOP-RATED CHASERS IN 2021-22

RPR	Horse
184	A Plus Tard
181	Allaho
	Shishkin
179	Energumene
177	Galopin Des Champs
176	Chacun Pour Soi *(below)*
	Clan Des Obeaux
172	Conflated *(above)*
	Minella Indo
	Protektorat *(right)*

A PLUS TARD

probably didn't shoulder the same burden of public confidence, while Russell's 2014 heroics on Lord Windermere came aboard a rank outsider. That's not to take away from those mesmerising steers, merely to illustrate the sheer audacity of Blackmore's endeavour.

In that context, all that went before amplifies the magnitude of what she achieved. Moreover, because of what happened a year earlier, the aftermath was coloured by sweet redemption.

Watch the ruin on Blackmore's face as she collapsed into her saddle and cursed the skies on pulling up aboard A Plus Tard in 2021. She had owned the week, announced her imperious talent to the wider world in spectacular fashion, yet she was distraught at the one that got away – the big one. Thwarted by a mount she had eschewed.

This time, having stewed on it and spent a year figuring it, she avenged that pain with a steer from the gods. "It has not quite been every day you'd be thinking about it – I'd be gone mad – but it's definitely in the back of your mind as this is what the whole week is about and what you're working for," Blackmore pondered of how much the 2021 defeat had consumed her.

Asked how the triumph ranked alongside her Aintree exploits, she said: "It's an incredible feeling when you do that over the back of the last at Cheltenham. These are such special days and I wouldn't swap the Grand National for anything, but this is the Gold Cup. He's a very talented horse and I'm very lucky to be on him."

De Bromhead has often spoken of how his relationship with Blackmore

has evolved as his confidence in her has grown over the years. In the aftermath of his second Gold Cup success, he was asked about the extent to which her tactical deliberations had underpinned A Plus Tard's stunning display.

"The great thing about Rachael, and [his wife] Heather always says this, is when she makes a mistake, she goes off, she thinks about it and she comes back," he said. "Now, I don't think she made a mistake last year, but she thought she did. She was kicking herself. So she analysed it and she came up with her plan.

"I had no idea what the plan was and I didn't question any of it too much. She told me about three weeks ago that she was going to ride him

▲ Sweet success: Rachael Blackmore and groom Johnny Ferguson celebrate Gold Cup victory; inset, the following day's Racing Post front page; below, A Plus Tard jumps the last and powers up the hill

more for speed and I said, 'Grand, whatever.' And then she started rabbiting on before the race and I turned to her and said, 'Rachael, you do whatever you want, you're the boss.' We're just so lucky to have her – she's a savage rider."

She's all that, and so much more. As had been the case on the Tuesday when she returned to a raucous winner's enclosure aboard Honeysuckle, on A Plus Tard Blackmore surfed back in to a cascading din of appreciation.

The Prestbury Park faithful had arrived in the Cotswolds desperate to atone for their 2021 absence. Blackmore's singular Gold Cup performance gave them one last, glorious cause to do so.

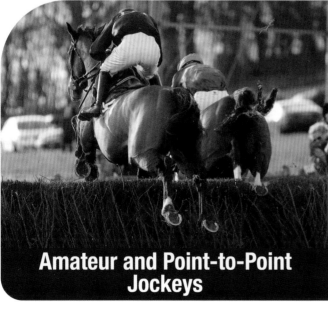

SWEET HONEY

Honeysuckle retained her title in the first leg of a second Champion Hurdle-Gold Cup double in a row for Henry de Bromhead

By David Jennings

ANOTHER impeccable campaign stretched Honeysuckle's winning sequence to the sweetest 16 and, in the celebrations of her second Champion Hurdle victory, the argument intensified over who is the greatest mare of all time. For many, she is beginning to get up in that debate.

The Henry de Bromhead-trained superstar remains addicted to winning and her predictability is precious. She won the same four races last season as she had the season before, and each of her four campaigns has brought the same number of wins. Four times four equals 16.

Desert Orchid and Moscow Flyer both won seven on the spin, Arkle managed nine, as did Denman, Hurricane Fly, Quevega and Un De Sceaux. Annie Power, Faugheen, Istabraq and Sprinter Sacre all got to ten; and then there were Buveur D'Air (11), Bula (13), Douvan (14) and Sir Ken (16). By the end of last season, only Big Buck's (18) and Altior (19) had a longer winning streak than Honeysuckle.

Of her 16 in succession, the most recent 11 came in Grade 1s. She has won the last two Champion Hurdles by an average of five lengths and the last three Irish Champion Hurdles by a combined winning distance of 17 lengths. While the flair and flamboyance might be in shorter supply these days, she has never forgotten how to win. She only does enough of late, but enough was just fine again last season.

Yet some were still not convinced. Matt Chapman was cheerleading for the sceptics. "Tell me who she has beaten? She has yet to face a top-notch hurdler," the ITV and Sky Sports Racing broadcaster proclaimed in the lead-up to the 2022 Champion Hurdle.

It was billed as Honeysuckle's biggest test. Appreciate It was a question she had never answered before. He had won the previous year's Supreme Novices' Hurdle by 24 lengths and, while he had failed to appear since, was unbeaten in four runs over hurdles. If there were chinks in the mare's armour, many expected him to find them.

Yet Appreciate It had a big question

▸▸ Continues page 36

to answer himself on his comeback from a 12-month layoff and it was he who failed the test. He bowled along at the head of affairs but the writing was on the wall for him coming down to the second-last.

That was the moment Rachael Blackmore decided to unleash the beast. Honeysuckle loomed large, kicked a few lengths clear off the final bend, flew the last and stayed on strongly to beat 2020 winner Epatante by three and a half lengths. It was emphatic.

"Where's Matt [Chapman]? I haven't managed to find him yet. I'd love to have a word with him," De Bromhead joked afterwards. How dare anyone doubt the wondermare.

When asked to describe his emotions, the trainer said: "It's pure relief, it really is, and ecstasy as well in the sense that I just really hoped she would get the welcome back that she got. I'm always preparing myself for the day she'll get beaten, but I was really hoping she would get that roar."

She got the roar. She won the 2021 Champion Hurdle in silence, but this time the noise was deafening. Racing fans always let legends of the game know how they feel and Honeysuckle was showered in songs and superlatives.

★★★★

HONEYSUCKLE'S season started in the usual place at the usual time. The Hatton's Grace Hurdle at Fairyhouse has been the pre-Christmas highlight since 2019 and she was 2-5 favourite to complete a hat-trick in the race.

The Racing Post's Tom Segal wasn't so sure. In his Pricewise column on the day, he said: "If ever she is going to be beaten, I think it will be today." Her trainer was even inclined to agree with him, De Bromhead admitting afterwards: "I had myself convinced all week that she would get beaten this time."

Both forgot that the words 'beaten' and 'Honeysuckle' do not belong in the same sentence. Stormy Ireland tried to take her out of her comfort zone, scampering into a huge early lead, but Blackmore never flinched. Her reliable mount was alongside Ronald Pump three out and clear from early in the home straight. She got lonely but only because she was so far clear. She won by eight lengths.

'You can make the dream come true'

Eimir Blackmore on her daughter Rachael's second Champion Hurdle victory with Honeysuckle

"I was nervous, I'm always nervous, but I'm working very hard on it and I'm getting better. It's amazing and the crowd has been fantastic, so thanks to everybody for making it so special.

"The support Rachael has had and the good feeling that has come out of this has really been fantastic. It shows that if you have a dream, you can make the dream come true. I'm very proud that she's given people something to cheer about at a time when there's a lot of unhappiness in the world."

▲ Winning machine: Honeysuckle rounds off her fourth unbeaten season at Punchestown; below, Rachael Blackmore salutes a third Irish Champion Hurdle; top, with the Punchestown trophy; previous pages, a second Champion Hurdle triumph at Cheltenham

"She probably gave me a fright in this race last year, so maybe we did a little bit more this year for it. I let a lot of my horses progress but when you have only so many runs, we had her pretty straight today," De Bromhead stressed.

Next stop Leopardstown in February. It was a demonstration of the new version of Honeysuckle. The one where races are won in between the second-last and the last and the run-in is little more than a lap of honour. She was about eight lengths clear coming down to the final flight, steadied into it and coasted home six and a half lengths in front of Zanahiyr.

"I pay the bills, but these people all around us own her," said owner Kenny Alexander as he pointed to the perimeter of the parade ring, which was four or five deep with adoring fans.

Reflecting on the race, the former chief executive of bookmaking giant GVC added: "I think she always had it under control. I was reasonably confident throughout, but I get very nervous when she's running now. The only reason I can afford these horses is because I used to run a company that got 1-5 shots beaten every day of the week. They do get beaten and I know that more than anyone."

This one didn't and she didn't get beaten at Cheltenham either or at Punchestown, where she once again wrapped up her campaign in the Paddy Power Champion Hurdle. There was talk of Constitution Hill coming over for that, his owner Michael Buckley having floated the idea before Cheltenham kicked off, but the clash never materialised.

Honeysuckle was 1-5 again at Punchestown and, while she wasn't at her peak, she still got the job done. That is what the best horses do.

Perfect mare breaks new ground

Honeysuckle became the 16th mutiple winner of the Champion Hurdle and the first mare to land the race twice. A hat-trick would match the record held by Hatton's Grace (1949-51), Sir Ken (1952-54), Persian War (1968-70), See You Then (1985-87) and Istabraq (1998-2000).

CHAMPION HURDLE-WINNING MARES

1939 African Sister
1984 Dawn Run
1994 Flakey Dove
2016 Annie Power
2020 Epatante
2021 Honeysuckle
2022 Honeysuckle

HONEYSUCKLE'S RECORD UNDER RULES AT THE END OF THE 2021-22 SEASON

Starts 16
Wins 16
Best RPR 172 (includes 7lb mares' allowance)
Prize-money £1,317,181
Shortest SP 1-5 (2022 Irish Champion Hurdle, 2022 Punchestown Champion Hurdle)
Longest SP 9-4 (2020 Mares' Hurdle)
Biggest winning distance 12 lengths (Fairyhouse maiden hurdle, November 2018)
Narrowest wins Half a length (from Darver Star, Benie Des Dieux, Ronald Pump)
Total winning distances 88 lengths

'Our hearts are truly broken'

Jack de Bromhead, the son of trainer Henry de Bromhead and his wife Heather, died aged 13 in a freak fall at Glenbeigh horse and pony races on September 3. The Racing Post reported the tragedy in a series of moving articles

By Richard Forristal
and Mark Boylan

A PALL of unbearable sadness hangs over the racing and broader sporting communities following the tragic death of Jack de Bromhead, the "larger-than-life" 13-year-old son of Henry and Heather de Bromhead who was killed in a freak fall at Glenbeigh horse and pony races.

A statement from the family described the teenager as "a one-of-a-kind child who touched all our lives in the best way possible", with the devastated parents adding: "Our hearts are truly broken."

Tributes poured in from across the world of sport for the pony racing fanatic, who was characterised as a "very outgoing person who loved life" by family friend Peter Molony.

Gigginstown House Stud manager Eddie O'Leary paid tribute to De Bromhead as "a thoroughly lovely young man" touted to be a "future star" by pony racing followers.

A twin brother to Mia and older sibling to Georgia, the rider was already a familiar face to racing fans having featured in various television interviews as the likes of Honeysuckle, A Plus Tard, Minella Indo and Minella Times carried all before them for his father's County Waterford stable.

He was known as a pleasant and humble boy who was regularly seen by his father's side at the races, and had begun to carve his own career on the horse and pony racing circuit over the past couple of seasons, making a big impression by riding a handful of winners this summer.

On Saturday he was participating at the historic Glenbeigh races two-day event, which takes place on Rossbeigh Strand in County Kerry.

De Bromhead was riding in the fifth race when his mount veered into the sea as they rounded a bend and fell, landing on top of him. An air ambulance was summoned to attend the stricken rider but despite the best efforts of all the emergency services he died at the scene.

"Jack was a larger-than-life type of person," said Molony, who operates as racing manager to Kenny Alexander, owner of De Bromhead-trained superstar Honeysuckle.

"He always had a smile on his face and just loved racing, loved horses, loved ponies. Pony racing was his life. He absolutely lived for it. He was a very outgoing person who loved life. I think unimaginable is the only way to describe how everyone must be feeling right now.

"Jack and his sister Mia, a wonderful girl, have been front and centre in supporting Honeysuckle. We'll especially miss him being there during the season with her running."

He added: "I think one of the best ways of describing his love for racing was a story Henry has been telling for the last couple of years. He'd tell us how Jack spent most of his evenings on the back of the sofa riding finishes to whatever races were going on, and all Henry could hear was the noise of him in full flow during the finish.

"Last Christmas they got him an Equicizer [mechanical horse] and it was just pure delight for him. I can remember one day we were all down there and Rachael [Blackmore] gave him a lesson on the Equicizer. It was fantastic."

Prayers were said for De Bromhead's family and friends during Sunday morning mass at Glenbeigh church, with a host of messages, flowers and teddy bears left on Rossbeigh Strand in his memory.

O'Leary said: "Anybody who spoke about Jack spoke of him as a future star. He seemed to be a thoroughly lovely young man. We just feel so sorry for all his family and friends at such a tough time."

Recently retired Cheltenham Gold Cup and Grand National-winning jockey Robbie Power became familiar with the teenager through his link with the Knockeen stable, and hailed both his horsemanship and demeanour.

"Jack was a lovely young man, as well as being a very capable rider," said Power, who assists the leading trainer as a race planner. "I rode out with him at Henry's on a few occasions and you could see how much he loved racing and just loved horses. He had an unbelievable enthusiasm for the game. Your heart bleeds for the De Bromhead family. We're all thinking of them."

Legendary Irish rugby international Ronan O'Gara was among those to post messages of support on social media, tweeting: "Thoughts and prayers with the De Bromhead family. A 13-year-old boy taken doing what he loved. The poor family. The heart hurts."

A statement from the Irish Jockeys' Association said: "The tight-knit family of jockeys, many of whom have come through the world of pony racing, are devastated at the tragic loss of Jack de Bromhead, a kindred spirit. Our heartfelt sympathies to Jack's beloved family and his very many friends."

De Bromhead became the first fatality on an Irish course since Jack Tyner, only son of Robert and Mary Tyner, died after sustaining injuries in a fall at Dungarvan point-to-point in 2011, while fellow amateur rider Lorna Brooke was killed after a fall at Taunton last year.

Record-breaking amateur JT McNamara died in 2016, three years on from a fall at the 2013 Cheltenham Festival that left him with life-changing injuries.

This is an edited version of an article that appeared in the Racing Post on September 5

JACK DE BROMHEAD

'A one-of-a-kind child who touched all our lives in the best way possible'

Henry and Heather de Bromhead's tribute to their son Jack

ON SEPTEMBER 3, we said goodbye to our extraordinary, beautiful 13-year-old-son, Jack.

A one-of-a-kind child who touched all our lives in the best way possible – he will be forever present in our lives. Always cherished, always loved, frozen in time with a beautiful young soul.

He was an amazing son who told us he loved us every day. He had an over-brimming heart of loyalty, empathy, patience, pluck, courage, and how he made us laugh!

Not only the perfect, funny, loving son but also an incredible loving brother to our beautiful daughters, his twin sister Mia and his little sister, Georgia. He always had their back and was fiercely loyal and kind. Our hearts are truly broken.

He made so many friends wherever he went and they felt his special, unique and loyal touch on their lives, too. We ask that they please celebrate and love him as we know he would have wished.

Jack has lived so many more years than the thirteen – he filled every moment of his days, always busy, forever curious, grasping at life and new interests.

The passion he had for his family and friends extended to all his hobbies and interests, too many to fit into 13 years and he was certainly too busy to spend more than a minute more than he had to in the classroom!

It started with his work on the farm, the tractor, the cattle, the ponies and horses. He was a passionate expert on them all by the time he was ten. By 11, he was offering expert advice and consultation to his father on training horses as he developed his father's passion for all aspects of racing.

He recently started at a new school and by day two had already made a huge number of new friends to add to all his closest

friends from home. Jack's friendships were of the deep and loyal kind, and were treasured by him.

Jack, you will be with us always at home in your family and friends' hearts. Always present, always cherished, with so many memories

from your packed, extraordinary life.

Deeply loved and missed by your parents, Henry and Heather, your sisters Mia and Georgia, your grandparents Andrew, Marian, Harry and Sally, your aunts and uncles, extended family and friends.

Our precious Jack

"And he will raise you up on eagles' wings
Bear you on the breath of dawn
Make you to shine like the sun
And hold you in the palm of his hand"

ELLIOTT

BRITISH SCULPTOR CHARLES ELLIOTT - ELLIOTT OF LONDON

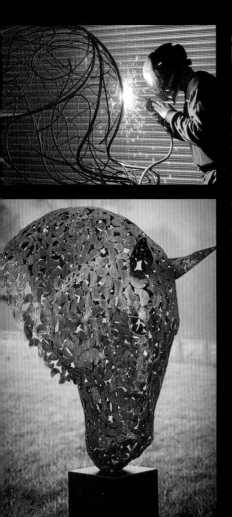

HANDCRAFTED SCULPTURES

All commissions welcome. Studio visits by appointment only.
For more sculptures please vist our website.

www.elliottoflondon.co.uk

Email: info@elliottoflondon.co.uk Studio: 01494 758896

Farewell to a young man who captured everyone's hearts

By David Jennings

AT NOON, in the shadows of the gallop where Honeysuckle, Minella Indo and A Plus Tard were moulded into superstars, we said goodbye to the most precocious talent to have ever emerged from Knockeen. At the same time, we learned all about the one-of-a-kind teenager who squeezed so much into his 13 years.

The funeral mass of Jack de Bromhead took place at the Church of the Nativity of the Blessed Virgin Mary in Butlerstown four days after his fatal fall at the Glenbeigh horse and pony races, a heartbreaking tragedy which shook Irish racing to its very core.

Ruby Walsh made the walk down the narrow country road towards the church with his wife Gillian and three of his children, while in his slipstream was Sir Anthony McCoy. Rachael Blackmore, Barry Geraghty, Charlie Swan, Davy Russell and Norman Williamson were also in attendance. Seven of the greatest jockeys Ireland has ever produced were paying their respects to a young man many believed was destined to be another.

Parish priest Father Pat Fitzgerald said pony racing sensation Jack was "an incalculable loss, a young man who captured the hearts of not just a parish but of a nation, and far beyond" and for the best part of two hours we were given the most glorious snapshot of a life jam-packed with love and laughter.

Parents consoled their children. Children consoled their parents. We cried together, but we laughed too. It is what Jack would have wanted.

With wife Heather by his side, Jack's heartbroken father Henry somehow found the strength to deliver a eulogy that brought us on the most beautiful journey through his son's life. We learned how 'Jacksie' was into everything – driving tractors, football, hurling, rugby, riding ponies, showjumping and even surfing.

After telling us a hilarious story about Jack's first proper rugby match, where he "tackled everything that moved, including his own teammates", we heard about how he woke his mother and father up at 6am one day to tie his stock for a hunt happening hours later.

But pony racing became his biggest passion. Henry told us: "Last summer all he wanted to do was ride in a pony race. All I could think of was how all the places where these pony races are held are nearer New York than Waterford!

"Anyhow, the Shark [Hanlon] rang me one day to sponsor a race at Thomastown so I said, 'Of course I will.' Thomastown, only half an hour away. Happy days. Shark even gave Jack a pony to ride, Silent Star.

"I'll never forget it. They weren't going much of a gallop and midway through the race he went from last to first and picked it up. In my mind it was exactly the right thing to do and for someone who had never ridden in a race before it was uncanny. He was just beaten on the line but it was the right thing to do."

After a few minutes Henry stopped and wondered: "I hope I'm not going on too much?"

Not a bit of it, Henry. Carry on.

He continued: "The other Sunday we went to Cahersiveen. We spent a great four hours in the car on the way down. Jack slept the whole way. We got there anyway and he was second on the first lad and got a bollocking because he should have won. Not off me. He was fourth on the next lad, then he won, and then he got a fall. He was fine but he was sensible. He said, 'You know what, Dad, I don't want to ride the last one, I don't think he has any chance.' That was fine so we jumped into the car.

"Four hours home. On the way home he just said out of the blue, 'Dad, I love pony racing. I get such a buzz out out of it.' I said to him, 'What about the fall?' He said, 'Henboy [the nickname he used to call his father], if you can't take the falls, you shouldn't be doing it'."

After the laughter came the love.

"One of the greatest comforts Heather and I have in his passing is he knows how much we loved him," Henry said. "All our kids, they just know how much we love them and we know how much he loved us. I just ask any of you, whoever you love, make sure to tell them.

"If something like this happens to you, something so tragic, it's a great comfort. If you could take that away with you, we would really appreciate it."

Then, standing side by side, Henry and Heather told us what Jack used to say to them each and every night before he went to bed: "Night Mum, night Dad, love you."

And with that tears rolled down cheeks.

There had been lots of love and laughter before that as Heather's father and Jack's grandfather Andrew Moffat spoke beautifully of his grandson.

Moffat said: "As Jack grew and matured, the bond between him and I suddenly changed, with my status reduced from Jack calling me 'grandpapa', downgraded then to 'grandad', then to more affectionately 'gramps', and now to my present form of address, 'grandyboy'. I wasn't the only person downgraded. His most esteemed father was referred to as 'Henboy'.

"Jack, the grandson we all adored, had a serious number of interests beyond his fame as a horse rider. His interest in driving and diggers commenced at the age of four. On a visit to Marian and I, a digger was working on a site nearby.

"He took me and we stood for an hour watching the digger work. Shortly after, a birthday present Henry and Heather bought him was a large-pedal John Deere tractor. Marian and I then supplied the matching trailer, and in no time he had [twin sister] Mia in the trailer, hurtling around the stable yard at reckless speed.

"Marian and I had custody of a rather grand mobility scooter. On being introduced to the scooter at about six years old, Jack soon discovered the power control switch and had it up to full power from the very beginning. The scooter was then attached to a trailer that he made, and all the grandchildren participated in its use. Roller-skating became a passion, and the grandchildren soon had ropes attaching them to the scooter to pull them at breakneck speed around the laneways of our house."

There were many more stories that brought smiles to faces before he concluded by saying: "Our 13 years with our beloved Jack will never be forgotten, by his family and all our friends and colleagues who knew the happiest, loving child you could ever hope for. Jack, you will live in our hearts – and memories – forever."

Jack's younger sister Georgia paid tribute to her brother, saying he "was the kindest, most caring big brother I could ever ask for. He was never scared to stand up for people and was always there for you no matter what".

Jack's twin sister Mia also spoke from deep inside her heart, saying: "Jack, you were the best brother ever, I got so lucky when you were born with me. I will miss your cheeky smile that made all my friends fall in love with you."

Jack de Bromhead packed a vast amount of love and laughter into his 13 years.

Farewell, Jack. You made some impression.

This is an edited version of an article that appeared in the Racing Post on September 8

Take the stress out of training...

**HIGHLY STRUNG, DIFFICULT TO TRAIN HORSES | STARTING PROBLEMS
PARADE RING EXCITEMENT | SALES & YEARLING PREP | BAD TRAVELLERS**

Nupafeed MAH® Calmer

Patented MAH® magnesium. Pharmaceutically developed for sharp or stressful behaviour. Supports healthy nerve and muscle function during times of stress.

No drowsy additives. LGC screened and fully race compliant.

"We have several horses on Nupafeed MAH Calmer. It's used on those that are, like their Trainer, rather highly strung!! I find it a real help to keep them switched off and relaxed."

James Fanshawe

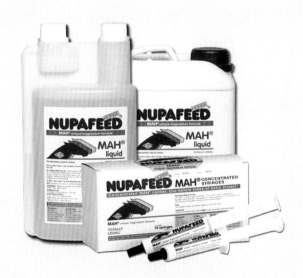

 · 01438 861 900 · **nupafeed.co.uk** · info@nupafeed.co.uk

IN THE PICTURE

Sawbuck jumps into racing history books with 300-1 stunner

SAWBUCK earned a place in racing history at Punchestown on May 24 when he won a 2m½f maiden hurdle for four-year-olds at odds of 300-1, equalling the record for the longest-priced winner of a race in Britain or Ireland. His winning odds were the biggest ever in a British or Irish jumps race.

Trained by Conor O'Dwyer and ridden by his son Charlie, Sawbuck was one of four 300-1 shots in the 22-runner field but, while the others predictably made no impression, he achieved a stunning four-length success from joint-second favourite Ballybawn Belter. The 100-30 favourite Vocito was third.

Sawbuck, who started at 999-1 on Betfair, was having just his third run over hurdles. The other two had also been at Punchestown the previous November when he was sent off at 125-1 and 250-1 and was beaten 43 lengths and 55 lengths. He had most recently finished tenth of 12 when tried on the all-weather in a 1m2½f Dundalk handicap in early April.

The winning rider said Sawbuck had been in good form at home and he was expecting a better effort back over hurdles but not to be involved in the finish. "After his two previous runs over hurdles, if he left here with a nice run and finished somewhere in the middle I'd have been delighted," he said. "But from the drop of the flag he travelled great. He did it handily enough."

Sawbuck's victory was a good result for the bookmakers, although Coral's John Hill reported: "Not many punters looked twice at the horse, but we tip our hat to the customer who placed £2 each-way on the winner. They clearly saw something others had missed." William Hill's Tony Kenny said: "A total of 28 punters chose him, accounting for just 0.14 per cent of all stakes placed on the race."

In his next race, a novice hurdle at Wexford, Sawbuck was pulled up and then he was ninth of 12 at 50-1 in a handicap hurdle at Cork in August, beaten 40 lengths. He went back to the Flat later that month and was 12th of 13th at Navan as a 16-1 shot.

Sawbuck holds the record for the longest-priced winner alongside the Luke Comer-trained He Knows No Fear, who set the mark when winning a mile maiden on the Flat at Leopardstown on August 13, 2020. Before that, the Irish record had been held by 200-1 shot Killahara Castle when triumphing by five lengths in a Listed novice hurdle at Thurles on December 17, 2017.

The British record is held by Equinoctial, who started at 250-1 when landing a novice hurdle at Kelso on November 21, 1990.

Picture: PATRICK McCANN (RACINGPOST.COM/PHOTOS)

INSTANT CLASSIC

Shishkin and Energumene produced one of the great jumps races with an epic battle in the Clarence House Chase at Ascot in January

By Nick Pulford

THE race of the season, a race for the ages. Shishkin v Energumene in the Clarence House Chase at Ascot in January promised so much and delivered even more, going right to the wire in a compelling contest between the star two-milers from Britain and Ireland. Shishkin won, Energumene lost, but both emerged with their reputations enhanced. It was an instant classic.

The rematch two months later in the Queen Mother Champion Chase was quite the opposite. Shishkin could not perform to the same astonishingly high level and was pulled up, leaving Energumene to take the crown. In terms of their rivalry it was as unsatisfactory as the first clash had been unforgettable. The damp squib at Cheltenham merely served to emphasise how lucky we had been to witness the Ascot fireworks.

There is always a certain level of angst that goes with the anticipation in the build-up to these big clashes. So many head-to-head showdowns have ended with one of the contenders underperforming – not just in racing but in other sports too – that there is a widespread tendency to dial down the excitement as a guard against deflation and disappointment. In fact, virtually right up until raceday, some found it hard to believe the Clarence House meeting would materialise.

It was a point addressed by Chris Cook in his Saturday preview in the Racing Post, with hours to go until battle was due to commence. "What a cynical lot we are, to have been so convinced this would never happen," he wrote. "All week, the most frequently expressed opinion was that the clash between Shishkin and

▶ *Continues page 48*

Energumene would not happen, that their two trainers were bluffing and eventually one of them would blink. And yet, look! They're both still running."

What lay in store was an old-fashioned Anglo-Irish clash of the type that rarely happens away from the big festivals. Representing Britain was the 5-6 favourite Shishkin (although he was Irish-owned and Irish-bred), who had won ten of his 11 starts for Nicky Henderson, with the only blot being a novicey fall at the second flight on his hurdling debut. The previous season's Arkle Chase winner was fresh from a comfortable reappearance victory at Kempton over Christmas, which had pushed his official rating up to 172.

From Ireland came the 5-4 challenger Energumene (British-owned and French-bred), who was likewise unbeaten over fences and had suffered only one defeat in his career when third on his bumper debut. Up to now Willie Mullins had kept him on Irish soil, where he had been a Grade 1 winner twice as a novice chaser and had made a smooth seasonal debut at Cork in December. His official rating was 171 and he was also just a pound behind Shishkin on Racing Post Ratings, which had them on 175 and 174.

To most eyes it was a match race, although there were two other runners. One was the 80-1 rank outsider Amoola Gold but the other was the previous year's Clarence House winner First Flow, who had run to an RPR of 170 that day. His virtual dismissal at 16-1 in a four-runner contest emphasised the high quality of the big two who were grabbing all the attention.

★★★★

IN THE day's Ascot selection box, listing a range of tipsters from the Racing Post and other newspapers, there were ten votes for Shishkin and four for Energumene. That reflected the difficulty many envisaged for Paul Townend's front-running tactics on Energumene against the stalking Shishkin under Nico de Boinville. Shaking off Shishkin, or even drawing the sting from his finish, looked an immensely challenging task. Townend and his willing partner almost pulled it off.

Energumene was in front from the off and quickly jumping economically, with Shishkin doing likewise in company with First Flow a couple of lengths behind. Amoola Gold went straight to the rear and stayed there, collecting £8,000 for going round in his own time to finish fourth. The first big moment came down the far side at the sixth fence, an open ditch, where Shishkin pecked on landing, drawing a collective "ooh" from the distant stands. Townend was making sure this would be a test like no other for the favourite.

Going to the last of the open ditches, four out, there was another sign of difficulty when De Boinville started to push a little on Shishkin as Townend's mount maintained his smooth rhythm in front. Off the bend with two to jump, at which point First Flow started to lose touch with the rising pace, De Boinville's urgings became more insistent as he tried to keep tabs on the leader. It wasn't unusual for Shishkin to hit a mid-race flat spot before finishing strongly but this was the moment, the only one De Boinville said later, where he thought: "We're cooked here and we're going to have to pull out something special." The noise from the stands rose in step with the growing intensity of the battle. This was, as Henderson said afterwards, "a proper race".

The gap was perhaps a length and a half over the second-last and had increased a little at the final fence, but now De Boinville threw everything at Shishkin. With one crack of the whip with his left hand, and two more with his right, De Boinville got the response he wanted as his mount started to claw back ground on Energumene. Townend was not beaten easily, with Energumene still fighting hard against the rail, but he was finally overtaken in the final 50 yards. Victory went to Shishkin by a length.

★★★★

EVERYONE knew something special had just happened. From his spot on the grandstand roof, TV cameraman Stuart Alexander reported: "That was everything I wanted and more. I've not heard a cheer like that for ages." Down on the ground, as racegoers

▲ Battle scenes: Paul Townend on Energumene and Nico de Boinville on Shishkin drive for the line, and the jockeys exchange a handshake; opposite page, De Boinville stands tall as he is led in on Shishkin; below; Shishkin's proud head; previous page, Shishkin (right) and Energumene at the finish

rushed to greet the prize-fighters back to the winner's enclosure, one woman exclaimed: "That was glorious." And it was.

The winning jockey savoured the moment, standing tall in his irons as he was led in on Shishkin, with some racegoers chanting "Oh, Nico de Boinville" to the tune of Seven Nation Army. "That was some horserace," De Boinville said. "It was the greatest thrill simply to be involved in the race, let alone to win it. Even if I had come second I would be saying that was the best race I've ever ridden in."

Having slept on it, De Boinville was still on a high the following day. "It was like being at the football and fabulous to be taking part," he said. "It created such an atmosphere. The crowd really responded to it and the whole place was rocking and rolling. It was a special place to be."

Mullins agreed, despite being on the wrong end of the result. "A lot of people said to me they had never seen such a welcome back into the winner's enclosure for a horse who had finished second, as well as the winner. I think everyone appreciated it," he said.

Gracious in defeat, Ireland's champion trainer was proud of Energumene's leading role in the epic, saying: "The horse ran his heart out and Paul gave him a terrific ride. Nico

de Boinville was excellent on Shishkin and, of course, Shishkin did what he always does. He pretends to be beaten and then he nabs you on the line, although, to be fair, he usually does it a bit earlier than that."

Henderson, whose long list of top two-mile chasers features Sprinter Sacre and Altior, also hailed this episode with his latest star as something extraordinary. "The only sad part of it is there didn't deserve to be a loser. That was the only bit that seemed unfair," he said. "But it lived up to the billing and it was an epic. It was one of the races we'll never forget."

Brough Scott, the esteemed writer and broadcaster, has seen it all over many decades and he was also in no doubt Shishkin v Energumene was in the highest rank. In the following day's Racing Post, he wrote: "You always need two to make a race and that's what we got here. I don't think there's been anything better and I feel very lucky to have been there. For me, in my 80th year, it was like with Mill House and Arkle or Grundy and Bustino." There could be no greater accolade than comparison with those great rivalries of the 1960s and 70s.

Thoughts immediately turned towards a rematch in the Queen Mother Champion Chase and indeed Shishkin and Energumene lined up again, but hopes of another thrilling battle were quickly dashed. Energumene was on his A-game in a comfortable victory, but Shishkin was out of sorts from the start and De Boinville pulled him up sharply after the eighth fence.

On the day blame was pinned on the soft ground, which was changed to heavy after the Champion Chase, but within a few weeks an unusual bone condition was diagnosed, which put Shishkin out of training until a scan came back clear in the summer. It was a setback that emphasised just how blessed we had been to see both Shishkin and Energumene at the top of their game at Ascot.

Those days when the stars align perfectly are rare and special. The Clarence House lasted barely four and a quarter minutes, but the memory of that epic battle will live on for many years.

SMOOTH OPERATOR

Energumene topped another incredible season for Willie Mullins by giving him a long-awaited victory in the Queen Mother Champion Chase

By David Jennings

I T WAS an outrageous oddity. How could the most successful trainer in Cheltenham Festival history, the man who had won 11 Champion Bumpers (soon to be 12), nine Mares' Hurdles, seven Supremes and four Champion Hurdles, not have a single Queen Mother Champion Chase on his CV? Add in the fact that there were four Arkle victories too and it became even more bizarre.

Gilt-edged chances had been missed. Open goals when it looked easier to score. Douvan was 2-9 in 2017 but one of the most accurate jumpers of the modern era chose the biggest day of all to clatter into every other fence. He was seventh and found to be lame afterwards.

Un De Sceaux was 4-6 in 2016. He, however, turned into the fall guy to facilitate the Sprinter Sacre fairytale. Then there was Chacun Pour Soi in 2020. He had been trading at around 6-4 but had some pus in his foot on the

morning of the race. It was only a 24-hour recovery, but it was 24 hours that Mullins didn't have.

And, so, all that history meant Mullins had the strangest of stats following him around the place like a bad smell. A stench he couldn't get rid of, no matter what. Not even the delicious fragrance that was Douvan could dilute the odour.

Enter Energumene in Tony Bloom's blue and white colours. The strapping French-bred had looked a bit of a freak in his novice

chasing campaign, a tearaway who told Paul Townend what he was going to do, not the other way around. He won his beginners' chase by 18 lengths at Gowran Park without coming off the bridle. He then disposed of the classy Captain Guinness at Naas before adding the Irish Arkle at Leopardstown by ten lengths. That was his first Grade 1.

Energumene didn't get to Cheltenham in 2021, depriving us of a scintillating first showdown with Shishkin in the Arkle, but he

did recover quickly to notch a second Grade 1 at Punchestown.

The promise was there. Could he be the one to set the record straight for Mullins at long last?

★★★★

WE FINALLY got to see Energumene v Shishkin in the Clarence House Chase at Ascot in January, an epic encounter that will live long in the memory, and it was 1-0 to the star striker on the Seven Barrows team heading to Cheltenham.

The rematch would kick off at 3.30pm on March 16 on a soggy pitch at Cheltenham following torrential rain on the morning of the big game. Surely the downpours would not dampen a spectacle of such magnitude. Both horses were proven on soft ground anyway. But, alas, the thrilling end-to-end contest never materialised.

The battle began in strange fashion. Energumene, the proven pacesetter who had always worn his heart on his sleeve, was not sent straight to the front as had been the case in each and every one of his previous six starts over fences. Instead, Townend threw a curveball by dropping him in at the back of the field. We didn't see that coming and we definitely didn't predict what came next.

Shishkin was sluggish over the first and could not shake off the lethargy. Nico de Boinville gave him a shake of the reins, an ominous early sign that all was not well with the previously unbeaten 5-6 favourite. A mistake at the sixth followed by a slow jump at the eighth ended his challenge. He was out of the equation before the field had even got to the fifth-last.

When De Boinville put Shishkin out of his misery and pulled him up, Chacun Pour Soi was still bowling along merrily at the head of affairs under Patrick Mullins. He was loving it. Well, until he took off too early five out and parted company with the champion amateur.

Energumene's two biggest

▸ Continues page 52

ENERGUMENE

dangers were now gone and, quickly realising what was unfolding around him, Townend decided to make his move coming down the hill. Having been last through the early stages, he found himself disputing it by three out and was coming clear by the time he reached the second-last. A slick leap at the final fence sealed the deal and the most outrageous oddity in jump racing had been rectified. Willie Mullins had trained the Champion Chase winner.

He was emotional afterwards, a clear indication of how much it meant to him. The hoodoo had been broken. The one marquee jumps race to have eluded him no longer did. The relief was tangible and his normally impeccable composure escaped him for a few moments.

"I'm surprised I'm feeling how I am, but there we are," he said with a lump in his throat. "That shows how much it means to me."

It was a brave call to change tactics. Energumene was a powerful pacesetter, sickening horses with his long stride and slick jumping, but Mullins made the decision not to stick to the usual script. He tore it up and wrote the most unpredictable of scenes.

Explaining the tactical manoeuvre which completely changed the complexion of the contest, Mullins said: "We just felt we had completely the wrong tactics at Ascot and we needed to change things up. We needed to do something different and that's what we did."

Townend said: "The first headache was trying to decide whether to ride him or Chacun Pour Soi, and then we had to decide what to do. It didn't work for us at Ascot, so we rolled the dice and took a chance. We had to think about it and every day is a school day. As it turned out today, it probably didn't matter because Shishkin was never going. I knew going away from the stands he wasn't, and I had to react to that and chase the race."

Asked about the distinction of delivering a first Champion Chase to Closutton, he added: "Ruby [Walsh] didn't leave too many behind him for me to be the first to do and we're glad to pick up what scraps he left. It's great when something like that works out."

Mullins later admitted the biggest factor was that the two main challengers exited the contest. "It wasn't so much about tactics in the end," he said. "Shishkin just didn't handle that ground and Nico wisely pulled him up. I was really disappointed about Chacun Pour Soi. I thought he was absolutely loving it out there, so that was frustrating, but of course I'm delighted to win this race. I haven't done things as dramatically as Henry [de Bromhead] did last year [completing the Cheltenham triple crown] but yes, we're getting there!"

Getting there? Now there is the understatement of the century. Mullins got there a long time ago and the Champion Chase was merely a snag that needed fixing. Energumene sorted that out with an emphatic display. The race was there for the taking and he grabbed it by the scruff of the neck.

▲ Winning team: Willie Mullins and owner Tony Bloom greet Paul Townend after Energumene's Queen Mother Champion Chase triumph; below and previous pages, Townend out on the track

★★★★

MULLINS held the whole jumps season in his grip and the Closutton chapters in the record books continued to be added at a rapid rate. He now has 88 Cheltenham Festival winners on his jam-packed CV as well as 16 Irish trainers' championships. Once again, he provided the ammunition for Paul Townend to win his fifth jockeys' title and for his son Patrick to be champion amateur for the 14th time.

The stable housed a multitude of established and rising stars headed by the top-rated Allaho. In the Anglo-Irish Jumps Classifications he led the middle-distance chase division for the second consecutive year, Energumene was level with Shishkin at the head of the two-mile chase division, Galopin Des Champs was the top novice chaser overall and Gentleman De Mee led the two-mile

▶▶ Continues page 54

RoR
Retraining of Racehorses

Racing to a new career at ror.org.uk

RoR Source a Horse
Retraining of Racehorses

sourceahorse.ror.org.uk

A new website for selling or loaning a horse directly out of a trainer's yard and for all former racehorses.

Owner/Trainer Helpline

A dedicated helpline to assist in the placement of horses coming out of training.

Rehoming Direct

RoR has compiled a checklist to safeguard your horse's future when moved directly into the sport horse market.

Retrainers

RoR has a list of retrainers recommended by trainers who can start the retraining process and assess each horse.

Visit
ror.org.uk
for rehoming options and advice

Equine Charities

Retrain former racehorses for a donation, as well as care for vulnerable horses with the help of RoR funding.

RoR is British horseracing's official charity for the welfare of horses retired from racing.

T: 01488 648998

novice chase category. Facile Vega was the season's best bumper horse.

Punchestown is perhaps Mullins' favourite playground of all and he sent out 14 winners at the 2022 festival. Nine came in Grade 1s, including Energumene in the Champion Chase, where he took care of Chacun Pour Soi with the minimum of fuss. He also won six of the eight Grade 1s on offer at the Dublin Racing Festival at Leopardstown in February.

Mullins trained 202 winners last season in Ireland, where he had a 26 per cent strike-rate and earned a whopping €5.88 million (£4.8m) in prize-money. He had only 89 runners in Britain but won with 15 of them (17 per cent) and prize-money earnings of £1.73m (€2.1m) put him fourth in the trainer standings. There was a record ten-winner haul at the Cheltenham Festival (beating the mark of eight he had established) and he took the King George VI Chase at Kempton with Tornado Flyer. It was a stunning season in every sense.

As ever, the man behind those astronomical numbers wanted to deflect all the praise elsewhere.

"I've got some very loyal owners and they have the wherewithal to provide these horses if we can spot them," he said. "When you have the likes of my wife Jackie, Patrick, Ruby [Walsh], David Casey, it's not just one person. It's the whole lot put together that makes a huge difference. Our staff as well – they ride out in all weathers and are at home working away while we're here [at the races]. I'm very lucky to have them all."

He added: "I love the game, it's not work to me. It's what I know and it's not a job when you're enjoying it. I'm very lucky. Like any football team, if you can have young talent coming through that's a great basis for a proper team later on and that's what we try to replicate."

There is an endless supply of young talent in Closutton and they are being managed by a master.

Same as it ever was.

Dominant force

Willie Mullins' incredible numbers in the 2021-22 season

16th Irish trainers' title

202 winners in Ireland (26% strike-rate)

€5,883,515 (£4,842,406) prize-money in Ireland (more than Gordon Elliott and Henry de Bromhead combined)

4th in the British championship (from 89 runners)

10 Cheltenham Festival winners (record)

23 Grade 1 wins in Ireland (62% of total)

14 Punchestown festival winners

9 Grade 1 wins at the Punchestown festival (75% of total)

6 Grade 1 wins at the Dublin Racing Festival (75% of total)

£356,182 Prize-money won by top earner Energumene

5 horses in the top seven on Racing Post Ratings

181 RPR for Allaho, his top performer

2 champion riders (Paul Townend and Patrick Mullins)

▼ Willie Mullins and his team at Closutton with his record ten Cheltenham Festival winners: clockwise from left, Billaway, The Nice Guy, Energumene, Stattler, Facile Vega, Sir Gerhard, Allaho, State Man, Vauban and Elimay

Horseboxes – Uprating and Downplating

Uprating Horseboxes

As you may be aware, the DVSA is paying close attention to the horsebox industry and in particular, to lightweight horseboxes which they suspect may be operating overweight.

We have seen cases of horseboxes being stopped, checked and impounded on the roadside, owing to running overweight. The horses in transit have to be loaded into a different box and taken away, and the resultant fines are ever increasing in size. Yet, there is an alternative.

SvTech is keen to promote its uprating service for lightweight horseboxes (3500kg), whereby the horsebox can gain an extra 200-300kg in payload. This provides vital payload capability when carrying an extra horse and/or tack and offers peace of mind for the owner.

SvTech has carried out extensive work and testing on lightweight models and has covered uprates for most lightweight vehicles.

It is worth noting that some uprates require modifications or changes to the vehicle's braking, tyres and/or suspension, for which SvTech provides a simple

purpose-built suspension assister kit. This will take between 1-2 hours for you to fit. Your horsebox will then go for a formal inspection to bring it into the 'Goods' category, and, depending on the vehicle's age, may also require fitment of a speed limiter, for which there are one or two options. Most importantly, vehicles registered after May 2002 must be fitted with manufacturer's ABS, if going above 3500kg.

If you're unsure, or don't believe that you need to uprate your lightweight horsebox, try taking it to a public weighbridge when you're fully loaded with your horse, tack, passenger, hay, etc. and weigh off each axle individually and the vehicle as a whole. There could be a distinct chance that you've overloaded one of the axles, even if you're within the GVW. If there is a problem, we can help. Call us to discuss your options.

Due to recent changes at DVSA, we are no longer required to make a mechanical change to the vehicle and, once downrated, we will be supplying you with a revised set of Ministry plating certificates, or if exempt, plating and testing, a converter's plate and certificate at the lower weight.

Depending upon vehicle usage, it is at the discretion of DVSA as to whether they will require a formal inspection of your vehicle.

DOWNLOAD AND FILL IN THE ENQUIRY FORM AND RETURN IT ALONG WITH THE INFO REQUESTED

Downplating Horseboxes

Do you own a 10 - 12.5 tonnes horsebox and do you want non-HGV licence holder to drive it? Your horsebox could b downplated to 7.5 tonnes so that any driver with a licence issued prior to 1st Jan 1997 could drive it.

● You are paying too much Vehicle Excise Duty.

● You want to escape the need for a tachograph.

The most important aspect when downplating is to leave yourself suitable payload to carry your goods. The Ministry requires that for horseboxes of 7500kg there is a minimum payload of 2000kg. Hence, when downplating to 7500kg, the unladen weight must not exceed 5500kg. For 3500kg horseboxes, you must ensure that you have a payload of at least 1000kg, thus, when empty it cannot weigh more than 2500kg.

SvTech
Special Vehicle Technology

T +44 (0)1772 621800
E webenquiries@svtech.co.uk

ALL CONQUERING

Allaho had another dominant season capped by a sensational first chase win over three miles in the Punchestown Gold Cup

By Alan Sweetman

A FEW years ago a non-racing friend came across an article of mine in which I used the cliche about a horse having "questions to answer". "That poor horse," he messaged. "Imagine going to bed every night wondering if Jeremy Paxman is going to pop his head over the stable door in the morning."

I remembered the witticism when reflecting on the flawless campaign enjoyed by Allaho last season. We can safely say that the Willie Mullins-trained eight-year-old answered every question asked of him in compiling four wins from four races, including three Grade 1 victories achieved by an aggregate margin of 30 lengths.

After a second consecutive success in the Ryanair Chase at the Cheltenham Festival, he signed off an immaculate campaign with a quite spectacular performance in the Punchestown Gold Cup. This was an exhibition of sheer exuberance from start to finish. Taking on a field of established three-mile performers, including two previous winners of the race, two Cheltenham Gold Cup winners, the King George winner and the Savills Chase winner, Allaho was utterly dominant.

It mattered not a jot that he showed a familiar tendency to jump to the left. He was always travelling powerfully and in rhythm under Paul Townend. Three out, it looked as if the 2021

winner Clan Des Obeaux had some sort of chance of making a race of it but Allaho simply sauntered away from the Paul Nicholls-trained gelding, who had won the Betway Bowl at Aintree for the second time only three weeks earlier.

It was a stunning finale to a season in which Allaho cemented his position as one of the top chasers in Britain and Ireland, with the distinction of having only the 15-length Cheltenham Gold Cup winner A Plus Tard ahead of him on Racing Post Ratings.

The previous season, when he delivered arguably the most impressive performance of the 2021 Cheltenham Festival in trouncing the excellent Fakir D'Oudairies by 12 lengths in the Ryanair, Allaho topped those ratings, despite having been mastered by his stablemate Chacun Pour Soi when dropped to two miles for his final start of the season in the Grade 1 Champion Chase at Punchestown.

★★★★

AGAINST a background of such outstanding achievement, it hardly seems fair to return to the theme of interrogation. But we have to go there because the really exciting thing about Allaho's career is that it is still evolving.

How much further can he go? You can interpret that question in two ways. What fresh heights can he reach in the essentially prosaic matter of ratings? Or, more romantically, is there a chance he

can find the resources of stamina to win the Cheltenham Gold Cup?

Mullins is well used to speculation about Allaho's trip requirements. He summed up his thoughts in reaction to the gelding's explosive display in the 2021 Ryanair. "He was just awesome, his galloping and his jumping, he put the two together," he said. "I was hoping he could do that over three miles, but if he's only a two-and-a-half-mile horse that will do for me if he can repeat that performance."

In winning a three-mile race of the calibre of the Punchestown Gold Cup in commanding front-running style, Allaho showed stamina consistent with the early days of his career when he arrived at Closutton after finishing second in a two-and-a-quarter-mile hurdle at Auteuil in March 2018.

Mullins started him off in a bumper at Leopardstown's Christmas fixture at the end of that year, a choice of race that implied he was regarded as one of the yard's best youngsters. Apparently paying the price for getting involved in a prolonged duel with the Gordon Elliott-trained Fury Road, he faded into fourth.

What happened next gives us a retrospective insight into the trainer's early impressions of the young recruit. It's rare enough for Mullins not to give a second chance to a bumper horse who has come up short of expectations at the first attempt. But, on this occasion, there was an immediate change of emphasis. Moreover,

Mullins steered away from the orthodox in his choice of race for the No Risk At All gelding, whose year-older half-sister Shanning had won her first two races over hurdles for the stable the previous season.

Rather than find Allaho an opportunity in a maiden at two miles or two and a half miles, Mullins sent him to Clonmel for a three-mile Grade 3 novice hurdle that he had won in four of the previous six seasons, including with the subsequent RSA Chase winner and Cheltenham Gold Cup third Don Poli.

Despite running a bit freely in the hands of Ruby Walsh, Allaho picked up strongly after getting the second-last wrong and strode clear to win by four lengths from the Henry de Bromhead-trained Minella Indo, a point-to-point winner the previous season and also having only his second outing over hurdles.

It seemed like an auspicious performance, but Minella Indo exacted emphatic revenge when relegating Allaho to third in the Albert Bartlett at Cheltenham and confirmed his superiority in a 'decider' at the Punchestown festival. When the pair clashed again in the following season's RSA Chase, Minella Indo again had the upper hand, although neither could match the strong-finishing Champ.

That marked a tame conclusion to a three-race novice chase campaign for Allaho. When he resumed on a visibility-restricted

▸ *Continues page 58*

afternoon in the John Durkan at Punchestown at the beginning of December 2020, it seemed like an apt metaphor, signifying an uncertain future in the senior ranks. In a race in which Mullins supplied the first three finishers, he trailed in last after reportedly jumping poorly in the fog.

Nonetheless, Allaho's reputation was such that he was sent off the shortest-priced of the stable's five runners in the Savills Chase at Leopardstown after Christmas. When he could manage only fourth behind Henry de Bromhead's A Plus Tard in the same Cheveley Park colours, Mullins was forced into rethinking his likely optimum trip.

Within a month, the process of rehabilitation was well under way with a reassuring victory in the Grade 2 Horse & Jockey Hotel Chase over two and a half miles at Thurles. It was a turning point. Before that race, Allaho's career record showed two wins from ten starts. But from there to his Punchestown Gold Cup victory at the end of last season, he won six out of seven and lost only on that drop to two miles against Chacun Pour Soi.

✷✷✷✷

HIS Punchestown Gold Cup performance was sensational, put in perspective by the post-race reaction of Harry Cobden, who rode runner-up Clan Des Obeaux. "Christ, Allaho is an absolute machine. I was flat out everywhere and he was doing a half-speed. He's a seriously classy horse."

Although Allaho's display categorically answered questions about his ability to stay three miles, Mullins, characteristically pensive, was not prepared to commit him to a possible Cheltenham Gold Cup challenge in 2023.

"I don't know," he replied. "He has a huge engine and he's going to be more mature again next year. But another quarter of a mile is tough, although I think he would probably be better going left-handed, so I just don't know. When you see what he can do over two and a half miles, you wonder."

Questions, questions, Mullins has plenty to ponder. He and Cheveley Park could be forgiven if they decide

to play it safe again. Allaho could return to Cheltenham in March bidding to become the first horse to win the Ryanair Chase for a third time. It would be a niche distinction in that race's relatively short history and bring a certain cachet.

▲ Easy does it: Allaho and Paul Townend clear the last at Cheltenham before strolling home to take a second Ryanair Chase; previous pages, winning scenes from the Punchestown Gold Cup

Another exhibition of stylish swagger in the Ryanair would confirm his stature in the chasing ranks. But the Gold Cup remains the supreme challenge for any staying chaser and leaves no room for evasion. It's the ultimate question to answer.

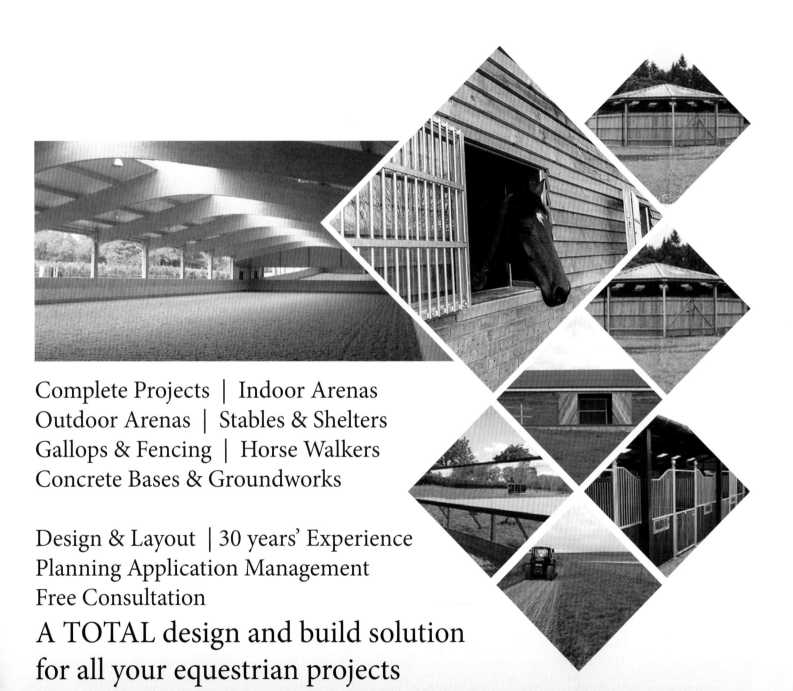

EXTRAORDINARY

Galopin Des Champs brought the wow factor to his novice chase campaign – even in defeat at Cheltenham

By David Jennings

WILLIE MULLINS' mask rarely slips. Hype has never consumed him. He deals in cold, hard facts. Official ratings. Rock-solid form. Horses who can do it on the big days in the big races. Beginners' chases are merely stepping stones to somewhere else, somewhere bigger.

Yet not even Ireland's 16-time champion trainer could keep his emotions in check in the aftermath of the Ballymaloe Relish Beginners Chase at Leopardstown last Christmas. He was swept away in a wave of wonderment along with the rest of us.

"I thought it was extraordinary what he did there," was Mullins' reflex reaction to the chasing debut of Galopin Des Champs. "I thought he was good but I didn't think he was that good. That was just something else. He was so effortless over all his fences. He did everything right and galloped away through the line and beyond it."

Harold Kirk, Mullins' right-hand man for the last few decades, opted for the word "awesome". Just to remind you, this was only a beginners' chase.

There were only eight runners. It was only December. But it was glorious.

There was something almost surreal about the way Galopin Des Champs attacked his fences down Leopardstown's back straight. He met each one on the perfect stride and made good horses look distinctly average. Floueur, a 140-rated hurdler, was beaten 38 lengths. Blue Sari, runner-up in the 2019 Champion Bumper, was 40 lengths adrift and Crosshill, a 141-rated hurdler, was beaten double that distance. Column Of Fire, who looked the most likely winner of the 2020 Martin Pipe Handicap Hurdle when falling at the last, trailed home 108 lengths behind the winner. He embarrassed the whole lot of them.

To put the performance into perspective, Galopin Des Champs clocked 5min 29.9sec. The same race 12 months earlier was also run on officially yielding ground and went to the 150-rated hurdler The Big Getaway. He won by ten lengths in a time of 5min 42.5sec. Galopin Des Champs was 12.6 seconds quicker.

According to Racing Post Ratings, it was the best chasing debut of the modern era. His RPR of 163 was better than horses who have since become household names. Sprinter Sacre got 154 for his 24-length romp at Doncaster; Kauto Star was given 152 for his first go over fences at Newbury; Vautour was also 152; Best Mate 151. Altior got closest to Galopin Des Champs. He earned 160 for beating Black Corton by 63 lengths at Kempton in 2016.

★★★★

SO, THEN, where did this dark and handsome beast come from? Well, he won the previous season's Martin Pipe Handicap Hurdle under Sean O'Keeffe off a mark of 142, getting the better of a seriously well-handicapped rival in Langer Dan. He backed that up by winning his first Grade 1 – the Irish Mirror Novice Hurdle at the Punchestown festival – by a dozen lengths.

He had been a slow burner over hurdles, though. He was a beaten odds-on favourite on his Irish debut at Gowran Park, was pulled up next time in a Grade 2 event at Limerick when evens and finished sixth to stablemate Appreciate It in the Grade 1 Chanelle Pharma Novice Hurdle at the Dublin Racing Festival when allowed to go off at 100-1. Yes, 100-1.

But it was blatantly obvious from what we witnessed at Leopardstown last Christmas that Galopin Des Champs was going to be a completely different proposition over fences.

After bolting up in his beginners' chase it was back to Leopardstown less than six weeks later for the Ladbrokes Novice Chase. It was a Grade 1 but, such was the impression he had created on his chasing debut, he was 4-9. He won easily again, this time by nine lengths, although there was an error at the eighth fence and he was a shade keener than ideal in the early part of the race.

That keenness meant the Brown Advisory Novices' Chase over three miles was now off the table at Cheltenham. He would instead clash with the brilliant Bob Olinger in the Turners Novices' Chase. It was billed as one of the most eagerly awaited showdowns of the entire festival.

Both were unbeaten over fences and had been almost flawless in their chase outings to date. Punters kept changing their minds. Bob was favourite one minute, Galopin the next. There were only four runners but this was one race where quality superseded quantity.

What transpired was not a rumble in the Cotswolds jungle

▸▸ *Continues page 62*

but a rout. Galopin Des Champs took Bob Olinger out of his comfort zone with a jumping display that had us drooling. He was about a dozen lengths in front and going further clear as Paul Townend found the perfect stride coming into the 16th and final fence.

"Galopin Des Champs is away and clear and he's over safely," proclaimed racecourse commentator Mark Johnson, only to reverse rapidly. "No, he's not."

Galopin Des Champs knuckled on landing, bringing loud gasps from the disbelieving crowd. Perhaps it was Henry de Bromhead, trainer of one of the luckiest winners in Cheltenham Festival history in Bob Olinger, who summed it up best of all.

Looking disillusioned and dejected despite having trained the winner, he said: "I didn't think I'd ever see a horse who would make Bob Olinger look like that. Fair play to Galopin. That was some performance. I was surprised to see Bob Olinger off the bridle so soon. As I say, I never thought I'd see a horse do that to him."

Mullins somehow managed to take the freak incident on the chin. "It's just one of those things," he said philosophically. "Galopin Des Champs was doing everything right the whole race. He landed properly and just slipped after landing." He was no doubt consoled by what could be to come. He had a sound horse who was none the worse for his unfortunate spill.

★★★★

A MONTH later we got another treat from Galopin Des Champs. Mullins resisted the temptation to step him up to three miles at the Punchestown festival and instead opted for Fairyhouse's Easter meeting. The BoyleSports Gold Cup Novice Chase had another small field but his three rivals were rated 149, 153 and 154.

Master McShee, a Grade 1 winner at Christmas, tried to pester Galopin Des Champs rounding the final bend but was swatted away in a few strides. The race was over a long way out. This time the winning distance was 18 lengths and the RPR was 177.

▲ Golden potential: Galopin Des Champs and Paul Townend after their victory in the Grade 1 Ladbrokes Novice Chase at Leopardstown; inset top, Townend with his trophy for the BoyleSports Gold Cup Novice Chase at Fairyhouse; previous page, action from the Turners Novices' Chase at Cheltenham in which he fell at the final fence
▼ Galopin Des Champs puts in a perfect jump on his chasing debut before being pictured with Townend in the winner's enclosure

There was only one thing we needed to know afterwards and Mullins didn't hesitate in telling us. "I reckon Galopin Des Champs is a Gold Cup horse," he said. And there it was. The sentence we craved so much.

He added: "I'll have to discuss that with Greg and Audrey [Turley, owners] but he looks a horse for the Gold Cup. Once he changed gear between the last two it was all over bar jumping the last.

"He just seemed to be on a wrong stride and Paul let the horse decide. He put down lovely and got over it. He quickened away after the last and Paul couldn't pull him up going around the bend."

Townend couldn't pull him up after his "extraordinary" chasing debut at Leopardstown either. How good could he be? Perhaps only A Plus Tard has the potential to give us an answer to that.

St Patrick's Day, 2023. A Plus Tard v Galopin Des Champs in the Cheltenham Gold Cup. The master against the most precocious apprentice we have seen for some time. What a prospect.

WHEN WE RACE.
EVERY
BODY
WINS.

THE
BIGGER
PICTURE

The Katy Price-trained Premier D'Troice and Ben Poste plough on through the mud to come home fourth of the five finishers in a gruelling 3m5f handicap chase at Lingfield in February

EDWARD WHITAKER (RACINGPOST.COM/PHOTOS)

Constitution Hill capped an incredible first season for Nicky Henderson
with a stunning runaway triumph in the Supreme Novices' Hurdle

THE SPECIAL ONE

By Nick Pulford

THE four days of Cheltenham 2021 were dark times for British trainers. Even Nicky Henderson, for so long the best festival trainer of them all, could not escape the gloom. Amid a virtual Irish clean sweep, one of the most worrying signs for the health of the home team was that the Seven Barrows maestro could not muster a single runner in the Grade 1 novice hurdles for the first time since 1998.

For Henderson, however, the brightest of lights was about to appear. On the weekend a sobering 2020-21 season drew to a close in Britain, a four-year-old gelding by Blue Bresil made a promising debut in Ireland at the Tipperary point-to-point course, finishing a head second for trainer Warren Ewing. In partnership with Barry Geraghty, Ewing had bought the foal who came to be named Constitution Hill at the age of eight months, and now Henderson's former stable jockey was instrumental in persuading his

old boss to add the once-raced pointer to his string. Four weeks later, at the Goffs UK Spring Sale, the deal was done for £120,000.

Henderson had bought a gem for a relative bargain sum in today's high-rolling jumps market. Ewing knew it already – "he was always a special one," he said later – and Henderson was soon to realise what a rare talent had arrived at Seven Barrows. Within the space of just three runs, culminating in a devastating performance on the opening day of Cheltenham 2022, Constitution Hill announced

himself not just as the best of his generation but as one of the standout novice hurdlers in any era.

★★★★

SOME of the early signs had not been so good, as Henderson divulged when he first talked about Constitution Hill at length following a winning debut at Sandown in December. "He holds the whole string up every morning when we're walking and trotting," he said. "After two months I phoned Warren and Barry and said, 'What on earth have you sold

me? He's not even a racehorse.' But then when he pulls out and you press the button, he just disappears."

The Sandown field included the promising Might I, already a smart winner on his debut, but Constitution Hill disappeared from his view too as he raced 14 lengths clear in remarkably impressive fashion. Harry Fry, Might I's trainer, had a good yardstick and knew Constitution Hill measured up well. "To see him beaten 14 lengths was something of a shock. It would appear we may have run into something rather special," he said.

A Racing Post Rating of 148 was in the top bracket for a racecourse debut over hurdles and the time was nearly seven seconds quicker than the Listed handicap hurdle later on the card. Constitution Hill was already 10-1 for the Supreme and Henderson's post-race comments made clear there would

be much more to come.

"He can't be fit as he's fatter than me," he said. "He's the most extraordinary creature I've come across in years. He'll go back to his stable and go to sleep now. You love horses like that. It's fascinating trying to work horses out, that's the fun of the game."

Five weeks later the special one was back at Sandown for the Grade 1 Tolworth Novices' Hurdle and massively expected to win despite the heavy ground. On only his second start the 2-5 favourite was the cover star of the Saturday Racing Post, which posed the question: "Is this jumping's next big thing?"

Henderson had his own query. "The ground is a definite question mark," he said. "It's up in the air whether he'll handle it. The ground will be horrible." He added that he was hoping Constitution Hill's first run "wasn't a flash in the pan" but

there was no danger of that, nor of the Sandown gluepot having any effect, with rider Nico de Boinville reporting that he knew within ten strides of setting off to the start that it wouldn't be a problem.

The new star of Seven Barrows raced well clear again to score by 12 lengths and Henderson, who wasn't at Sandown as he was self-isolating with a bout of Covid, called it an "extraordinary" performance. "You have to say he's a very good horse," he added, "but how good he is I just don't know – he's just seriously good."

Among the many experts impressed with the now 2-1 favourite for the Supreme was Geraghty, who had seen the

development of Constitution Hill for three and a half years before he was passed on to Henderson. "You have to be very impressed with him and even as a foal we were happy from the day we got him," Geraghty said. "He always impressed with everything he did. At all stages through his breaking

▶ *Continues page 68*

▼ Glorious isolation: Constitution Hill wins the Supreme Novices' Hurdle by a yawning 22 lengths

◀ Shining star: Michael Buckley with Constitution Hill at Nicky Henderson's owners' day in September

and pre-training he was good. His schooling was always good. He was always going the right way and maturing physically. He was turning into the type of horse you hoped he would be as a foal."

✶✶✶✶

MICHAEL BUCKLEY, Henderson's great friend and a long-standing owner at Seven Barrows, had another star in his white and black colours, perhaps one to rank even higher in time than his 2012 Queen Mother Champion Chase winner Finian's Rainbow. But the rise of another top novice inevitably brought back memories of those he had lost such as Spirit Son, who was struck down by a freak virus after his one season over hurdles brought Aintree victory over Cue Card and a close second in the Supreme, and most especially The Proclamation.

Constitution Hill's Tolworth was close to the 32nd anniversary of The Proclamation's death following a fall at Ascot on his second start over fences and that desperate time was at the forefront of Buckley's mind in the Sandown winner's enclosure. "Even now it feels painful," he said. "I remember getting a letter from Nicky the following week with tear stains on it. We've had a lot of tears together as well as some great times."

It was Buckley that Geraghty first alerted to Constitution Hill's potential. "Michael and I talk regularly and he asked me if I had any nice young horses. This was back when Constitution Hill was a three-year-old. I told him I had a nice horse by Blue Bresil who I thought was very smart. It grew from there," said Geraghty, who rode Finian's Rainbow to Champion Chase victory. "I rode lots of winners for Michael over the years and he was always a great supporter. Even through tougher times, injuries and the like, he was always there for you. He's someone I'm very close to and I'm delighted with the way it's working out."

✶✶✶✶

THE story would soon take the most thrilling twist at Cheltenham. All season Henderson had talked about his "extremely exciting" team of novice hurdlers – in sharp contrast to the previous season's empty hand – and in the unbeaten Jonbon he had a serious rival to Constitution Hill in the Supreme, while the ever-dangerous Willie Mullins fielded Dysart Dynamo, who went off 9-4 joint-favourite with Constitution Hill.

In his two Sandown victories Constitution Hill had won by a combined total of 26 lengths and now

▸ *Continues page 70*

Supreme mark on Racing Post Ratings

Constitution Hill was given a Racing Post Rating of 172 for his devastating Supreme victory in a fast time, replacing Altior (166) as the highest-rated winner of a Cheltenham novice hurdle in the history of RPRs.

He was the top-rated hurdler of the season overall on RPRs and in the Anglo-Irish Jumps Classifications. His official rating of 170 was the highest for a novice hurdler since the classifications were introduced in 1999-2000, eclipsing the 168 given to Iris's Gift after he was second in the 2003 Stayers' Hurdle behind Baracouda.

TOP-RATED HURDLERS IN 2021-22

RPR	Horse
172	Constitution Hill
169	Flooring Porter
168	Honeysuckle*, Klassical Dream
166	Epatante*
165	Champ, Sire Du Berlais, Teahupoo

*Includes 7lb mares' allowance

Did you know farriery is a registered profession?

It is illegal in Great Britain to practice farriery if unregistered

For the welfare of your horse or pony ask to see your farrier's registration card or check the Register at **www.farrier-reg.gov.uk**

frc@farrier-reg.gov.uk

01733 319911

Farriers Registration Council

he was so dominant that he almost matched that in one fell swoop on what is supposed to be the most demanding stage of all.

The big three pulled well clear of their rivals but the front-running Dysart Dynamo crashed out at the third-last, leaving the race between Henderson's pair. As a contest it did not last long, with De Boinville soon easing Constitution Hill to the front and going further clear with every stride. The winning margin was a yawning 22 lengths and the clock stopped at 3min 34.35sec, three-quarters of a second quicker than Annie Power's Old course record in the 2016 Champion Hurdle. "Staggering" was De Boinville's verdict.

It was a sensational opening to the festival and no wonder Buckley was making big plans in the Cheltenham winner's enclosure. "He's obviously a hugely talented horse," the excited owner said. "He's only five, so he's very young. So why not win the Champion Hurdle and then one day win the Gold Cup? That's the sort of double that not many horses do. I just pray he stays in one piece."

This was a day for dreaming and Henderson, back with a bang in the Grade 1 novice hurdles, was as awestruck as anyone. "Jonbon is a very good horse, so to do that to him is remarkable," he said. "It's extraordinary that he's a genuine two-miler. He'd stay two and a half miles standing on his head, I think, but he has an enormous turn of foot. It's as if he's racing two gears below everything else because it's all so easy for him. And the turbo works. You press a button and it works."

Push-button brilliance of this ilk is so rare that many had to go back to the ill-fated Golden Cygnet's acclaimed Supreme victory in 1978 for a valid comparison. A mark of 172 for Constitution Hill made it the best performance on Racing Post Ratings in any festival novice hurdle and, for good measure, there was a notable form boost three weeks later when Jonbon won the Grade 1 Top Novices' Hurdle at Aintree.

Special. Extraordinary. Staggering. Constitution Hill deserved every plaudit. This wasn't hype, this was hyper achievement.

'We can dream about anything now'

Nicky Henderson was not alone in mounting a British fightback in the Grade 1 novice races at the 2022 Cheltenham Festival. Alan King and Venetia Williams also turned back the clock to more successful times for the home team by producing a pair of classy winners in a highly competitive chasing division.

King had last won at the festival in 2015 and has turned increasingly to the Flat in the years since, but he arrived this time holding a favourite's chance with Edwardstone in the Arkle Chase.

The 5-2 shot might have been in the race the year before but he unseated on his first attempt at chasing in December 2020 and was sent back over hurdles, finishing fifth in the County Hurdle at the festival.

A second attempt at chasing last season also started disappointingly when Edwardstone was brought down at Warwick but this time King persevered with him. Less than a fortnight later Edwardstone got off the mark over fences at the same track and that started him on a roll. Next he won the Grade 1 Henry VIII at Sandown, followed by a pair of Grade 2s, and went into the Arkle on a five-timer.

The eight-year-old delivered in style, seeing off Irish outsider Gabynako by four and a quarter lengths to end King's festival drought and give jockey Tom Cannon his first winner at the meeting.

Patience had been key. "We didn't start racing Edwardstone until he was five. He was just two or three years in the making," King said. "I always thought he was very good but these good horses don't happen overnight. It has been a team effort."

The revitalisation of the British chasing ranks was confirmed with a one-two in the Brown Advisory Novices' Chase when L'Homme Presse, the 9-4 favourite, and Ahoy Senor went off as the first two in the betting and finished in the same order in the race.

The Williams-trained L'Homme Presse had a similar profile to Edwardstone, arriving at the festival on a five-timer after an impressive rise that included a Grade 1 victory at Sandown, in his case in the Scilly Isles in February. He looked even better stepped up to 3m½f for the first time at Cheltenham, jumping impressively despite the testing conditions. Staying on powerfully, he scored by three and a half lengths, although the form was emphatically turned around by Ahoy Senor in the Grade 1 Mildmay at Aintree three weeks later.

This was a first Grade 1 winner at the festival for Williams, who had not scored there since 2013, and, like Cannon on Edwardstone, it was jockey Charlie Deutsch's first success at the meeting.

Williams' high regard for L'Homme Presse was clear in her post-race comments. "I haven't felt so sick in a race," she admitted. "I can't be more thrilled. It was lovely to hear the crowd cheer every time he put in one of his spectacular leaps. We can dream about anything now."

The ultimate dream is the Cheltenham Gold Cup. With British pride restored by last season's top novice chasers, the big prizes are back in sight.

▼ Britain's got talent: L'Homme Presse soars to his first Grade 1 victory in the Scilly Isles Novices' Chase; above, Edwardstone jumps the last in the Arkle

IN THE PICTURE

Carberry in winning form on Dancing With The Stars

NINA CARBERRY handled the pressure of being favourite with her usual aplomb to win Ireland's Dancing With The Stars competition in the live TV final on March 27, comparing her success to her memorable Irish Grand National triumph on Organisedconfusion in 2011.

Carberry, 36, who retired from the saddle in 2018 after being one of the most successful amateur jockeys of all time with 423 winners, was immediately installed as 3-1 favourite when she was announced among 12 celebrity contestants for Dancing With The Stars. Paired with professional dancer Pasquale La Rocca, she played down her chances at first.

"I took it on thinking it would be fine but, no, it's the hardest thing I've done in my whole life," she said after two weeks of training before the show opened on RTE Television in January.

"It's a complete culture shock, but I'm really relishing the challenge and excited to give it a go. I have a bit of balance from riding horses, but dancing is all about posture and it's very difficult."

The seven-time Cheltenham Festival winner quickly found her feet, shortening to 2-1 after an impressive first dance, and continued to sparkle throughout the show's 12-week run. With the Irish racing community rallying support, most entertainingly with the TikTok dance videos performed by eight-time champion jumps trainer Noel Meade and his wife Derville, Carberry was hot favourite for the final and delivered a near-perfect performance. She lifted the glitterball trophy after earning 59 points out of 60 with her Viennese waltz and show dance.

After the final she said: "The support from this industry has been amazing. Between Noel and Derville doing the TikTok videos, the jockeys and the trainers wishing me well, it's like winning the Irish Grand National all over again. The reception we got was similar to winning the Irish National.

"Everyone comes together in racing and that was driving me on. I wanted to do everyone in racing proud. I'm delighted I was able to dance well and repay everyone's faith in me."

The mother of two said her daughters, Rosie, 4, and Holly, 2, got a big kick out of following her progress. "It's been unbelievable, a weird but very exciting journey," Carberry said. "It's been something different for the girls. A bit of glam, make-up and dresses – they're really into that and only remember me as a dancer now. They don't remember me as a jockey at all."

Pictures: RTE

FLYING

MACHINE

Nature Strip jetted in from Sydney to blow away the opposition in the King's Stand and give trainer Chris Waller a treasured Royal Ascot triumph

By Lee Mottershead

BASED solely on what we witnessed at Royal Ascot, one might have been left wondering who really did deserve to be called the world's best racehorse.

For although Baaeed was ruthlessly dominant in the race that got the party started, the defining moment of that memorable Tuesday afternoon came just over an hour later. It was produced by a horse who won by further than Baaeed, with even more authority and with an abundance of star quality. The truly smashing, positively dashing hero of the Ascot opening day was Nature Strip.

We hailed the horse but also his trainer. Chris Waller, the Sydney-based New Zealander who so meticulously prepared Winx to win 33 consecutive races, the final 25 of them at Group 1 level, is the dominant force in Australian racing. As he prepared to saddle Nature Strip in the King's Stand Stakes, he had amassed no fewer than 136 Group 1 victories since breaking his top-flight duck in 2008.

He had not, however, won a race in Britain. He had barely even had a runner in Britain, having reluctantly decided against bringing Winx to the royal

meeting in 2017. Indeed, not since he was represented in 2015 by Royal Ascot runner-up Brazen Beau had Waller sent a horse to the other side of the world. Win, lose or draw, this trip was always going to mean a lot to him.

★★★★

ON the Friday morning prior to the week of the royal meeting, Waller brought both Nature Strip and Platinum Jubilee Stakes contender Home Affairs for an early Ascot sighter. Together with compatriot Artorius, they galloped individually up half a mile of the straight track. Waller and his English assistant Charlie Duckworth watched from the steppings of the grandstand, surrounded by some of Nature Strip's many syndicate owners. They liked what they saw.

So, in an additional sense, did members of the British racing press. For while his two star sprinters cooled down in the pre-parade ring, Waller orchestrated his own photoshoot, standing between the speedballs and giving the cameras exactly what they wanted.

"This is a rarity in racing – a trainer actually helping to organise the photos," said photographer Steven Cargill, the object of whose admiration then made clear his desire to assist those who would be

writing about his horses. "Thanks everyone for coming here this morning," said Waller, inserting for good measure: "If you need anything from us during the week, you'll find us very accessible."

He was not just accessible but also strikingly honest. That was evident later that morning when Waller sat down with the Racing Post for a lengthy interview, during which he revealed he had already been shopping in London and, on the strong advice of Duckworth's father, purchased a new top hat to replace the one that had travelled with him from Sydney.

"Mr Duckworth advised me it was time for a change," said Waller, with a smile. Over the hour that followed there were more smiles but also tears, for as anyone who has watched him in the minutes following a major triumph will know, he is a man in touch with his emotions.

Those emotions rose to the surface when he spoke about the pressures of training Winx, the importance of his team and much more besides, including being spoken of in the same breath as Aidan O'Brien, Sir Michael Stoute and Andre Fabre.

"I don't let myself think I should be compared alongside those great trainers," he said, quite obviously meaning every word. "I would just rather not think that way. It's easier

not to. That's why I get emotional talking about it."

By now, his voice was choked. Rare indeed are the racing professionals willing – or perhaps even able – to be so refreshingly open.

"History. Tradition," he said when asked what other things cause him to wobble. It felt like every word was wrapped in sincerity. "I also don't think in advance about winning big races," he continued. "When the horse crosses the line in front, it hits you in the face. If that happens next week, it will be the first time I'll think about winning at Royal Ascot."

Then he paused, a simple "yeah" coming a second or two later to emphasise the point.

★★★★

UNLIKE Waller, Wesley Ward already knew all about winning at the royal jamboree. Ascot's favourite American also knew all about talking up his Ascot raiders. There was certainly no lack of confidence behind his King's Stand challenger Golden Pal, a Coolmore-owned four-year-old who had positively smashed his way out of the gates when landing the 2021 Breeders' Cup Turf Sprint. He would be a tough nut to crack. The Europeans in the
➤ *Continues page 76*

NATURE STRIP

RPR view

Nature Strip produced an extraordinary performance to win the King's Stand Stakes by a whopping four and a half lengths, looking better than ever in returning an RPR of 129. To win by so far in a fast time was some effort and he rates the best winner of the race since it was upgraded to a Group 1 in 2008. *Paul Curtis*

King's Stand field would turn out to be extremely soft nuts.

In their defence, Nature Strip made his British debut below only Baaeed in the sport's global rankings. He had bagged 20 of his 37 races, eight of them in Group 1 company. There had also been an exceptionally lucrative success in The Everest, whose £3.79 million first prize rather dwarfed the King's Stand's £283,550 winning cheque. This, however, was not a mission about money.

"Whether or not I win this year or ten years from now, I just want to be part of it," had been another of Waller's insightful comments on the Friday. As the 16 runners entered the stalls, the betting market had concluded he was indeed going to be left waiting. Nature Strip drifted out to 9-4 in the minutes leading up to the off, while Golden Pal shortened to 15-8 favouritism. He was the one the punters wanted. They could not have been more wrong.

No cameras captured Waller watching it all unfold. He viewed the action in Ascot's weighing room, alone with his thoughts save for the company of Duckworth, their union a symbol of the Anglo-Australian camaraderie that would soon break out all around them. They saw Golden Pal start with the urgency of a horse running in the Queen Alexandra. They then saw him rushed to the front by Irad Ortiz but they also saw James McDonald – another Kiwi who has made Sydney his home – enjoying a gloriously easy time aboard Nature Strip. What came next was even more enjoyable.

As Golden Pal went backwards, Nature Strip surged forwards. "The way he quickened on the rise and executed his gallop was unbelievable – the feeling coming up that rise was something else," McDonald said when reflecting on how his mount had

stormed further and further clear after grabbing the lead with just over two furlongs to run. At the line, four and a half lengths separated him from runner-up Twilight Calls. Khaadem was closer but he had left Jamie Spencer behind in the stalls.

"I got a bit of a scare at the 50 [metres] when the horse came to me," McDonald said. "I didn't think any horse could cope with him, so when a horse did come to him I was so surprised. It was a relief there was no jockey on!"

★★★★

IN THE weighing room, Waller and Duckworth had fixed their glare on a television whose sound was muted. No audio accompaniment was needed.

"It was incredible," Duckworth remarked. "I said to Chris: 'Well done.' He said back to me: 'No, well done to us both.' He was blown away. I don't think he believes it's really happening, a bit like a dream you don't believe can possibly come true."

This was a dream that did come true. From their position on the running rail, four men proudly unfurled a large Australian flag. Two of them were holding tinnies. At one end of the paddock, another group of Aussie racegoers repeated their pre-race cry of "Go, the Strip!" Very much not an Aussie, the former All Blacks coach Sir Steve Hansen, one of the winner's many jubilant owners, provided positive proof that big boys do cry.

"It's a privilege to be part of this," he said, struggling to get out the words. Remarkably, his trainer had managed to remain composed through a series of television appearances. Then, reminded of his insistence in the Racing Post interview that he would not contemplate winning until he won, the feelings rushed out of him.

"I didn't dare think about it, even after the race," he admitted, now allowing himself to well up. "It's very special. Obviously I get emotional when horses win, but to win here really is a dream for a trainer, a strapper, a jockey or an owner. It means a lot."

He was so very happy. It was so very easy to be happy for him.

Naval Crown leads Godolphin one-two

The Australian raiders were repelled in the Platinum Jubilee Stakes on the final day of Royal Ascot as Godolphin's Naval Crown caused a 33-1 upset in a one-two finish with stablemate Creative Force.

The Charlie Appleby-trained pair were separated by a neck, with Naval Crown (*below*) sticking to the stands' rail under James Doyle from his high draw and William Buick's mount Creative Force just beaten in a photo from stall one.

Artorius, from the Melbourne stable of Anthony and Sam Freedman, was half a length back in third and the other Australian challenger, Chris Waller's 5-2 favourite Home Affairs, was a disappointing 20th in his bid to follow up stablemate Nature Strip's triumph in the King's Stand.

"We thought we'd be following in the Australian horses based on what happened earlier in the week," admitted Appleby, who said the narrow margin at the line reflected what had happened in the build-up.

"William rode in a piece of work involving the two of them the other day and came back and said, 'Charlie, I'm going to have a job splitting them'. There really wasn't a lot between them at home," he said.

Remarkably, this was the second year in a row that the two Appleby horses had finished first and second at Royal Ascot. In 2021 the roles were reversed when Creative Force took the Jersey Stakes from Naval Crown.

HIGH SUMMER

Bred out of a castoff, unsold at auction and a slow starter in her racing career, Highfield Princess rose to stardom with an incredible winning spree in the Group 1 sprints

By David Carr

STRANGE times bring strange stories and the past year was full of remarkable tales that strained the edges of credulity.

Think of the diner at a restaurant in China who spotted a set of footprints in the outdoor courtyard. Experts arrived and it turned out they were left by a couple of dinosaurs around 100 million years ago. Or the Los Angeles woman using a vending machine to buy a lottery ticket who got nudged, accidentally pressed the wrong number . . . and ended up winning $10 million. Or the man on horseback who stunned onlookers as he rode up to the drive-in window of a McDonald's in east London and trotted off again with 100 Chicken McNuggets in his saddle bag.

Yet those seem almost common or garden compared to the extraordinary saga of a mare from North Yorkshire that is more the stuff of Roy of the Rovers than the Racing Post. Indeed, it lends itself perfectly to a comic book because this fairytale is an editor's dream with each episode ending on a genuine cliffhanger. Nor is it hard for a reader to root for such an engaging cast, each with a backstory that belies Flat racing's reputation as a game for toffs and millionaires.

Take Jason Hart. From the hotbed of riding talent that is Hawick, he was a passionate rugby player whose life changed when he ditched a club tour to ride in pony races instead and who showed that was the right career choice when he was crowned champion apprentice in 2013. Many a successful claimer takes time to establish himself when his allowance disappears and it was only in 2021 that the personable Scot really hit the heights that had looked within his grasp, riding 100 winners in a season for the first time.

John Quinn was already proven at the top level, not that he is the sort to shout about it – or about anything at all. The genial Irishman learned plenty as a conditional jockey with Edward O'Grady and then Jimmy FitzGerald, as he has shown since taking out a training licence nearly 30 years ago. Over the decades his softly spoken brogue has been heard innumerable times in winner's enclosures across Britain and beyond, often at Royal Ascot and the Cheltenham Festival.

The owner of his Malton yard is the other unlikely hero of this story – indeed, the man whose action caused it to be written. John Fairley, who was in charge of Channel 4 Racing in the heyday of the sport's coverage on television, is a breeder as well as a broadcaster.

He started something special when he paid 18,000gns for Pure Illusion at the Tattersalls December Sale in Newmarket in 2016, motivated in part by the desire to replace a mare who had died suddenly when in foal. That was not an obvious bargain at the time, with Godolphin clearly happy to get rid of a mare whose first five foals were nothing out of the ordinary, but the following year her sixth offspring, Cardsharp, sprinkled stardust on the pedigree by winning the July Stakes and being placed in the Gimcrack and Middle Park.

But it was really lucky number seven: the foal that Pure Illusion was carrying when she went under the hammer, a bay filly born the following May. Not that Fairley's good fortune was obvious straight away. The new arrival failed to sell when she returned to Tattersalls as a yearling – the bidding stopped at 29,000gns.

★★★★

NOR did his luck change when he put the youngster into training with Quinn. The newly named Highfield Princess pulled a muscle behind and could not run as a two-year-old. When she made it to the track the following summer, she was beaten a minimum of eight lengths in three Class 5 events – albeit she bumped into future Prix du Moulin winner Dreamloper when fourth in what must have been the best fillies' novice stakes ever run at Redcar.

She was awarded a BHA mark of 57, which meant the official handicapper rated her barely good enough to win an average seller, and she finished only third when racing off it for the first time at Doncaster. But that placing was a step forward – earning a rise of a whole pound – and she built on it by scoring a first win in a seven-furlong handicap at Ayr next time out.

Three further successes followed at Chelmsford as the three-year-old climbed another 22lb up the handicap and earned a crack at a Listed race at Deauville, where she faded into 11th after forcing the pace under a local jockey.

Job done. After squeezing four wins out of a cheaply bred filly with a good pedigree, the sensible thing would have been to head to the paddocks. But there is nothing sensible about this story and the next chapter began with Quinn believing there was more improvement to come and being proved right when she scored again at Haydock in May 2021.

Then came a stroke of luck on which all good tales turn. Highfield Princess was the very last horse to make the cut for the Buckingham Palace Stakes at Royal Ascot and she grabbed her chance to shine on the biggest stage by winning eased down – not a sight you often see in a 28-runner handicap.

"I thought she was at the top of her mark, but clearly not!" Hart said after riding his first Royal Ascot winner. His willing partner proved the point by following up in a Listed race at Chelmsford and running a string of good races in smart company, culminating in sixth place in the British Champions Sprint at Ascot when dropped to six furlongs for the first time.

She ended her second season exactly 50lb higher in the BHA handicap than when first assessed, a seven-time winner with black type aplenty. An outstanding breeding prospect.

But Roy of the Rovers doesn't quit when the biggest prizes are in sight. Quinn told Fairley he felt Highfield Princess could win a Group 3 race in 2022 as she was still improving. So she raced on

▸ *Continues page 80*

HIGHFIELD PRINCESS

and a £77,000 first prize in the seven-furlong fillies' and mares' race on All-Weather Championships finals day at Newcastle on Good Friday meant she was well ahead of the game even before the turf season had properly started.

Next she dropped back to six furlongs again to win the Group 2 1895 Duke of York Stakes, showing an astonishing cruising speed and seeing off established sprinters to score by nearly three lengths.

What a perfect ending to the story. A new high and a glorious victory on her local course. As Fairley marvelled at the time: "We bred her and she's in our own stables, I see her out of the window literally every day. Living in Yorkshire as long as I have, to win a Group race like that, at York, is tremendous."

Except that anyone familiar with this tale was wary of saying we had reached the 'lived happily ever after' stage. That 'ending' at York was actually just a warm-up for the most memorable summer a sprinter has enjoyed in many a year.

The obvious next step was a Group 1 and Highfield Princess made her first attempt in the Platinum Jubilee Stakes at Royal Ascot, finishing a close sixth behind Naval Crown. That was encouragement enough to go for the Prix Maurice de Gheest at Deauville, where she faced Naval Crown again as well as Commonwealth Cup winner Perfect Power.

In true comic book fashion, Highfield Princess rose to the challenge in breathtaking style. Not at all troubled to match strides with some of the top six- and seven-furlong horses around, she came home readily clear of subsequent Haydock Sprint Cup winner Minzaal.

▶ *Continues page 82*

▶ On a roll: Highfield Princess takes the Duke of York Stakes; top, trainer John Quinn; previous page, an easy win in the Flying Five at the Curragh

IRISH INJURED JOCKEYS

Help when the going gets tough

— 2022 —

Irish Injured Jockeys, would like to thank everybody for their generosity and support throughout the year. A random selection of our supporters is displayed above. All your efforts are really appreciated and are vital to enable our goals.

Thank you from all in IIJ!

Email: info@irishinjuredjockeys.com

www.irishinjuredjockeys.com

HIGHFIELD PRINCESS

▶ Northern powerhouse: Jason Hart shows his delight as Highfield Princess lands the Nunthorpe Stakes; below, John Fairley leads his mare into the York winner's enclosure

★★★★

AFTER the race, Quinn's son and assistant Sean was asked about future plans. "She's in the Nunthorpe in 12 days," he said, "but that'll probably come too soon . . ." But why worry about a 12-day turnaround and just a second-ever try at five furlongs, in Britain's biggest race at the trip, when you have a wondermare on your hands?

Not only did Highfield Princess turn up at York, she coped with the shorter distance as though she had been racing at it all her life, tracking the brilliantly speedy two-year-old The Platinum Queen before leaving her for dead in the final furlong to score by two and a half lengths.

The Flying Five Stakes at the Curragh took place just three weeks later, on ground softer than she had shown her best form previously and with no fewer than 19 runners. Yet if anything Highfield Princess was even more impressive, always looking to be cruising and just pushed out to triumph by more than three lengths.

It completed an astonishing Group 1 hat-trick in just five weeks. Winning three top-level sprints in a row over any time period is something special: think of Dayjur, Black Caviar, Blue Point and Muhaarar – and none of those did it after being beaten off 57 on their handicap debut.

How did she do it? Quinn believes that some horses simply get quicker as they mature and find their strength. Linford Christie showed how human sprinters can peak late in their athletic life. And just before Highfield Princess embarked on her Group 1 winning spree, Jamaican Shelly-Ann Fraser-Pryce underlined the point by proving too fast for her younger rivals in Eugene, Oregon and landing her fifth 100m world championship gold at the age of 35.

Quinn certainly understands the true significance of Highfield Princess's incredible tale. Asked to sum up what the whole remarkable story means, he said: "It gives everyone hope."

'A fairy story'
What the three main players said about Highfield Princess

John Fairley, owner-breeder

"I've suddenly been terribly lucky on the track. This is easily the best horse I've had. It's the ups and downs of this wonderful business, isn't it? It's a fairy story, a complete fairy story."

John Quinn, trainer

"Wow. What a mare. She's unbelievable. Apart from my family, she means everything to me. I love her. It's phenomenal what she's done."

Jason Hart, jockey

"To get a first Group 1 on home soil on her means so much. It's really emotional because it's what you strive to do from the first moment you sit in the saddle."

IN THE PICTURE

Buick in total control as he ends long wait for first championship

CHAMPIONS DAY 2021 was fraught and ultimately fruitless for William Buick in his championship quest when he lost out by two winners to Oisin Murphy despite a determined late surge. Twelve months on, Ascot's end-of-season highlight was altogether more relaxed for the Godolphin rider *(pictured with his son Thomas)*.

Buick, 34, was crowned Britain's champion Flat jockey at last and he could enjoy the occasion without pressure, having long since had the title wrapped up. With Murphy serving a 14-month ban for Covid-19 and alcohol breaches, Buick dominated the title race from the start and finished on 157 winners, 66 clear of runner-up Hollie Doyle.

It was the most one-sided contest since Ryan Moore defeated Richard Hughes by 70 winners in 2008 – the same year in which Buick shared the apprentice title with David Probert. Then 20, Buick was seen as a future champion but had been left waiting, having finished runner-up in 2015, 2020 and 2021.

"Eighteen-year-old me would say 'what's taken you so long?'" Buick told Great British Racing as he finally got his hands on the trophy. "It's something I've really wanted to achieve for quite a long time and obviously it's taken me a few years, but it's fantastic.

"My father was an eight-time champion jockey in Scandinavia, so it's great to be able to achieve it, and I feel I've done it in the way that I would like to do it – to balance it with the big races, the big meetings, my main employer Godolphin, making sure that's at the forefront of my focus."

Buick's big-race victories for Godolphin in Britain included the St James's Palace Stakes on Coroebus, while he travelled abroad for Classic wins on Native Trail (Irish 2,000 Guineas) and Modern Games (Poule d'Essai des Poulains). He will have plenty of ammunition again for next year's Classics, including his Gimcrack winner Noble Style.

With Murphy returning early in 2023, Buick's agent Tony Hind was already thinking about renewing rivalry with the three-time champion. "It doesn't matter what sport you're in, you always have to defend your crown and that's what we'll be aiming to do," Hind said.

Joining Buick as a title winner on Champions Day was Benoit de la Sayette, who took the apprentice crown after a hard-fought battle with Harry Davies. Both are graduates of Britain's thriving pony racing scene.

De la Sayette, 19, who is attached to John and Thady Gosden's powerful stable, racked up 61 winners to take the title by six from Davies. He joins Buick, Murphy, Tom Marquand, David Egan, Jason Hart and Cieren Fallon on the recent roll of honour.

Picture: EDWARD WHITAKER (RACINGPOST.COM/PHOTOS)

STAYING POWER

Kyprios took control of the long-distance division with a string of impressive displays from Ascot to Longchamp

By Lewis Porteous

WHAT a difference a year makes. Royal Ascot 2021 was an unpleasant experience for Kyprios. A leading fancy for the Queen's Vase, he was spooked in the starting gate and ended up squeezing out from underneath the doors of his stall. Not only did he have to be withdrawn that day, he wasn't seen again for the rest of the year after badly bruising his back in his act of escapology.

Fast forward 12 months and Kyprios went back to Royal Ascot in June, fully recovered and ready for the biggest test of his burgeoning career in the Gold Cup. This time everything went smoothly. He had to battle to the end but his half-length victory confirmed him as the new staying star for Aidan O'Brien, giving the Ballydoyle trainer a record eighth Gold Cup in a sequence started by four-time hero Yeats.

Far from disappearing from view, as he had the previous year, Kyprios continued to shine bright. He cemented his supremacy in the staying division with a thrilling victory over Stradivarius and Trueshan in the Goodwood Cup and followed that with Classic success in the Irish St Leger and a most extraordinary display in the Prix du Cadran on Arc weekend. As he came down the Longchamp straight in glorious isolation, scoring by 20 lengths despite veering across the full width of the track, his dominance was absolute.

It was the most incredible end to a perfect six-race season. What a difference a year makes.

★★★★

AFTER two comfortable wins in Ireland, and with O'Brien's Gold Cup record impossible to ignore, Kyprios was sent off the 13-8 favourite in the Royal Ascot showpiece. Three-time winner Stradivarius was just behind him in the market at 2-1 and the others given a serious chance in the field of nine were Princess Zoe (13-2), second to Subjectivist the previous year, and St Leger runner-up Mojo Star (15-2).

In a contest Kyprios's rider Ryan Moore would later describe as "messy" and far from enjoyable to ride in, there was plenty of in-running drama. What should be the ultimate test of staying prowess in Flat racing turned into a trappy, tactical affair. One in which racing on the pace was the place to be.

For Moore that meant giving up his preferred inside position to move to the outer leaving Swinley Bottom – "I don't like doing that" – but however bad he thought his trip was going, it wasn't half as painful as it was for Stradivarius and Frankie Dettori. In similar fashion to the 2021 race, they found themselves closer to the back than the front and were forced widest of all to get a run in the straight.

Moore also had to fan to the centre of the track to make his move but Kyprios was always in front of Stradivarius, with Mojo Star sitting on his shoulder and ready to pounce. The two four-year-olds kicked first in the home straight, with Dettori having to wait momentarily until those rivals had progressed before finding daylight on the outside.

The gloves were off now, with Kyprios hitting the front before Mojo Star counter-punched. While the front two went toe-to-toe, Stradivarius closed in from behind. Deep in the final furlong, when stamina was finally called into play, it was Kyprios who found extra, inching clear of Mojo Star as Stradivarius's run petered out.

The three-time winner may have been luckless in running but at the line – where it matters most – the horse travelling strongest and with most purpose was Kyprios. "It wasn't a nice race to ride," the winning jockey said. "It wasn't a true test today but he was much the best and there will be lots of good days with him."

O'Brien, more animated than is often the case in the winner's enclosure, also conveyed a real sense that the team behind Kyprios were convinced he was the new force in the staying division. "He's brave, genuine and a great horse," he said. "Ryan gave him a marvellous ride and had belief in him. When he really wanted him, he answered. We think he's a horse to look forward to."

★★★★

WHAT everyone could look forward to next was a rematch between Kyprios and Stradivarius in the Goodwood Cup, where they were joined by the previous year's winner Trueshan. This was the ultimate showdown between the division's three heavyweights.

Trueshan had been Stradivarius's main rival for a couple of years but they had rarely met, owing to their different ground preferences. Once again Trueshan had been taken out of the Gold Cup because the going was too fast – instead running a career-best in the Northumberland Plate on the all-weather a week later – but good ground for day one of the Glorious meeting offered a level playing field.

Kyprios was the 6-4 favourite, with Trueshan 2-1 and Stradivarius 9-2. Stradivarius had a new rider, a result of the fallout from Ascot, but ultimately it made no difference to the end result. He was closer to Kyprios at the finish this time but crucially he was still behind him. So was Trueshan, but only after a thrilling battle where all three played their part.

Moore was keen to be handy on Kyprios and determined to make Stradivarius and Trueshan pass him if they were going to win. Hollie Doyle on Trueshan was the first to play her hand, rushing past Stradivarius on the right-hander into the home straight to join Kyprios in the front rank. The knock-on effect was that Stradivarius was trapped behind the first wave of runners, leaving Andrea Atzeni waiting for the cutaway with two furlongs to run before he could make his move.

▶▶ *Continues page 88*

Just inside the final furlong, as Kyprios turned Trueshan away, Stradivarius momentarily edged ahead on the inner but, as he had proved at Ascot, the final half-furlong is where Kyprios is at his strongest. As Moore asked for more, his partner answered and at the line they were a neck in front of the staying legend, with Trueshan a further length and a quarter back in third.

"What a race" yelled commentator Simon Holt and he wasn't wrong. Things may have been a little uncomfortable early in the straight for Stradivarius, who had been bidding for a fifth win in the race, but he was in the clear with enough time to spare. He lost precious little in defeat to a horse half his age and primed to be the benchmark in the staying division for years to come.

"The horse keeps plenty and is very lazy," O'Brien said. "If you want him to stay in first gear, he will. That's the way he is and always has been. He's got a lot of quality and stayers like him, with that class, are very special. I'd say we're only starting to see what's in there."

✶✶✶✶

THERE was further evidence of what lies beneath the bonnet when Kyprios dropped back to a mile and three-quarters for the Irish St Leger in September. For such a strong stayer, this was a different test but he had at least 6lb in hand on official ratings and confirmed that advantage. Responding gamely to Moore's urgings both as the stalls opened to take up a prominent position and in the closing stages, he was well in control by three-quarters of a length from the game but outclassed Hamish.

His three Group 1 wins on the bounce had all been secured by less than a length, without ever really looking like he would be beaten, but his fourth in the Prix du Cadran at Longchamp was of a different order entirely.

Back over two and a half miles and on very soft ground, by far the most testing surface he had encountered all year, Kyprios was asked to stride on before reaching the home turn. "It was just to try to keep him going really," Moore explained afterwards,

but the upshot was that his mount kept going and going, leaving his rivals gasping for air.

Victory seemed secure early in the straight as Kyprios opened up a yawning gap but he injected some late drama. With 200 metres to run he was on the far rail but from there he started to drift left. By the 100-metre mark he was halfway across the wide track and at the line he was on the stands' rail, albeit still 20 lengths in front. O'Brien revealed Kyprios had lost his off-fore shoe halfway up the straight. "Maybe that was a little bit of the reason [for the drift], maybe it wasn't, but I think he was just left in front too long," he said.

On Racing Post Ratings it was the best performance by a stayer in the 21st century with a mark of 128. That took him past the peak RPR of 126 Yeats achieved for his Goodwood Cup wins in 2006 and 2008 and which

▲ Golden rule: Kyprios (left) beats Mojo Star and Stradivarius (right) in the Gold Cup at Royal Ascot; below, his victories at Glorious Goodwood and Leopardstown in a six-race winning streak

Trueshan earned for his weight-carrying win in this year's Northumberland Plate. It was also superior to the best efforts of Stradivarius and Order Of St George (both 125).

On the jaw-dropping manner of victory, O'Brien said: "Ryan rode him handy all the way and his opponents just fell away as they turned into the straight. He has an unbelievable capacity for covering any amount of distance. He obviously has an incredible heart and lungs."

Brian Ellison, trainer of third-placed Tashkhan, offered his own view. "The winner's a machine, isn't he? Just a different ballgame," he said.

The game will continue in 2023 when Kyprios resumes at the age of five. Already on a six-race winning streak, he is the dominant player in his division. Next year could belong to him too.

THE ENTERTAINER

Stradivarius packed a record feat, Ascot drama and
a brave swansong into his final year on the track

By Lewis Porteous

THE news was summed up in six words. "The music has stopped for Stradivarius," was the perfect parting phrase from owner-breeder Bjorn Nielsen in September as he announced the retirement of his star stayer. A career of remarkable achievement, longevity and popularity was at an end. Yet his virtuoso performances will linger long in the memory.

The facts and figures were phenomenal. Nielsen's homebred chestnut won 20 of his 35 starts over seven seasons for racecourse earnings of £3,458,968. His 18 Group wins was a record by a horse trained in Europe and included four Goodwood Cups, three Ascot Gold Cups, three Lonsdale Cups and the Doncaster Cup twice. His haul of seven Group 1 races matched Yeats's record for a stayer. He also earned a £1 million bonus twice for winning the Stayers' Million series of races in 2018 and 2019 – a bonus that was discontinued as a result of his supremacy.

Numbers can tell only part of the story, however. What they fail to capture is the connection Stradivarius made with so many people, from Nielsen to trainer John Gosden and jockey Frankie Dettori and to the racing public who adored him.

The roars when he made his race-winning moves and the ovations on his biggest days were long and heartfelt. He could be hot-headed at times but his quirks only added to his appeal. He was a horse with character, individuality and spirit to go with his ability. A born entertainer.

Earlier in the summer Nielsen had revealed how he always had a sense that there was something different about Stradivarius. "The only picture I have with any horse I've bred is with Stradivarius," he said in a Racing Post interview. "It was in August 2014, six months after he was born, and it just so happened he was lying in the paddock and I took a photo with just me and him. It's the weirdest thing. I've bred around 20 horses a year for the last 20 years but he's the only one I've done that for. I suppose it was fate."

On the day the music stopped, Nielsen reflected again on what fate had brought him. "It was a fairytale from start to finish," he said.

★★★★

EVERY year seemed to start the same as the one before with Stradivarius but, with the thought of retirement still on hold, he set out at the start of 2022 with the principal objective of winning a fourth Gold Cup.

At the age of eight, history was against him but he started the season on a high by landing a third Yorkshire Cup and taking his unbeaten record at York to six, a winning streak that had begun in May 2018. If ever there was a needless announcement it was the request on the York public address to "please show your appreciation for Stradivarius".

As if anyone did not know they were in the presence of greatness. You could tell that by the neck-craning as he paraded back up the track, the cheers on his return to the winner's enclosure and the applause as he did a lap of honour in the parade ring.

While the old boy had shown his trademark turn of foot was still in full working order on the racecourse, his joint-trainer gave a glimpse post-race of the challenges he faced trying to prepare an eight-year-old entire for duties on the track rather than the breeding shed.

"He was a bundle of fun to saddle in the stables, on his hind legs," said Gosden, latterly sharing training duties with his son Thady. "Every time he saw a filly he started showing off. But he came over here and was as professional as ever. It's great to win six from six on the Knavesmire and be the leading Group-winning horse of all time in Europe. That takes some doing – if he was a gelding it would be a bit easier."

With his 18th Group win in the bag, breaking the record of 17 for a European-trained horse he had previously shared with Cirrus Des Aigles, Stradivarius headed on to Ascot for a chance to equal Yeats as a four-time winner of the Gold Cup.

Winner of Royal Ascot's marquee event in 2018, 2019 and 2020, he had endured a nightmare passage in 2021 that ended his domination of the race but, with the ground good to firm and just eight rivals in his way, the stars appeared to have aligned this time. Punters narrowly preferred Kyprios in the market at 13-8 but Stradivarius was not short of support at 2-1. Now all that was needed was a clean fight.

It started well, with Stradivarius sharply away on the inside under Dettori, but by the time the runners had completed the home straight for the first time, he had been shunted down the order behind a pace that was mediocre at best.

It made what followed somewhat predictable but no less painful to watch. Forced off the heels of the leaders and to the wide outside to launch his challenge, Stradivarius was already on the back foot when finally finding daylight in the home straight and, try as courageously as he did, he was never quite getting to the younger pair of Kyprios and Mojo Star. He was left just over a length adrift in third as Kyprios took the crown.

Dettori blamed Father Time for catching up with Stradivarius, but Gosden and Nielsen saw things a little differently. "There are younger horses there who were first and second, but I just wish we had been a little handier and not had to go around a wall of horses," Gosden said.

"I was a bit surprised after being in the box seat that we dropped back so far. The problem is, when they sprint you've got to get a run and he had to come widest of all, so his head was turned around to get a run. He had a chance in the last furlong but the race just slipped away on him. They had gone a pretty steady pace."

Nielsen, who looked ten years older than he had done five minutes earlier in Ascot's parade ring, left little doubt at whose hands he felt the defeat lay. "Let's just say the horse wasn't to blame," he said.

Soon after, Gosden and Dettori had the briefest of "sabbaticals" from their long-standing partnership but Nielsen decided it was time for change, turning to Andrea Atzeni for the ride
▸ *Continues page 92*

on Stradivarius in the Goodwood Cup.

Dettori was still present at Goodwood and even joined owner, trainer and new rider in the paddock before the Group 1, but there he stayed as Atzeni headed into battle. When it was time to return, Stradivarius did so as the gallant runner-up, failing by just a neck to beat Kyprios in a performance that proved Father Time had not quite caught up with Stradivarius.

★★★★

YET the clock was ticking louder. A bruised foot prevented Stradivarius from going for a seventh York success in the Lonsdale Cup and, with the setback taking longer than anticipated to dissipate, Nielsen decided it was finally time to retire his pride and joy.

Asked whether it represented a sad day for him personally, Nielsen said: "Yes and no. It has been a great thrill to watch him racing all these years but you always know they can't go on forever. We contemplated stopping him at the end of last season but he showed us he wanted to go again, which was remarkable in itself."

Stradivarius's incredible longevity at the top level had stretched from his first Group 1 appearance in 2017, when he won the Goodwood Cup, to his last in the same race five years later. There was so much to be grateful for.

"Even if I'm fortunate to win the Derby or the Arc at some point, I know I will never have another horse like him," Nielsen added. "He was hugely appreciated by the public. He had great presence when he went to

'The most extraordinary racehorse'

John Gosden, who trained Stradivarius throughout his career, paid a heartfelt tribute on the retirement of his staying star

"Stradivarius was the most extraordinary and unique racehorse. He always maintained his total commitment and enthusiasm. He exhibited joy in his training and has given enormous pleasure to everyone, both on and off the track.

"His constitution has been a marvel to behold and his exciting style of travelling easily in a race, and then quickening to pounce, reflected his character.

"As everyone noticed, he could be very vociferous and playful before a race and quite often put in a buck cantering off to the start. He was always an entertainer but with a tough, competitive mind, who was all business when the starting stalls opened.

"To his owner-breeder, to everyone at Clarehaven Stables and to his loving public, he has been a constant source of pleasure and excitement. He goes to stud with an amazing race record and enormous affection."

◀ Record breaker: an emotional Frankie Dettori after Stradivarius had won the Yorkshire Cup in May; right, more scenes from York; Bjorn Nielsen with a picture of him and Stradivarius as a foal; the 'people's horse' at home

Various records for star stayer

Stradivarius earned a place in racing history in May when breaking the record for the most Group wins by a horse trained in Europe since the Flat Pattern was created in 1971. Bjorn Nielsen's eight-year-old's victory in the Yorkshire Cup was his 18th Group win, breaking the record of 17 he had previously shared with Cirrus Des Aigles, *writes John Randall.*

Those 18 successes included four consecutive victories (2017-20) in the Goodwood Cup, equalling the record for the most wins in the same European Group 1 event held by Vinnie Roe (Irish St Leger), Yeats (Ascot Gold Cup) and Goldikova (Prix Rothschild). His Goodwood Cup four-timer made him the most prolific winner of a race that dates from 1812, surpassing Double Trigger, who won it three times in the 1990s.

Stradivarius also recorded an unprecedented nine wins in the traditional Cup races that make up the stayers' triple crown. His three wins in the Ascot Gold Cup, four in the Goodwood Cup and two in the Doncaster Cup enabled him to beat the record of seven set by Double Trigger. He won all three races in 2019, becoming only the seventh horse to complete the stayers' triple crown in the same year.

Among the most prolific Ascot Gold Cup winners, his three wins (2018-20) rank him joint-second with Sagaro, behind four-time winner Yeats.

Many racefans insist Stradivarius was a great champion, but it is superficial to judge horses merely by the prestige of the races they win. Ratings are by far the best way of comparing champions, and by that criterion he fell well short of greatness. His peak Racing Post Rating of 125 ranks him far below genuinely great champions.

In the last golden age of Flat stayers in Europe in the late 1970s and early '80s, Sagaro, Buckskin, Le Moss and Ardross would have been rated in the 130s, but the standard of the Cup races has declined since then because most of the prize-money, prestige and stud value is now earned at middle distances.

Double Trigger, Persian Punch, Kayf Tara, Royal Rebel, Yeats (who is not in Aidan O'Brien's top 20) and Stradivarius won multiple Cup races by default because their best potential rivals did not run in them.

MOST GROUP WINS BY HORSES TRAINED IN EUROPE

18 STRADIVARIUS (2017-22)
17 Cirrus Des Aigles (2009-15)
15 Goldikova (2008-11)
13 Brigadier Gerard (1971-72)
13 Ardross (1979-82)
13 Acatenango (1985-87)
13 Persian Punch (1997-2003)
13 Famous Name (2008-12)
13 Vazirabad (2015-18)
13 Enable (2017-20)

Since creation of European Flat Pattern 1971
Includes Pattern wins outside Europe

the races, which the crowds loved, and his overall soundness was rare to see in any horse – never mind one of his age."

Dettori, who had been on board for 15 of the record 18 Group wins, including the three Gold Cups, also had the fondest of memories. In his Sporting Index blog, he said: "He's an absolute legend. He's been a huge part of my life for the last six years, a good friend and a wonderful horse that I've spent so many wonderful times with. He was the people's horse, a real fans' favourite."

Next for the people's horse was a move across Newmarket to the National Stud to start a new life as a stallion. Nielsen will send mares to him and look forward to seeing the babies. But he knows there will never be another Stradivarius.

THERE was no Group 1 for Trueshan in 2022 but it was nevertheless a record-breaking campaign for Alan King's doughty stayer. This time his standout form did not come at the top level, as it had at Goodwood and Longchamp the previous year, but in one of Britain's heritage handicaps. In ratings terms, his incredible weight-carrying performance in the Northumberland Plate was the best of his career.

The six-year-old was arguably the stayer to beat heading into the season. The previous year had ended with two convincing defeats of Stradivarius at Longchamp and Ascot and there was a feeling the best might be yet to come. The proviso with Trueshan is that he needs a soft surface to show his best. A big, powerful galloper, he hits the ground hard and therefore appreciates some cushion.

Good to soft at Nottingham in April for the Listed Further Flight Stakes was an ideal starting point and he reappeared in rude health to dispatch subsequent Group 2 Lonsdale Cup winner Quickthorn by three lengths.

Then came the summer drought, meaning Trueshan missed engagements in both the Gold Cup and the Queen Alexandra Stakes at Royal Ascot. While frustrating for Trueshan's connections and fans at the time, the prolonged dry spell meant King was forced to look to the all-weather and the Northumberland Plate to get a run into his stable star.

Officially rated 120, at least 19lb superior to everything else in the field, Trueshan was perched on 10st 8lb at the head of the weights for the famous handicap. He was still sent off the 3-1 favourite but we were into the realms of Desert Orchid and Denman over jumps when it came to modern weight-carrying feats. Just one horse since 1988 had run in a handicap off a mark this high on the Flat and that had ended in defeat.

What followed was one of the great handicap performances of the modern era but it was hard earned. Nudged along by Hollie Doyle

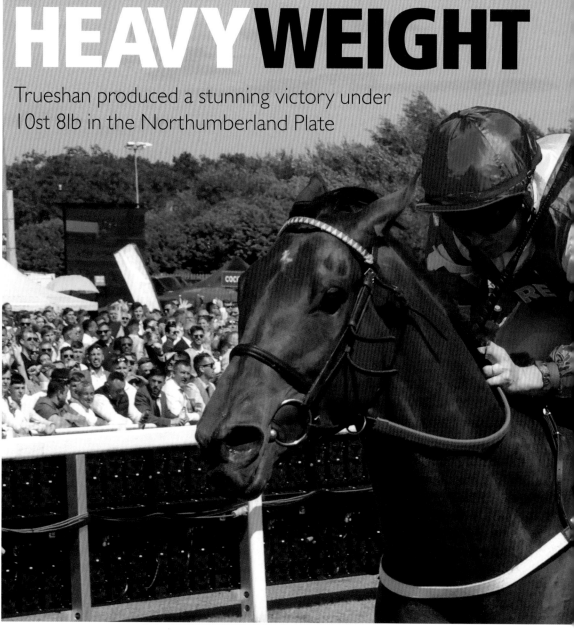

HEAVY WEIGHT

Trueshan produced a stunning victory under 10st 8lb in the Northumberland Plate

from five furlongs out, Trueshan started his progress.

Three furlongs later, Doyle was down in the drive position as Trueshan continued to build momentum. Making a strong challenge inside the final furlong, he claimed the lead with only 100 yards to run, squeezing past runner-up Spirit Mixer, who was carrying exactly 2st less.

The victory was the best Flat handicap performance in Britain ever measured by Racing Post Ratings, which were introduced in 1988, and shouldering 10st 8lb meant Trueshan had shattered the weight-carrying record for the race. That had stood since Barcaldine carried 9st 10lb to victory in 1883 and was subsequently matched by

Karadar (1984), Bold Gait (1995) and Tominator (2013).

Trueshan had been sixth off a 2lb lower mark in the race the previous year, which underlined that his win was a career-best. "That is unreal," said Doyle, perfectly summing up the sense of amazement. "I had to give him a squeeze and I don't usually have to do that.

"He's never had to battle hard to win a race, he's always won so easily. But his ears were pinned back and he really knuckled down. He wasn't getting beaten."

Only one of Trueshan's three owners made the trip to Newcastle and King was also absent, which perhaps tells its own story. The trainer was still in shock 24 hours

after the history-making run. "It was something quite special to see," he said. "I thought he'd run very well but I was thinking I'd have been very happy if he was in the first four or first six. I couldn't really see him winning off that mark."

On having the courage to run a Group 1 horse off a mammoth weight in a handicap, King added: "The jumps boys do it – if you think of Desert Orchid and Denman and going right back to Arkle in the Hennessy. And I had no option, I had to get a run into him."

The Plate was a prep race for the Goodwood Cup, so big things were expected when Trueshan turned up on the Sussex Downs

for his bid to repeat his 2021 victory. With the ground officially described as good, King was happy for Trueshan to take his chance and saw his warrior put up another brave fight.

Doyle made a bold move on the final right-hander into the straight, ranging upsides Kyprios and ready to strike. However, whether it was the ground or the calibre of opposition, Trueshan could never quite propel himself to the front. Kyprios edged out Stradivarius in a thriller, with Trueshan far from disgraced in a close third.

Back on good to soft, he then suffered a shock defeat as the 2-9 favourite in the Doncaster Cup. Truth be told, Trueshan did not look happy from early in the home straight, carrying his head to one side before hanging right and then left as he narrowly failed to chase down Coltrane.

The Northumberland Plate heroics appeared to have taken the edge off him at that stage, but King was inclined to blame himself for running on good ground at Goodwood. With questions to be answered, King took him away, sharpened him up again and brought him back on Champions Day at Ascot five weeks later.

This was familiar territory for Trueshan, who was going for a third Long Distance Cup in a row on the late autumn ground that suits him so well. There was a familiar rival too in the shape of his Doncaster conqueror Coltrane, and once again the race came down to a head-to-head battle between them.

It was nip and tuck all the way from the two-furlong pole. Two or three times it seemed Coltrane was about to seize the initiative but Trueshan and Doyle kept fighting back. Finally, in the last 100 yards it was Trueshan who edged in front to win by a head.

King was pleased to prove the doubters wrong. "I felt the pressure today," he admitted, "but for the horse we wanted to get him back and that was a proper battle. Luckily he's got all winter to get over it and so have I!"

On the preparation for Ascot, he added: "In the Doncaster Cup he was remembering Goodwood and wouldn't let himself down. He had a week on the water treadmill, which he absolutely loves, and it just loosens him up. As you saw today, it's got him back."

Trueshan turns seven in the new year but, as a gelding, it is hoped he will be around for a few more seasons yet. Whether he will ever make it to the Royal Ascot showpiece is another question.

"The one thing we've learned is not to run on quickish ground again," King said. "I just want a very wet June because I'd love to run him in the Gold Cup."

It would be great to see Trueshan there at last but, as the latest season proved, there are other arenas where he can show his talent and toughness.

THE
BIGGER
PICTURE

A scene from the hottest summer in England on record as the runners in a 1m3f handicap at Kempton on August 10 race into the home straight. Victory went to the Charlie Fellowes-trained Tequilamockingbird

EDWARD WHITAKER (RACINGPOST.COM/PHOTOS)

Luxembourg made his mark with a battling Irish Champion victory but misfortune beset the rest of a year that started with the highest hopes

SAVING GRACE

AIDAN O'BRIEN had a road map for Luxembourg, a route criss-crossing Europe with stopovers for a number of big attractions. "The original plan was that he would go to the Guineas, the Epsom Derby, the Irish Derby and then he would have a break and go to the Irish Champion Stakes and then the Arc," O'Brien said. That was the plan. It didn't work out as hoped.

The reality was that Ballydoyle's best three-year-old colt made it to only three of the five targets and won just one of them, close to home in the Irish Champion. The two he missed during a frustrating four-month absence carried the title that has echoed loudly through the County Tipperary stable for 60 years. The opportunities for Luxembourg to run in a Derby came and went, never to return.

At the start of the season there were even whispers that Luxembourg might be the one to end the long wait for a Triple Crown winner since Nijinsky, a great of the Vincent O'Brien era at Ballydoyle, achieved the feat in 1970. Ten years ago, Luxembourg's sire Camelot had faltered in the third and final leg, missing out by three-quarters of a length in the St Leger. Luxembourg did not make it through the first leg.

Third place in the 2,000 Guineas – beaten by the Godolphin pair Coroebus and Native Trail – was highly encouraging, however. It put Luxembourg bang on course to become the 15th Derby winner to emerge from Ballydoyle, a roll of honour stretching back to the Vincent O'Brien-trained Larkspur in 1962. The first O'Brien landed the Derby six times in 20 years from that point; the second (no relation, the usual caveat) has saddled a record eight winners since his first with the great Galileo in 2001.

"It was a lovely starting race for him," O'Brien said after Luxembourg's Guineas effort, which was all the more commendable given that he had clipped heels and stumbled shortly after the start. Ballydoyle's next big thing hardened as Derby favourite, now a best-priced 11-4, but it was a position he did not hold for much longer. Just a week later, he was out of the Derby after suffering a setback on the gallops.

It would be the best part of four months before we saw him again.

In that time the Derby days at Epsom and the Curragh passed by without Ballydoyle success, just as the British and Irish Guineas had.

★★★★

UNUSUALLY, to say the least, O'Brien was still waiting for a European Group 1 win with one of his three-year-old colts by the time Luxembourg was ready to return in mid-August. O'Brien desperately needed him back and he asked a lot of the colt to get him ready for the Irish Champion, via a detour from the road map in the Group 3 Royal Whip Stakes at the Curragh.

A neck victory at odds of 2-9 over a rival rated 10lb inferior was not the most impressive return but the important thing was that Luxembourg was back on track. Leg four of the original plan was another four weeks away. There was still time for him to leave a mark on the season.

Luxembourg took his place in the Irish Champion as joint-second favourite alongside Mishriff at 7-2. Jean-Claude Rouget's Eclipse winner Vadeni headed the market at 7-4 while the second French challenger, Onesto, was 11-1. In a select field of seven, all of those key rivals were officially rated above Luxembourg.

"I think you'll see a better version of him," jockey Ryan Moore said before the race, and he was right.

The pace was set by Stone Age, who in Luxembourg's absence had carried Ballydoyle's main hopes at 7-2 in the Derby but was now 28-1 after falling well short all summer. Onesto was the first to get serious in pursuit up the Leopardstown straight but Moore followed his run on Luxembourg and the pair were locked in battle for the lead with a furlong to go.

With the held-up Vadeni failing to get a clear run up the rail, the race was left to them and it was Luxembourg who proved the stronger for a half-length win.

O'Brien at last had a Group 1 with a three-year-old colt, restoring pride for Ballydoyle and Ireland in general in a season when Luxembourg was the sole Irish-based runner to make the frame in a British colts' Classic and both the Irish 2,000 Guineas and Derby went for export for the first time since 2005. What was also important for O'Brien was the reception for Luxembourg on the first Irish Champions Weekend with full crowds since 2019, and with emotions still raw just seven days after Jack de Bromhead's tragic death.

"To win a race like that, I don't think we've had an atmosphere for Flat racing in Ireland like that in a long time," he said. "He got applauded as he was going out – that's very rare. But that's racing people, when things are going well everyone is up for it and when there are sad times, everyone feels it. That's the way racing people are."

Turning to Luxembourg, O'Brien revealed just how much the colt had needed to find after the Royal Whip. "I promise, he had 20 to 30 per cent to improve from there, and you usually don't run a horse in a Group race like that," he said. "The plan was to go there, then come here and then the Arc, so that was the dream. All credit to the horse, we set him a fairly stiff task. And the pace was fairly solid here, so you were going to find out."

A couple of weeks later, just before the Arc, O'Brien spoke again on the theme, saying Luxembourg was asked to do "unnatural work" to get to the Irish Champion and it had been "a massive risk". It paid off with an 11th victory in the marquee race for O'Brien, and his fourth in a row, but there was to be no third Arc triumph.

Luxembourg was seventh at Longchamp, beaten seven and a half lengths, although O'Brien revealed the following day there was a valid reason for what had seemed a disappointing effort.

"Luxembourg stepped awkwardly from the stalls and pulled a muscle just off his hip," he said. "He's a very brave horse, we've always seen that from him, and he put his head down and battled all the way to the line, but he was very lame after the race."

There was also good news in the Ballydoyle bulletin. "The plan is for him to stay in training," the trainer added. "We obviously didn't get a clear run with him this year, so we hope that things will go a bit smoother next year."

New year, new plan, new hope.

▼ Marquee victory: Luxembourg scores by half a length from Onesto in the Irish Champion Stakes

F RIDAY at Epsom's big meeting belonged to Tuesday and Aidan O'Brien. On another day it might not have. In a thrilling Oaks, the Ballydoyle filly held on by a short head but runner-up Emily Upjohn was widely seen as a most unlucky loser after jinking coming out of the stalls – literally putting her on the back foot at the start – and almost making up all the lost ground.

Emily Upjohn might have been the moral winner for many, but it was Tuesday's name that went on to the roll of honour dating back to 1779. Of most significance for the history books was that this was O'Brien's 41st British Classic success, giving him the outright record ahead of 19th century trainer John Scott.

It was a year when O'Brien did not have his usual impact on the Classics but this milestone may rank as his greatest achievement. He beat Scott's trainers' record of 40 British Classic wins that had stood for 159 years, and which O'Brien equalled when Snowfall ran away with the Oaks in 2021. O'Brien had his first victory in this category with King Of Kings in the 1998 2,000 Guineas, and his score of 41 has been achieved with 38 different horses, his dual winners being Camelot, Minding and Love. He holds the trainers' record for both the 2,000 Guineas (ten) and the Derby (eight).

The Ballydoyle trainer also holds the Irish Classic record with 47 victories and has won 97 European Classics. Among many other distinctions are a world record number of Group 1 victories and a unique 1-2-3 in the Prix de l'Arc de Triomphe.

Tuesday became O'Brien's tenth Oaks winner and there was no surprise in her performance despite the arguments over whether Emily Upjohn should have taken the spoils. Oaks day was actually Tuesday's third birthday, making her the youngest in the field, and she was building on her Classics form at a mile, having finished third in the 1,000 Guineas and runner-up in the Irish 1,000.

Tuesday's Oaks win gave Aidan O'Brien the outright record for a trainer in British Classics history

AIDAN'S DAY

She was bred for the job, being a sister to Minding, who did the Guineas-Oaks double in 2016.

The John and Thady Gosden-trained Emily Upjohn, though, headed the betting at 6-4 after an impressive victory in the Musidora Stakes at York and her stablemate Nashwa, a similarly rapid later developer, was next at 4-1. Tuesday went off at 13-2. As soon as the stalls opened, the favourite was in trouble.

A freeze-frame of the start showed Emily Upjohn back on her hind legs after slipping badly at the off. Losing all momentum from the jump out of the stalls, she set off last of the 11 runners. "She lost her footing completely, the front and the back, and the race was gone then," her jockey Frankie Dettori said afterwards.

The counter-argument was that Tuesday was also near the back, having not started too well either, and once Emily Upjohn slotted in at the tail of the field the two rivals raced together for most of the first mile. As Dettori pointed out,

▼ In the blue corner: Tuesday holds off the fast-finishing Emily Upjohn (red) to give Aidan O'Brien (left) a landmark success

in-running problems, the two fillies certainly produced a thrilling finish as they drew clear of third-placed Nashwa. Tuesday had first run down the centre, taking the lead just inside the final quarter-mile, while Emily Upjohn had come around the outside and was launching her run near the stands' rail. Dettori still had two lengths to make up going into the final furlong and rapidly closed the gap but Moore and Tuesday fought hard to repel Emily Upjohn's late surge by a short head.

History belonged to O'Brien. "It's an honour for me to be in this position. Everybody puts in so much work, so it's unbelievable for the whole team to be able to enjoy this," he said. "Ryan gave her a brilliant ride. He rode her very cold. She was a long way back, but the next thing she was challenging. What she did there was classy."

On the day it certainly looked a high-class Oaks, with Emily Upjohn even made favourite for the Prix de l'Arc de Triomphe such was the impression she left in defeat, but the form did not hold up as well as expected in the rest of the European Group 1 season. Nashwa did her bit with two victories at the top level including the French Oaks, but Tuesday and Emily Upjohn ran into difficulties.

Tuesday went off joint-favourite when she took on the colts in the Irish Derby but was a well-beaten fourth. Her best run afterwards was a one-length second to Alpinista in the Yorkshire Oaks but that was not backed up in two autumn trips to Longchamp.

There was more bad luck for Emily Upjohn when she had to miss the Irish Oaks after a bird strike hit the plane that was meant to fly her over. Rerouted to the King George VI and Queen Elizabeth Stakes a few weeks later, she finished last of six. Eventually, after a three-month break, she came back to form to land the Group 1 British Champions Fillies & Mares Stakes at Ascot.

As a spectacle, the Oaks remained one of the races of the year. And, after all the arguments, the result was there in black and white. British Classic number 41 for O'Brien.

however, he was positioned on the outside, while inside him Ryan Moore was covering less ground on Tuesday.

"I was way too far back," Dettori said. "Ryan had the rail and knew the field would open up on the inside. I had to go round them. Bless her, she took me there in great style but the damage was done. She was a very unlucky loser."

Moore is a master at holding his position in running and he did not cede much ground either in his post-race view, arguing that Tuesday also had to overcome difficulty. "She was awkward at the start," he said. "I wasn't quite in the spot I wanted to be, but Frankie was with me and the pace was even. She gave herself every chance very quickly but was a little babyish when she hit the front and became a little bit unbalanced down the middle of the track. I always felt she was holding on and, although it was a bit closer than it should have been, I felt there was another bit there."

Whatever the arguments about

IN THE
PICTURE

Hanagan's winning ride on The Ridler poses big questions

WHEN The Ridler passed the post first in the Norfolk Stakes at Royal Ascot on June 16, it wasn't the end. It was merely the beginning of a long-running saga that dragged on for another two and a half months until the result was finally settled.

On the day The Ridler (*red*), a 50-1 shot, crossed the line a length and three-quarters in front of 7-4 favourite Walbank (*purple cap*), with Crispy Cat (*white cap*) and Brave Nation (*green and yellow*) close behind in third and fourth, but Paul Hanagan's winning ride was immediately mired in controversy.

Having hit the front inside the final furlong, The Ridler veered violently left and badly hampered Crispy Cat and Brave Nation, leading to a ten-day ban for Hanagan for careless riding and reigniting the arguments over whether the interference rules did enough to discourage a win-at-all-costs mentality.

The Royal Ascot stewards were "satisfied that the interference had not improved the position of The Ridler" but within a couple of weeks an appeal was launched by Kia Joorabchian, whose Amo Racing colours were carried by Walbank and Crispy Cat. He had already made plain his view of the incident, saying: "If that's not a mistake we may as well give up. For an experienced jockey to wipe out four horses in the field, I don't even know what to say to that."

There was a two-month delay before the appeal was heard. Rory Mac Neice, representing Joorabchian, argued that Hanagan had ridden dangerously and his mount should therefore be disqualified. Failing that, he should be demoted to third behind Crispy Cat, who would have prevailed with a clear run.

The arguing over the result of the 60-second race lasted six hours – and then it was another seven days before the appeals panel delivered its verdict. The claim of dangerous riding was rejected and The Ridler was allowed to keep the race, although the panel was highly critical of Hanagan's ride, saying it was "poor, reprehensible and self-evidently culpable".

Still the arguments about riding practices rumbled on. In delivering its verdict, the appeals panel recommended a "broad review" of interference rules in British racing and suggested it should go further than being "merely confined to the matter of penalties".

A few days later, writing in the Racing Post, Hanagan called the "careless mistake" he made at Royal Ascot "the biggest of his career" but put his error and those being made by other riders down to the fact that "jockeys have been getting away with too much for too long".

Rarely have 60 seconds of action stretched so far.

Picture: ALAN CROWHURST (GETTY IMAGES)

Amateur Sam Waley-Cohen won the Grand National with Noble Yeats on his final ride

FAIRYTALE FAREWELL

By Lee Mottershead

THE Grand National delivered yet again. Yet again over the Grand National fences, so did Sam Waley-Cohen. It was all a bit far-fetched and therefore all the more fabulous. On his swansong ride as a jump jockey and just six days before his 40th birthday, horseracing's most celebrated dental entrepreneur fulfilled his lifelong ambition. He finally captured the race he had dreamed of winning since the days when he rode a rocking horse over an imaginary Aintree racecourse.

On Saturday, April 9, 2022, Aintree was real and the rocking horse had turned into Noble Yeats, an animal whose own Grand National story was not much less remarkable than that of his partner.

First, the man. Waley-Cohen travelled to Liverpool as the most successful practitioner of a most difficult art. He was officially an amateur but over the iconic green fences this was the ultimate professional. True, he had never won the Grand National, but he had passed the post in second, fourth, fifth and eighth. In all those instances he donned the colours of his father, Robert Waley-Cohen, with whom he had teamed up to win six races leaping Becher's Brook, the Chair,

Valentine's and the Canal Turn. That ridiculous number of victories was made up of three Foxhunters', two Tophams and a Becher Chase. Here was the human equivalent of Red Rum.

Noble Yeats was nothing like Red Rum, at least not going into the Grand National. What comes next sounds daft because it was daft, albeit to his supremely shrewd and talented trainer Emmet Mullins it seemed perfectly reasonable.

Noble Yeats joined the 39 other runners as a horse who had been running in a bumper only 14 months earlier. He ran in and won his first start over hurdles in March 2021, no more than 13 months before he tackled the world's greatest steeplechase. In the interim he had contested just seven races over fences, winning one of them. He was a novice chaser, a boy in a man's world and also unusually young, given that not since Bogskar in 1940 had a seven-year-old conquered the Grand National. There was a lot against him.

In his favour was the man on his back – and for that man, this was always going to be the end of a rewarding road.

★★★★

WALEY-COHEN had high expectations of winning around his

favourite course on the opening day of the Aintree festival. Jett had got from start to finish and collected £11,250 when finishing the 2021 Grand National 47 lengths behind Minella Times. He was sent off 5-2 favourite to put his name on the Foxhunters' roll of honour but ran out of puff, eventually being pulled up before the penultimate fence. His rider returned to the weighing room and revealed that according to his own maths, that had been his 40th excursion over the Merseyside spruce. He also revealed that the 41st would be followed by his immediate retirement.

It was, however, just one of countless narrative strands that helped to create a typically fascinating edition of the race that outranks all others in the public consciousness.

Twelve months on from becoming the National's first female winning jockey, Rachael Blackmore was back for more on the Henry de Bromhead-trained defending champion Minella Times. Jockey and trainer were in fantastic form, Honeysuckle having won her second Champion Hurdle at Cheltenham, where A Plus Tard ran away with the Gold Cup.

Minella Times's owner JP McManus was represented by five of the 40 runners, one of them

being the 2021 third Any Second Now, this time sent off 15-2 favourite. In total, Ireland had just over half the field, with Gordon Elliott boasting one-third of his nation's 21-strong challenge.

Tiger Roll was not among them – Michael O'Leary, not for the first time, had been unhappy with the dual winner's allocated weight – but very much in the Elliott squad was Delta Work, who had spoiled the party when narrowly denying the Tiger a glorious victory on his farewell appearance in the Cheltenham Festival's cross-country chase. Having been the villain of Gigginstown's own pantomime, this was an opportunity for him to shine again under Jack Kennedy.

Neither Paul Nicholls nor Nicky Henderson were involved but the home team featured some genuine contenders, not least Fiddlerontheroof, charged with giving Colin Tizzard a popular success in the trainer's final crack at the race, and Snow Leopardess, who sought to become one of the Grand National's more unusual heroines, as a grey mare who was also a mother. Childcare responsibilities had already been passed on.

★★★★

THE winner was barely sighted on the first circuit. Sam Waley-Cohen
▸ *Continues page 106*

NOBLE YEATS

would later explain that Noble Yeats had been unable to go the pace. For Robert Waley-Cohen, this must have been somewhat disconcerting. He had bought Noble Yeats as recently as February, since when the novice had run just once for his new English owners when ninth in the Ultima Handicap Chase. He had been caught for toe on that occasion as well.

On the plus side, Noble Yeats seemed to be fine with the fences. Not a single mistake was made on the first lap of Aintree. As he embarked on lap number two, he was suddenly, noticeably and threateningly much closer.

By now, Minella Times had been brought down and Snow Leopardess pulled up. Fast forward to the final fence and three horses, all of them trained in Ireland, were in with a chance of winning. Come the Elbow, Delta Work was booked for third. It was between Noble Yeats – who had survived a slight peck five out – and Any Second Now, but soon enough it was apparent that this was to be another Grand National fairytale.

Noble Yeats was forging clear against the rail. Was this how it had felt aboard that rocking horse? His career now all but behind him, his destiny so close it could be touched, Waley-Cohen was about to do the thing he and his father had been desperate to do for so long. They had famously lifted the Gold Cup with Long Run in 2011, yet the Grand National towered above all other races in their estimations. Winning it felt every bit as good as they had hoped.

Following Tiger Roll and Minella Times, this was yet another Grand National winner filled with a feelgood factor. More than anything, it was about family.

So many of them were there. The winner's enclosure scene was one filled with euphoria, tears and Waley-Cohens. Sam was joined in the happy throng by wife Annabel and children. Felicity Waley-Cohen was marginally less emotional than her husband, Robert, who looked like a man unable to fully compute what had happened. More composed, and with a wide smile across his face (and binoculars hanging from an arm), was Sam's brother, Marcus. Not there in person,

▸ *Continues page 108*

▲ Family affair: celebrating with Sam Waley-Cohen are wife Annabel, children Scarlett and Max and his parents Robert and Felicity; previous pages, Waley-Cohen revels in the glorious end to his career

NOBLE YEATS

but present in spirit, was the boys' lost sibling, Thomas, who died from cancer, aged just 20, in 2004.

"This is a big family day and Thomas is part of it but obviously he isn't here with us," said Sam. He had ridden with his brother's initials on his saddle. "I always think about him on these days," he added. "You need a lot of luck – and maybe he was lady luck today."

As well as needing luck, to win the National you need a horse and jockey in perfect symbiosis. Noble Yeats and Waley-Cohen were such a union. That said, the soon-to-be-40-year-old attempted to convince us he was nothing special.

"You have to be on the right

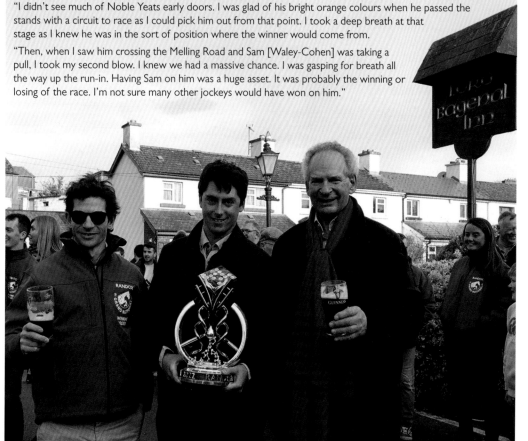

▲ National hero: Noble Yeats back home in his stable the day after; below, trainer Emmet Mullins (centre), Sam and Robert Waley-Cohen continue the party in Leighlinbridge, County Carlow

horses," he said. "I've also been able to ride a lot more over these fences than most of the other jockeys and experience does help. Honestly, though, I think it's luck.

"I also have to say thanks to Dad. He has supported me unwaveringly and lovingly when others said he should use another jockey. We've had a partnership and there has never been one cross word. It has only been for fun."

Never had it been more fun, certainly not for Waley-Cohen snr, a former Cheltenham chairman who adores jump racing with a rare passion. "I've nearly lost my voice from shouting too hard," he said.

"We've had such fun and an amazing time together. I'm so proud because he rode the most brilliant race.

"We've had so many wonderful, happy days together – the Gold Cup, two King Georges, the Becher Chase, two Tophams, the Whitbread – the list goes on and on. I'm really sad it's over. He's extraordinary over these fences. If you could bottle it, you would."

And what about the trainer? Had the jockey and owner not provided such a fabulous story, Mullins would have made more of the headlines. You sense, however, that staying out of the spotlight is exactly how he likes it.

"It was a long-term plan and it seems to have come off – I don't know how," Mullins said. "We were probably more confident a month ago. The closer we got to it everyone was talking up their chances, but the horse didn't know any different. The form was there – and that last circuit, everything just seemed to fall into place."

Happiness was all around. For two sets of connections, there would soon be deep misery. Discorama and Eclair Surf sustained what proved to be fatal injuries, the former while galloping, the latter when jumping. It was an awful postscript but nobody could begrudge the Waley-Cohens for continuing to rejoice in their day of days. The stewards deemed Sam's ride worthy of quite a few days – nine, to be precise – but his whip ban was rendered meaningless as he served it in retirement. Future Grand National jockeys will be more careful, for British racing's whip rules were beefed up only three months later, with the disqualification of serious offenders approved as the ultimate sanction.

Waley-Cohen made a brief return later in the year to take part in the Leger Legends charity race. He will forever remain a Liverpool legend.

"Honestly, you feel like you travel on goodwill at this place," he said when wearing his father's silks for the final time. "Aintree was a part of my childhood. The thing that kept me going year after year was knowing I could come back here and get a feeling like that."

He will not experience that feeling again. Fortunately, the last time was the best.

'I was gasping for breath all the way up the run-in'

Emmet Mullins, 32, has been a Cheltenham Festival winner as a jockey, guiding Sir Des Champs to victory in the Martin Pipe Handicap Hurdle in 2011 for his uncle Willie, and as a trainer with The Shunter in the 2021 Paddy Power Plate. He became a Grand National-winning trainer with his first runner in the race.

Speaking the day after the National back at his stables in Bagenalstown, County Carlow, Mullins said: "It could take you a lifetime to win a Grand National and I can't believe it's happened already. I've only twice been short of breath in my life. Saturday was the second time it has happened to me and the only other time was when The Shunter won at Cheltenham last year.

"I didn't see much of Noble Yeats early doors. I was glad of his bright orange colours when he passed the stands with a circuit to race as I could pick him out from that point. I took a deep breath at that stage as I knew he was in the sort of position where the winner would come from.

"Then, when I saw him crossing the Melling Road and Sam [Waley-Cohen] was taking a pull, I took my second blow. I knew we had a massive chance. I was gasping for breath all the way up the run-in. Having Sam on him was a huge asset. It was probably the winning or losing of the race. I'm not sure many other jockeys would have won on him."

THE STORY ROLLS ON

Six months apart, Racing Post writers saw Tiger Roll in the final chapter of his glorious racing career and enjoying his new life after retirement

'What a warrior he is. He's a legend'

March Lewis Porteous reports on a brave final effort at the Cheltenham Festival

DUAL Grand National hero Tiger Roll was denied a historic sixth Cheltenham Festival win by his own stablemate on his farewell appearance in the Glenfarclas Chase.

Not since Top Cees won the Coral Cup in 1998 had a festival victory been booed from the grandstand but such is the admiration among fans for Tiger Roll, there were sneers, jeers and a chorus of boos after Delta Work defeated the Cheltenham legend by three-quarters of a length.

Tiger Roll, trained by Gordon Elliott, raced with all the enthusiasm of the horse who won the Triumph Hurdle way back in 2014, leading from the 25th of the 32 fences in his bid for a third win in the cross-country chase.

He was still swinging turning in and was clear over the last but Delta Work, carrying the same Gigginstown House Stud colours as his legendary stablemate, came from the pack under Jack Kennedy to hunt Tiger Roll down in the final strides.

Owner Michael O'Leary, who announced beforehand that this would be the final appearance for the two-time National winner, tried to put a brave face on the result, but his deep disappointment was impossible to hide.

"I'm disappointed," he said, his voice already beginning to quiver. "I don't know what to say, I'm going to shoot Jack Kennedy when I see him! On ground that doesn't suit him and that's a Gold Cup horse that's beaten him, and only just beaten him, after over three miles on ground he wouldn't have liked and, ultimately . . . I'm sorry, I'm actually upset. I would have loved to see him win it."

He added: "If I could have controlled it I would have. You have to throw as many darts as you can at the dartboard here and hope something sticks. But, look, everybody here will get to celebrate Tiger today. This will be the last time they see him running on a racetrack and what a warrior he is. He's a legend."

A legend indeed and he departed like a legend. Back at his happiest hunting ground, flicking over Aintree-style fences, gobbling up the cheese wedges and skipping over the stuffed hurdles, he loved every single second of it. If he hated the ground he had a funny way of showing it.

By the time they got to the 25th obstacle, another railed hedge, Tiger Roll's rider Davy Russell couldn't wait any longer. Easysland, his conqueror in this race in 2020, had taken him as far as he could. The champagne was starting to be shaken; let's get this party started.

But, just as the final few words of the fairytale were being penned, Delta Work and Kennedy appeared out of the gloom to spoil all our fun. Tiger Roll did his very best to fight him off, he rallied once, twice, three times, but the younger and classier legs prevailed.

"I'd say a lot of people will hate me now but it doesn't really bother me," said the winning rider. "I thought I was always going to get there. To be honest, I thought the ground had gone for Tiger Roll and I was surprised at how well he was going, but I suppose it was in the back of my head that he might not get up the hill as good as my lad on that ground. I actually expected to pick him up a bit easier, but my lad just ground him down in the end.

"I was schooling Delta Work here the other morning and I said to my brother afterwards that I'm going to be the most hated man in Cheltenham on Wednesday evening. I was right. He's been very disappointing all season, but the switch to this cross-country racing rejuvenated him. I'm delighted."

Elliott was an emotional wreck afterwards. He looked as though he had gone the distance with Mike Tyson but somehow came out of the bout winning and losing. "To be honest, I'm not going to tell you a lie, I was shouting for Tiger coming down to the last," he said.

Asked if he regretted running Delta Work, he added: "No. If I was here today and the ground went that soft and I didn't have Delta Work running I would have been absolutely puking. The wrong horse won and it would have been a dream come true if Tiger had won but he did us proud and Tiger Roll made the race what it was. I wanted Tiger to win, I really did, but, look, Delta Work won and it was a great race."

It was indeed a great race, a fabulous one, which tugged on our heartstrings every step of the way. That is what Tiger Roll has done for his entire career. He has turned us all into soppy messes.

Too small, too slight, too slow. Successful staying chasers without size and scope are about as rare as candlelit dinners between O'Leary and BHA handicapper Martin Greenwood. Tiger Roll was always a bit different, though. He never stuck to scripts or did the things he was supposed to do. If he did, the "little rat of a thing", as O'Leary once infamously described him, would be long forgotten by now.

But Tiger Roll will never be forgotten. Not in our lifetime. Not ever. He will take up quite a few chapters of the history books and stay there too. You don't win at five different Cheltenham Festivals, land back-to-back Grand Nationals and not be remembered for a very long time.

Farewell, Tiger. Thanks for the memories.

This is an edited version of an article that appeared in the Racing Post on March 17

'He's been spoiled rotten'

September David Jennings spends a day finding out how life has changed for Tiger Roll

IN A field of dreams at Gordon Elliott's Cullentra House stables, dreams that have already come true, are the winners of three Grand Nationals, a Gold Cup and six Cheltenham Festival races. There is the tall, dark and handsome Don Cossack, the imposing Silver Birch and, standing small in between them, the biggest legend of the lot.

On a calm and clammy autumn morning, as the next generation begin their fitness regime for the forthcoming jumps season on the main gallop nearby, the best-known jumps horse of the modern era is proudly growing his gut and enjoying the early stages of a richly deserved retirement. His work here is done.

And what a job Tiger Roll did. He went from the stable skivvy to Cullentra's CEO in the space of eight glorious years and his leaving do at Cheltenham in March was quite the occasion too. Despite detesting the conditions, he gave every last drop of energy in his attempt to go out in a blaze of glory. If anything, he earned even more admirers in defeat.

That was March and this is September, so you may be wondering what Tiger Roll has been up to since you saw him last.

"He's been spoiled rotten," laughs Mary Nugent, his mammy, granny and nanny all rolled into one. "He still gets three scoops even though he shouldn't. But it's very hard not to give in to him. One, because he's always hungry. And, two, because he's Tiger Roll. He just loves his food. He's so fat, but he looks amazing, doesn't he? I think he looks savage. He came back here to parade for the open day we're having."

That open day is about to take place and you can guarantee Tiger Roll will be the busiest selfie server. He has certainly been popular in horse shows over the last few months as Wendy and Ted O'Leary, wife and son of Gigginstown racing manager Eddie

O'Leary, took it upon themselves to retrain him as a riding horse. That might sound straightforward but when you have spent your life trying to run as fast as you can, slowing down is not so simple, as they soon found out at their Lynn Lodge Stud.

Explaining what is involved in the transformation from racehorse to riding horse, Nugent says: "It's behaviour, conformation, their showpiece and how they ride. They have to walk, trot and canter in an outline. To go from a racehorse to a riding horse is actually quite hard for them. It's like humans who aren't natural runners because they have walked their whole life. Running is a bit alien to them because it's a completely different discipline. That's what it's like for ex-racehorses.

"To get them to put their head down and just do a semi-trot is not easy. In their head they just want to go fast all the time, so it's mentally challenging. It's hard work; it's just a completely different discipline. For the short time he had to retrain, it's phenomenal how well he's done really.

▲ Three kings: Tiger Roll (right) with Don Cossack (centre) and Silver Birch; below, Tiger Roll in his new life as a show horse; previous pages, Tiger Roll in retirement and in battle with stablemate Delta Work (blue cap) in his final race at Cheltenham

It's nothing short of a miracle. Wendy and Ted have done an incredible job with him."

That incredible job took patience. Wendy explains: "I think the biggest thing was to break his old routine. We needed him to realise that when he went out every day he wasn't going to work on the gallop and he wasn't schooling over fences. He's a very intelligent horse, so once he worked all that out he settled into his new role quite quickly.

"We took him to the Tullamore Show and he won. He performed impeccably that day, so we said we'd give it a go at the RDS [Dublin Horse Show]. But it was a huge ask in just 12 weeks. None of the other horses had been off the track for as little time as he had."

Tiger Roll came third in his class, which was won by former Irish Grand National winner General Principle. "To do what he did in the class he was in was amazing really given the short period of time he'd been preparing for it. I was so proud of him," Wendy says.

▶ *Continues page 114*

MOORCROFT

Equine Rehabilitation Centre
Charity No: 1076278

At the centre in West Sussex, we help many horses to return to soundness and then a better life. We have many years of real experience at rehabilitation, and we now help many other breeds too who need help after surgery, time off or lameness issues. If you are worried about your horse and feel you need help, please call us or come and see us. We are a charity set up to help when horses are in need, and we keep our costs affordable by fundraising and with the support of many who value what we do.

www.moorcroftracehorse.org.uk

Huntingrove Stud, Slinfold, West Sussex RH13 0RB Tel:07929 666408

TIGER ROLL

Ted, 17, was the lucky young man who got to ride him in the shows. "It was unbelievable to be even near him, never mind ride him," he says. "He's a horse of a lifetime and probably the most famous horse in Ireland. His brain is a bit wired but we eventually found a way to get through to him. In the first few days we weren't sure whether it was going to work out but it did in the end. We just stuck at it and it was worth it."

Nugent thinks Tiger Roll could do anything. Being successfully retrained as a riding horse is the latest in a long list of achievements that vary from the sublime to the ridiculous.

"Anything he puts his hand to, he's just really good at," she says. "Everything seems to come easy to him. He loved it when we brought him to the beach, he adored hunting, he took to the Grand National fences, he loved all the different obstacles in the cross-country races and, even the day he ran in a Flat race on the all-weather at Dundalk, he ran a cracker and finished second."

September brought another new experience. "We took him to the Curragh to parade as part of Irish Champions Weekend," Nugent says. "There were a few moments that were a bit hairy. He likes to put on a show, you see, and he's really good at bucking. He can do it effortlessly. His front legs don't move and his back legs just let fly. He did that a few times at the Curragh but once he went into the parade ring he was as good as gold."

Was he the centre of attention? "I'm biased but I'm going to say yes. Everybody always just seems so excited to see him."

So, then, after posing for endless selfies at Elliott's open day, what's next for Tiger Roll?

"He'll be heading back to Gigginstown with Don Cossack, Roi Du Mee and all those legends, but I'm sure he'll be making appearances here, there and everywhere," Nugent says. "He's in demand. I've been to Aintree with him, then the Mullingar show, then Tullamore, the RDS, and the Curragh. He's never short of an invitation."

This is an edited version of an article that appeared in the Racing Post on September 16

TIGER'S FEATS

Foaled March 14, 2010

Pedigree Authorized - Swiss Roll (Entrepreneur)

Breeder Gerry O'Brien

Owner Gigginstown House Stud

Trainer Gordon Elliott

Starts 45

Wins 13

Earnings £1,437,256

Grand National wins 2018, 2019 (right)

Cheltenham Festival wins 2014 Triumph Hurdle, 2017 National Hunt Chase, 2018 Glenfarclas Chase (above), 2019 Glenfarclas Chase, 2021 Glenfarclas Chase

First race Won Market Rasen juvenile hurdle, November 10, 2013, when trained by Nigel Hawke

Final race Runner-up in the Glenfarclas Chase, Cheltenham, March 16, 2022, beaten three-quarters of a length by Delta Work

Highest Racing Post Rating 174 (2019 Grand National)

Cheltenham Festival record 10111212

THE BIGGER PICTURE

Trainer Paddy Corkery with Master McShee on Connigar beach in Dungarvan Bay, County Waterford, in January. Last season Corkery's stable star won the Grade 1 Faugheen Novice Chase at Limerick's Christmas meeting and was twice runner-up to Galopin Des Champs in Grade 1 contests later on
PATRICK McCANN (RACINGPOST.COM/PHOTOS)

Racing's greatest patron

'The first six days marked in her diary each year were Derby day and the five days of Royal Ascot'

Her Majesty Queen Elizabeth II died on September 8 at the age of 96. These extracts from the Racing Post's extensive coverage reflect the importance of her high-profile role in racing and how much the sport meant to her

By John Randall

OF ALL the monarchs who have ever been involved in horseracing, Queen Elizabeth II was the most knowledgeable and the most enthusiastic. Her passion for the sport was evident to all and, with a keen appreciation of the Stud Book and of a horse's conformation, she was a true professional.

She was champion owner twice and won all the British Classics except the Derby, in which she had runner-up Aureole; he won the race named after her parents, the King George VI and Queen Elizabeth Stakes. She also had dual Classic-winning fillies Highclere and Dunfermline, with the latter triumphing in the Oaks and St Leger in her Silver Jubilee year, and her other outstanding winners included Carrozza (Oaks), Pall Mall (2,000 Guineas) and Estimate (Ascot Gold Cup).

Duty was always paramount, but the first six days marked in her diary each year were Derby day and the five days of Royal Ascot. She derived immense pleasure from spending time with thoroughbreds, not only on the racecourse but also on the gallops and with her mares and foals at stud. She had a natural eye for a horse and recognised every one of them. She relished visiting studs such as those of Alec Head in Normandy and Will Farish in Kentucky, and on her state visit to Ireland in 2011 a tour of local studs, including Coolmore, was a highlight.

At a very young age she was enthralled by her grandfather King George V telling how his filly Scuttle had won the 1928 1,000 Guineas. Her father was champion owner in 1942 thanks to Big Game and Triple Crown heroine Sun Chariot. At 16 she visited Fred Darling's Beckhampton stables with her parents to watch those champions work, and she felt so honoured to run her hand over Big Game that she did not wash for several hours. Princess Elizabeth got to know the mares and foals at the royal stud at Hampton Court, and in one of her early visits to the racecourse she saw her father's Hypericum win the 1,000 Guineas in 1946.

When she married in 1947 her wedding present from the Aga Khan was a filly foal, who was named Astrakhan and went into training with Willie Smyth. Lord Mildmay encouraged the princess and her mother to buy a jumper, and they went half-shares in Monaveen, trained by Peter Cazalet. Astrakhan and Monaveen both made their debuts in the princess's colours in October 1949, with Monaveen scoring over fences at Fontwell to become her first winner. Monaveen won the Queen Elizabeth Chase at Hurst Park that December and came fifth to Freebooter in the 1950 Grand National, but later broke a leg.

King George VI died in February 1952, and the new queen announced that she would breed and race on the same lines. This meant having her homebreds in training with Cecil Boyd-Rochfort at Newmarket, and those horses bred by the National Stud and leased to her for their racing careers (and sometimes known as the 'hirelings') in training with Noel Murless, who moved to Newmarket at the end of 1952.

Her first top-class horse was Aureole, who, like many of Hyperion's offspring, had a mind of his own. In 1953 he was fifth in the 2,000 Guineas and won the Lingfield Derby Trial by five lengths. On the morning of the coronation one of the Queen's ladies-in-waiting, thinking of the imminent ceremony, asked if all was well, and she replied that Boyd-Rochfort had just rung to report that Aureole had gone well in his last work for the Derby.

At Epsom four days later he came second, beaten four lengths by a great champion in Pinza, who was ridden by the newly knighted Sir Gordon Richards. In the King George at Ascot he was again second to Pinza, this time by three lengths. He refused to settle when third in the St Leger, then won the Cumberland Lodge Stakes.

As a four-year-old Aureole was ridden by Eph Smith because royal stud manager Charles Moore decided the highly strung colt went better for him than for stable jockey Harry Carr, and he proved himself the champion older horse in Europe. He won the Coronation Cup by five lengths and the Hardwicke by a short head, and in the King George he went one better than 12 months before, beating French raider Vamos by three-quarters of a length.

Aureole was the best colt owned by the Queen and he was also a champion at stud, heading the sires' list twice while based at the Royal Studs. His successful offspring in the royal colours included Apprentice and Hopeful Venture. Aureole was the main reason the Queen became champion owner in 1954, although Landau and Corporal also contributed to her prize-money haul. Landau, a son of Sun Chariot, won the Rous Memorial Stakes at Royal Ascot and the Sussex Stakes, and was Sir Gordon Richards' last ride in public when third in the Eclipse. Corporal became the only horse ever to beat his stablemate, subsequent Triple Crown winner Meld, when taking the Newmarket Foal Stakes.

For strength in depth the Queen enjoyed her best season in 1957, as she was champion owner for the second time. About a dozen of her 30 victories came in races we would now regard as being of Pattern standard. Mulberry Harbour won the Cheshire Oaks and carried her first colours in the Oaks, but it was her second-string Carrozza who prevailed, with Lester Piggott riding one of his strongest finishes to repel Silken Glider by a short head. Trained by Murless, Carrozza was Piggott's only Classic winner for the Queen.

▸ *Continues page 120*

Yet her best filly that year turned out to be Almeria, who won the Ribblesdale Stakes, Yorkshire Oaks (by six lengths) and Park Hill Stakes. During that annus mirabilis her other winners included Doutelle in two Classic trials and the Cumberland Lodge Stakes, and Pall Mall in the New (now Norfolk) Stakes.

As a four-year-old in 1958 Doutelle beat Ballymoss in the Ormonde Stakes, but in the King George Ballymoss proved himself a champion as Almeria and Doutelle filled the minor placings. Almeria then ran in the Doncaster Cup, and the temperamental filly would have won had she consented to go past her pacemaker Agreement, who sprang a 25-1 shock in the first of his two victories in the race.

The owner's star performer that year was Pall Mall, who was Boyd-Rochfort's second-string in the 2,000 Guineas, as the trainer also had the favourite Bald Eagle, who was far superior at home. Pall Mall, a 20-1 shot ridden by Doug Smith, led in the Dip and beat Major Portion by half a length with Bald Eagle unplaced. He then won the inaugural Lockinge Stakes by five lengths.

The Queen was suffering from a heavy cold and could not attend Newmarket. But winning a Classic with a homebred like Pall Mall meant more to her than victory with a horse leased from the National Stud, as Carrozza had been. Pall Mall was even better as a four-year-old, winning the Lockinge again and putting up a magnificent performance to be second under top weight in the Royal Hunt Cup, conceding 20lb to the winner. Also at Royal Ascot in 1959, the Queen enjoyed a double via Doutelle's half-brother Above Suspicion in the St James's Palace Stakes and Pindari in the King Edward VII Stakes. By Pinza out of Sun Chariot, Pindari was later third in the St Leger.

This golden age for the royal racehorses ended in 1960 and heralded a decade of disappointments and personnel changes. Charles Moore, the royal stud manager since 1937, retired

in 1962. Peter Hastings-Bass started to train for the Queen in 1964, but died of cancer a few months later and was succeeded at his Kingsclere stables by his assistant Ian Balding. Dick Hern, at West Ilsley, joined the trainers' roster in 1967.

In 1964 it was announced the National Stud would sell all its mares and foals and become a stallion station. This meant it would have no more foals to lease to the Queen for their racing careers.

Boyd-Rochfort produced two shock big-race winners for the owner-breeder in 1965. Canisbay, a son of Doutelle, was a 20-1 shot when scoring a short-head victory in the Eclipse, and Apprentice was the outsider of five when winning both the Yorkshire Cup and the Goodwood Cup.

The last of the 'hirelings' was Hopeful Venture, who Murless

trained to win the Princess of Wales's Stakes and come second to Ribocco in the St Leger in 1967. As a four-year-old the colt won the Ormonde and Hardwicke Stakes, and surpassed himself with victory in the Grand Prix de Saint-Cloud, with the great Vaguely Noble third.

The end of the 1968 season marked a decisive change in the royal racing operation, as its two main trainers ceased to be involved; the newly knighted Boyd-Rochfort had retired and Murless no longer had any National Stud-breds. For the next two decades Hern and Balding were the principal royal trainers, sharing the yearlings bred at the Royal Studs. At the start of 1970 Lord Porchester (later Earl of Carnarvon) became the Queen's racing manager. A prominent owner-breeder in his own right, he had been giving advice to his childhood friend for many years,

and the arrangement was now put on a formal footing. At the same time Michael Oswald became her stud manager.

A pair of royal fillies, Escorial and Highclere, won the two divisions of a maiden race at Newbury in 1973. Escorial then won the Fillies' Mile at Ascot – that inaugural running was called the Green Shield Stakes – and Highclere developed into a dual Classic winner.

A granddaughter of Hypericum, Highclere won the 1974 1,000 Guineas without a prep race. The blinkered filly held on by a short head from Polygamy, who went on to win the Oaks with Escorial unplaced. Highclere bypassed the Oaks because it was thought Epsom would not suit her and she ran instead in the French equivalent, the Prix de Diane, in which she beat Comtesse De Loir by two lengths. The Queen was at

◀ Troops in the colours: royal jockeys past and present line up in the Queen's silks on Derby day at Epsom as part of the Platinum Jubilee celebrations

Chantilly to witness her biggest triumph on foreign soil, and that evening Dick Hern, jockey Joe Mercer and their wives attended a family party at Windsor Castle in celebration. Her filly was then second to Dahlia in the King George.

Her other dual Classic winner, Dunfermline, came second in the May Hill Stakes and Fillies' Mile, and made a winning reappearance in 1977 in the Pretty Polly Stakes at Newmarket, ridden by Hern's new stable jockey, Willie Carson.

The Oaks favourite, Durtal, got loose in the preliminaries and had to be withdrawn. In the race Dunfermline kept on dourly to lead in the last 100 yards and beat Freeze The Secret by three-quarters of a length. She was then third in a slowly run Yorkshire Oaks.

In the St Leger the Vincent O'Brien-trained Alleged started odds-on favourite, but Lester Piggott sent him to the front early in the long straight, making the race a stiff test of stamina and setting it up for Dunfermline, who stayed on resolutely to lead below the distance and triumph by a length and a half.

Dunfermline thus became the only horse ever to beat subsequent dual Arc winner Alleged, and it was perhaps the best single performance by any of the Queen's horses – surpassing Aureole's victory in the King George and Pall Mall's second place in the Royal Hunt Cup.

It was the Queen's Silver Jubilee year and her heavy schedule of official duties prevented her witnessing either of those Classic victories in person. Yet they were particularly satisfying for the owner-breeder, as she had bought Dunfermline's granddam, Stroma (also dam of Canisbay), as a

▶▶ *Continues page 122*

Her racing life

First runner Astrakhan (trained by Willie Smyth, ridden by Tommy Burn) 2nd at Ascot, October 7, 1949

First winner Monaveen (Peter Cazalet/Tony Grantham) over fences at Fontwell, October 10, 1949 (owned jointly with her mother)

First big-race winner Monaveen (1949 Queen Elizabeth Chase, Hurst Park)

First winner on Flat Astrakhan (Willie Smyth/Tommy Burn) Hurst Park, April 15, 1950

First winner as Queen Choir Boy (Cecil Boyd-Rochfort/Harry Carr) Newmarket, May 13, 1952

First Royal Ascot winner Choir Boy (1953 Royal Hunt Cup)

King George VI and Queen Elizabeth Stakes winner Aureole (1954)

Classic winners Carrozza (1957 Oaks), Pall Mall (1958 2,000 Guineas), Highclere (1974 1,000 Guineas, Prix de Diane), Dunfermline (1977 Oaks, St Leger)

Coronation Cup winner Aureole (1954)

Gold Cup winner Estimate (2013)

Eclipse Stakes winner Canisbay (1965)

Sussex Stakes winner Landau (1954)

Yorkshire Oaks winner Almeria (1957)

Grand Prix de Saint-Cloud winner Hopeful Venture (1968)

US Graded stakes winners Unknown Quantity (1989 Arlington Handicap), Fictitious (2000 De La Rose Handicap), Call To Mind (2018 Belmont Gold Cup)

Group 1 winner as breeder but not owner Kingdom Of Fife (2011 Queen Elizabeth Stakes, Randwick)

Richest win £198,485 (Estimate, 2013 Gold Cup)

Placed horses in Derby Aureole (2nd in 1953), Carlton House (3rd in 2011)

Grand National runner Monaveen (5th in 1950)

Cheltenham Gold Cup runner Barbers Shop (7th in 2009)

Last winner Love Affairs, Goodwood, September 6, 2022

Top-rated horses (Timeform) Dunfermline (133), Aureole (132), Pall Mall (132), Landau (129), Highclere (129), Doutelle (128), Above Suspicion (127), High Veldt (126), Atlas (126), Almeria (126)

Trainers Peter Cazalet, Willie Smyth, Sir Cecil Boyd-Rochfort, Sir Noel Murless, Walter Nightingall, Tom Masson, Norah Wilmot, Peter Hastings-Bass, Ian Balding, Dick Hern, Earl of Huntingdon, Neil Graham, Neil Howard (USA), Roger Charlton, Sir Michael Stoute, Richard Hannon snr, Christophe Clement (USA), Nicky Henderson, Andrew Balding, Hughie Morrison, Henrietta Knight, Michael Bell, John Hammond (France), Gai Waterhouse (Australia), Richard Hannon jnr, William Haggas, Richard Hughes, John Gosden, Charlie Longsdon, Clive Cox, Thady Gosden, Harry Charlton

Racing manager/adviser Earl of Carnarvon 1970-2001, John Warren 2001-22

Stud manager Charles Moore 1952-62, Tony Wingfield 1962-63, Richard Shelley 1963-69, Sir Michael Oswald 1970-97, Joe Grimwade 1997-2013, Matthew Hill from 2013

Champion owner (money won) 1954, 1957

Royal Ascot wins 24

Group/Grade 1-class wins as owner 14

Most wins in a calendar year as owner 39 in 2021 (36 Flat, 3 jumps)

Total wins as owner 1,121 (GB Flat 1,022, GB jumps 71, abroad 28)

Compiled by John Randall

yearling for 1,150gns at Doncaster in 1956. Three weeks after the St Leger, Dunfermline finished fourth to Alleged over the shorter trip of the Arc. She failed to win as a four-year-old.

The Queen then had three Derby runners in four years, starting with Almeria's grandson English Harbour, who beat Ile De Bourbon in the 1978 Predominate Stakes but flopped at Epsom. Milford, Highclere's first foal, ran away with the Lingfield Derby Trial the following year but finished tenth behind stablemate Troy in the 200th Derby, although he later won the Princess of Wales's Stakes. And Church Parade was a distant fifth behind Shergar at Epsom in 1981.

Highclere's daughter Height Of Fashion won the May Hill Stakes and Fillies' Mile, and in 1982 she won the Lupe Stakes and bypassed the Oaks in favour of the Princess of Wales's Stakes, in which she beat older horses decisively. She was then sold for a reported £1.5 million to Hamdan Al Maktoum, and the proceeds enabled the Queen to buy West Ilsley Stables from the Sobell/Weinstock family. This seemed a reasonable decision at the time, yet Height Of Fashion turned out to be easily the best broodmare ever bred by the Queen, whereas ownership of West Ilsley caused huge problems.

Height Of Fashion's offspring included an outstanding champion in Nashwan, as well as Unfuwain, Nayef and daughters who carried on her line. If she had been retained at the Royal Studs, she would not have been mated with the stallions who sired her illustrious offspring because their fees would have been unaffordable on the royal budget, but she would have been a considerable asset.

In 1984 Dick Hern was paralysed in a hunting fall, and in June 1988 he underwent heart surgery. In August, amid concerns about his ability to continue training, his wife Sheilah was told by Lord Carnarvon that his West Ilsley lease would not be renewed

▶ *Continues page 124*

'She absolutely loved horses and they had an amazing way of relaxing in her presence'

John Warren, the Queen's racing and bloodstock adviser, spoke movingly in a revealing interview shortly after her death

▲ Happy times: the Queen and John Warren at the races

By Lee Mottershead

REMARKABLY, it was just two months before her death, a July day whose perfect yet poignant story can now be told. The Queen was in residence at Windsor, where a few weeks earlier she had watched the Derby and Royal Ascot on television. Mindful of the mobility issues that forced the sport's most revered individual to forgo the pleasure of attending those events in person, John Warren had arranged for her to receive some particularly special visitors.

Temporarily stabled in the royal mews were 15 of Her Majesty's latest crop of yearlings, superbly prepared by the teams at her studs. In normal times, the Queen would have relished travelling around those farms to inspect them. This time they had come to her. One or two had the sort of normal conformation issues well known to a breeder of such long standing, yet among the babies waiting to parade were thoroughbreds rich in quality, by super stallions and out of precious mares like Estimate, Memory and Diploma. In pedigree and appearance, they were an exceptional bunch.

Warren, the Queen's racing and bloodstock adviser for 21 years, has vivid memories of that day. The first thing he recalls is watching his 96-year-old boss driving herself in a Jaguar from the castle to the mews. After drawing up in the yard, she got out on her own and then looked at Warren with eyes that sparkled.

"Guess what!" she said to him, her face carrying an expression that will stay with him forever. "What, Ma'am?" he replied, sensing the delight with which the Queen was about to impart her news. "I'm not stiff," she said, causing Warren to inquire for what reason she might have been stiff. "I rode yesterday!"

declared the Queen, filled with pride that she had come down to the mews the previous day, ridden her horse in the indoor school and woken up the next morning without discomfort. It was a marvellous encounter that set the tone for what was to follow.

The Queen was shown each yearling, one by one. It had already become apparent to Warren that they were directly beneath the Heathrow flightpath, as a result of which Memory's daughter crouched down to inspect an aeroplane that suddenly appeared overhead. The Queen watched on, fascinated, enthralled and excited.

"To have such high-quality horses paraded in front of the Queen was a wow moment – it was a wonderfully warm feeling to see her so thrilled," says Warren, for whom this represented arguably the apogee of his employment with the sport's most famous owner-breeder. For years they had worked together to improve the quality of her broodmare band and the profile of the stallions the mares visited. Never before had the end results contained such justifiable hope of future glories.

"When horses aren't bred as well as these are, breeding often dictates the end result," says Warren. "In the past we've been excited about the physicality of the yearlings, but when they were by mid-range stallions you could kid yourself as to how high they might climb. I think the Queen was very proud to see the green shoots starting to properly come back. The record number of winners we had last year was tremendous and helped to invigorate the understanding that we're now a hair's breadth from getting some really lovely horses.

"The great tragedy for the Queen is I think she has bred her best crop of yearlings this year. History will prove me right or wrong, but I believe the current crop could go all the way. I really do think the

Queen has a serious chance of leaving a very important legacy."

On that summer day nobody could have known the Queen would die just two months later, yet she must equally have been aware her time could end before the racing careers of those yearlings began.

"If it crossed her mind, she never let on," insists Warren, who is confident the thought did not enter the Queen's head. As someone who had known her across four decades – his father-in-law, Lord Carnarvon, preceded him in his coveted role – it is more than reasonable to believe Warren is correct in his assessment.

Indeed, not only did he work for the Queen, the bloodstock industry stalwart and his wife Lady Carolyn Warren also had the regular honour of having the Queen stay as an overnight guest at their home Milford Lake House, just three fields from Highclere Castle. She sat on the sofa from which questions are being directed at Warren, who speaks with fondness and respect about a lady mourned the world over.

"The Queen has been coming to this house for 60 years," explains Warren. "She was at ease here. When she was in this house and having dinner with people we had invited from across racing, one was talking to a horsewoman. When I saw her on television, she was the Queen."

On average, they spoke every other day, while Warren would always arrange for the trainer of a royal runner to ring the Queen at an appointed time before any race.

"Some of the things she had to deal with as sovereign were not that nice but with the horses there was always hope and positivity," says Warren. "I think that gave her a real lift. If it was a chore, she wouldn't have wanted to speak when I phoned, but I can't remember a single occasion across all the years when she didn't take one of those calls.

"Racing was a very important part of her daily life. It's also absolutely true that she read the Racing Post every morning, without fail. It was a ritual – and when I say she read it, I mean she really did read it. You would never see her studying a racecard at the races because she had already done her homework and banked any relevant information."

Throughout her 70-year reign, racing fans have enjoyed being able to see the Queen at close proximity. The final chance to do that came last October on Qipco British Champions Day at Ascot, where she was presented with a memento to mark her induction into the sport's hall of fame. Sadly, she was this year unable to make her customary trips to the royal meeting, Newbury in April and the Derby, which was made part of the official Platinum Jubilee celebrations.

"The Queen was aware of her capabilities," says Warren. "She did run it to the wire, but the day before the Derby she realised it was going to be a step too far. Talking to her that night, I said that Carolyn and I didn't have to go to Epsom and asked if she would like us to watch the racing with her. 'Would you?' she asked, to which I replied, of course we would.

"We went over to Windsor and all watched the racing together, with copies of the Racing Post laid out everywhere. She was totally absorbed in every minute of the occasion, which was so special. Seeing Stoutey win the Derby with Desert Crown was also a real pick-me-up for the Queen, who then spoke to him on the phone.

"After tea, and just as we were leaving, the Queen asked if we were going to watch that evening's Platinum Jubilee concert. After we said yes, the Queen said, 'I really think you should make sure you watch the beginning of the concert'. Carolyn and I got in the car and wondered aloud why the Queen was so keen we should see it from the start. When we saw the Paddington Bear sketch, we knew why. She was so proud of that."

As an avid racing participant, she was never prouder than when winning the 2013 Gold Cup with Estimate, as was gloriously evident in the now iconic television pictures that showed the Queen and Warren willing the filly home from the royal box and then celebrating with glee.

It was special for so many reasons, one of them being the generosity of the Aga Khan, who seven years earlier had decided that as an 80th birthday present to the Queen he would give her access to ten mares from ten different lines, with the Queen taking ownership of the first filly produced by each mare. Estimate was one such filly. One year after winning the Queen's Vase, she returned to Royal Ascot, trained to the minute by Sir Michael Stoute. Ridden exquisitely by Ryan Moore, she emerged triumphant after a pulsating battle up the home straight, in the process making the Queen the first reigning monarch to win the Gold Cup.

"I know it was the Queen's most joyous moment because of the welling up in her eyes," recalls Warren. "I knew her for nearly 40 years and it was the only time I saw her like that. There were wins that I had seen make her highly excited, but this was just a bit different.

"The Queen went flat out to the winner's enclosure. Everyone was desperate to congratulate her but all she wanted to do was get over to Estimate and put her hand on the filly's head. I thought that was such a touching, serene scene. She didn't want to bask in her own glory because she knew her horse had put her heart and soul into the race."

That evening, Stoute, his late partner Coral Pritchard-Gordon, Moore and wife Michelle were invited to a special Windsor Castle dinner, where Warren gave a speech. "Prince Philip was so proud of her, which was incredibly touching," says Warren. "I don't say this lightly, but it was a joyous day."

The Queen had been obsessed with horses since childhood. "She absolutely adored horses," says Warren. "Whenever we went to see foals, all she wanted was to get closer and closer to them. I was worried towards the end that one of the horses might move a bit quickly and cause an accident but she just wanted to be close up with them.

"Horses had an amazing way of relaxing in her presence. I never saw a single one do anything silly around her. That was remarkable."

He uses the same word about the Queen herself. "I know she will be sorely missed by people all around the world who were so grateful to her for participating in our wonderful sport," he says. "She was revered by the major owners and breeders all around the world. I know that to be true and I cannot emphasise it enough.

"On a personal note, I'll miss my evening calls to her. They could last from five minutes to 45 minutes. I'll also miss the one-on-one conversations with her, discussing the horses – and as she was a friend of this family, we were able to talk well beyond horses.

"Throughout her life she possessed an unwavering dedication to duty. She could never be distracted from that. She was also a wonderful listener, exceptionally kind and unbelievably thoughtful. We have been very blessed."

In the concluding days of her life, the Queen continued to think about the next chapters of her marathon racing story. As usual, Warren had begun work on the mating plan for the Queen's stock straight after Royal Ascot. He took a draft of that plan to Balmoral.

"She was completely looking to the future," says Warren, who was with the Queen on the Saturday, Sunday and then Monday morning prior to her death on Thursday, September 8. "We had such a wonderful weekend, chatting together in her room. We also watched a little bit of racing. She really just wanted to be surrounded by family and to talk about horses."

The day after Warren left Balmoral, the Queen's colours were carried to victory one last time, by Love Affairs at Goodwood. Later that evening, she did as she always did after any runner and spoke with her closest racing lieutenant.

"Her death came as a complete shock," admits Warren. "I have so much respect for her. She did her duty until the bitter end."

Then, in a perfect summary, he brings our conversation to a close.

"My goodness," he says. "She went out on a high."

when it ran out in November 1989, although he was later informed that he could continue to live there indefinitely.

Hern's dismissal was not made public until March 1989, when an official announcement stated that the Queen had appointed as his replacement William Hastings-Bass – a son of Peter Hastings-Bass, brother-in-law of Ian Balding and Carnarvon's godson. The depth of the public's anger at Hern's treatment became manifest when Nashwan triumphed in the 2,000 Guineas and the trainer, in his wheelchair, was greeted with cheers in the winner's enclosure. Further proof of his undiminished ability to train was provided by Nashwan's victories in the Derby, Eclipse and King George – results that were all the more embarrassing because he was a son of Height Of Fashion.

Carnarvon bore the brunt of the criticism but the Queen's personal reputation was also damaged, even in the staunchly royalist world of racing. The perception was that she was kicking a man when he was down – sacking one of Britain's greatest trainers just when he was at his most vulnerable. This perception was diminished only slightly by the announcement that Hern would be allowed to train at West Ilsley until November 1990.

Just as the furore was fading, Hastings-Bass trained a top-level winner in the royal colours. This was Unknown Quantity, who was more than a stone below top class but in August 1989 won the Grade 1 Arlington Handicap in Chicago, carrying bottom weight against only four rivals. After moving to West Ilsley, Hastings-Bass – or the Earl of Huntingdon as he became in 1990 – trained several more Pattern winners for the Queen, most of them abroad, but in 1999 he gave up training and she sold the stables to Mick Channon.

In that same year Sir Michael Stoute and Richard Hannon both had their first royal runners. Stoute – based at Freemason Lodge, where Boyd-Rochfort had trained – saddled Flight Of Fancy, an unlucky second in the 2001 Oaks.

The Queen suffered grievous losses with the deaths of Lord Carnarvon and the Queen Mother. Carnarvon's death in 2001 ended a lifetime friendship; his son-in-law John Warren succeeded him as racing manager in all but name. On the Queen Mother's death in 2002 her horses were inherited by the Queen, who therefore owned her first jumpers since Monaveen. The best of them was the Nicky Henderson-trained Barbers Shop, who came seventh to Kauto Star in the 2009 Cheltenham Gold Cup.

By now the Queen's status in racing had suffered a steady decline from dual champion owner in the 1950s to bit-part player in the 21st century. The two main reasons were the decision by the National Stud to stop breeding horses – the source of Landau, Carrozza, Hopeful Venture and many others – and the unique financial constraints on the royal racing and breeding operation.

It had to be self-financing, and seen to be so, because there would have been a public outcry had she liquidated some of her assets in order to indulge in her favourite hobby, especially by buying yearlings. In addition, because of the troubles in Northern Ireland, it was politically impossible for the Royal Studs to use Irish stallions (the best in Europe) for more than two decades from 1973.

Height Of Fashion, the broodmare of a lifetime, was sold

Seal of approval

How the Queen responded to Estimate's victory – in Sir Michael Stoute's words

"Her Majesty made no secret of the fact the Gold Cup was the race at Royal Ascot she coveted most. She was very thrilled to win it with Estimate – very thrilled indeed.

"There was a very amusing postscript. After racing we went to see her. She said to Ryan [Moore, above]: 'I see you got two days for careless riding.' She then looked at him with a smirk on her face and simply said: 'Accidental?'

"Ryan looked back at her and replied: 'No, Ma'am.'

"When she heard him say that she beamed!"

to one of the Arab owner-breeders who spent billions of pounds on the sport and, in so doing, raised the standard of British racing. The rise of Coolmore made the top races even more fiercely competitive. Therefore, in a bid to revive her fortunes, the Queen entered into various deals with other prominent owner-breeders, and that policy produced Carlton House and Estimate.

Carlton House was bred by Darley and ran in the royal colours after an exchange of horses with Sheikh Mohammed. In 2011 he won the Dante Stakes and started favourite for both the Derby and the Irish Derby, finishing third and fourth respectively. He won the Brigadier Gerard Stakes as a four-year-old and then became the first royal horse to be trained in Australia when transferred to Gai Waterhouse in Sydney, although he never won again.

Estimate, bred by the Aga Khan, ran away with the Queen's Vase at Royal Ascot in her owner's Diamond Jubilee year, and in the 2013 Gold Cup she showed plenty of stamina and courage in a driving finish to prevail by a neck and make the Queen the first reigning monarch to own a winner of the race. She was the Queen's first Group/Grade 1 winner since Unknown Quantity 24 years before, and the first in Britain since Dunfermline 36 years before. She won the Doncaster Cup as a five-year-old.

Carlton House and Estimate were trained by Stoute, as was the Darley-bred Dartmouth, who in 2016 beat Highland Reel in the Hardwicke Stakes and finished third to that champion in the King George.

The owner enjoyed a mini-revival in terms of quantity if not quality. In 2014 she equalled her personal-best calendar-year score of 30 wins in 1957, and beat it with 36 in 2019 and 39 in 2021, Flat and jumps combined.

This section on Queen Elizabeth II features edited versions of articles that appeared in the Racing Post between September 9 and 20

THE
BIGGER
PICTURE

The 29 runners break from the stalls in the Buckingham Palace Stakes, the final race of day three at Royal Ascot in June. Nearest camera is Inver Park, the 12-1 winner for jockey Ben Curtis and trainer George Boughey

EDWARD WHITAKER (RACINGPOST.COM/PHOTOS)

UNLIKELY MONSTER

Pyledriver defied his unfashionable background again to slay some big beasts in the King George

By Peter Thomas

IN RACING'S top tier these days, tales of David versus Goliath very rarely have a biblical ending. Put a hulking great giant with a sword against a small boy with a catapult, and what you usually get is a long odds-on winner; pit a small Lambourn yard with 35 horses against a massive Irish breeding empire or a mighty Newmarket powerhouse, and the result tends to be equally predictable.

Except, of course, when Team David can call upon a glistening, dark monster of a horse to go into battle on their behalf; the type that would strike fear into the hearts of any mortal and offer rather more firepower than a slingshot and a few pebbles.

No matter that he was the product of the unlikely mating of a moderate French-bred jumping mare (beaten 74 lengths on the last of her five British starts) with an unfashionable sprinting stallion; nor that he was unloved at the sales as a foal and left to go home with his owners, who may once have nursed mixed feelings about the fact but are now counting their blessings.

Pyledriver, a son of Harbour Watch out of La Pyle, is a 'David' by situation only – a strapping beast who would have done justice

to any of the most exalted silks in the sport, had history taken him in that direction. As it is, pitched against the biggest and best in the sport, he has hit the opposition squarely between the eyes in successive seasons at a deserted Royal Ascot, in Epsom's Coronation Cup and in the heat of Britain's most prestigious all-aged mile-and-a-half contest, the King George, where he left an Arc winner, a pair of John and Thady Gosden fancies and the pride of Coolmore trailing in his substantial wake.

For his joint-trainers William Muir and Chris Grassick, not to mention the La Pyle Partnership that owns him, he has already been the horse of a lifetime. Maybe there's more to come.

★★★★

WHEN La Pyle was sourced from France by Phillip Hobbs, there may have been hope in the hearts of Guy and Huw Leach, but the brothers, partners in a Cardiff construction business, were quickly disabused of any notion that glory with the mare would lie on the racecourse.

She wasn't very good in that sphere, to put it mildly, so they sent her to old pal and mentor Kevin Mercer at his Usk Valley Stud in Monmouthshire, whence she was whisked to Tweenhills
▶ *Continues page 130*

PYLEDRIVER

Stud and did the deed with Harbour Watch.

Her first foal, who, for reasons lost in the mists of time, was nicknamed 'Dave' and nurtured at home, was cruelly overlooked when he went on an exploratory visit to Tattersalls December Sales as a foal in 2017. He was there for all to see, but nobody fancied him, which if it may not reflect badly on the insight of countless racing professionals, certainly says something about the fickle nature of the bloodstock business.

Their loss, however, was Muir's gain. The Leaches were his kind of owners; they liked a game of golf and a bit of fun, but they were ambitious enough, and they had a nice horse that they sent to Linkslade Stables, where, since 1993, the trainer had sent out a healthy annual total of winners, peppered with top-class animals like Averti, Enforcer and Stepper Point.

In short, if there was some latent talent lurking in a beast, Muir would very likely unearth it and make the most of it, but this time he didn't have to work too hard.

"From the very start, everything he did was natural," remembers the down-to-earth handler. "He was stunning to look at and did his work as well as anything, in a season when we'd had five first-time-out two-year-old winners, so when he made his debut on firm ground at Salisbury, I told the owners to have a few quid each-way at 66-1."

A big-priced winner will make loyal owners out of most people, which was lucky for Muir, who had seen promising youngsters like Pyledriver shine on the racecourse before being sold on for good money and continuing their careers elsewhere. It helped that this one was owned by a small group, including partner Roger Devlin, so that when he won in Listed company at Haydock, then the Group 2 King Edward VII and Great Voltigeur Stakes as a three-year-old, the seven-figure offers slapped on the table were less of a temptation than they would have been for one man.

Thus Pyledriver continued his happy, lively, bucking and rearing life with Muir and his wife Janet, and a four-year-old season of huge promise began, delivering in spades with that

➥ *Continues page 132*

RACE-PRO CUBES

Everything you want in a feed - the right control but with the right energy.

It's a winning formula!

» REDUCED STARCH

» HIGH ENERGY

» SUPER PALATABLE

MADE IN OUR OWN UK MILL

Baileys Horse Feeds

Will Humphreys Tel: +44 (0) 7731 997 580
will@baileyshorsefeeds.co.uk

Head Office Tel: +44 (0)1371 850 247
info@baileyshorsefeeds.co.uk

PYLEDRIVER

Coronation Cup win, moving on apace in a Listed race at Lingfield, and then turning very lucrative indeed with a £400,000 second place in the Hong Kong Vase.

It may have seemed greedy to wish for another campaign of equal magnitude, but Muir and the La Pyle people knew there was plenty more to come from their pride and joy.

★★★★

IF THERE'S a wicked witch in this racing fairytale, it's the one who shoved Martin Dwyer, the likeable Liverpudlian who had partnered Pyledriver to all his biggest wins, off his horse on the gallops one morning in March, leaving him with a nasty knee injury, the like of which doesn't do any favours to a 40-something jockey.

Dwyer, Muir's son-in-law, had been on board when the upwardly mobile five-year-old returned to action with a moderate effort from a wide draw in Saudi Arabia, but by the time the Dubai Sheema Classic came around, it was Frankie Dettori's privilege to steer him into a lucrative fourth place, followed by a distant second to Hukum in his bid for a Coronation Cup repeat.

If there were any Hollywood-style justice in the real world, Dwyer would have made a miraculous recovery against all the odds and been ready to reappear in the final reel, being legged up on the feisty entire as he left the parade ring at Ascot, ready for the gunfight at Swinley Bottom.

As it was, the sidelined jockey was enduring his rehabilitation at Oaksey House, pausing only long enough to issue timely advice to PJ McDonald, the man lucky enough to be reunited with Pyledriver for the King George, three years on from their only other liaison: the Listed two-year-old win at Haydock.

Muir – and now the second name on the licence, Grassick – knew they had on their hands a horse who was prepared to "take off his coat, roll up his sleeves and show you what he can do", but this was shaping up to be the biggest moment of Pyledriver's – and Muir's – career and it was important that all available information should be shared for the common good.

"We feel sorry for Martin, but he told PJ exactly what to do, and it was

brilliant," enthused the trainer. A happy ending was brewing, even if the cast list wasn't quite as it had been imagined.

★★★★

ANYBODY who tries to suggest it wasn't a vintage King George will get short shrift from Muir. There may have been only six runners, but we had the previous year's Arc winner, the previous year's Juddmonte International winner, the Hardwicke Stakes winner Broome, the Irish Derby winner Westover and the narrow Oaks runner-up Emily Upjohn, and they finished in that order behind Pyledriver, on proper summer ground, as it should be.

To recap, that's the winners of eight international Group 1s, from the biggest yards in Europe, put in their place by an 18-1 shot who was brought home from the sales by his owners for 10,000gns. If all the others underperformed, then the La Pyle partnership probably didn't care all that much; if Torquator Tasso was highly likely to turn the tables if they met on heavy ground in the Arc, then so be it; perhaps Mishriff, beaten nearly 11 lengths, isn't as good as he was, but so what?

In short, this was the day and Pyledriver seized it. If there are reasons to think others let the side down, there are other reasons to think this wasn't a bad effort at all.

The pace, for sure, was strong and robust, with Westover racing a shade keenly but being followed closely by a wary Ryan Moore on Broome. Mishriff, raggedly slow from the gates, made life hard for himself, but Torquator Tasso sat easily in mid-division and was, as they say, "close enough if good enough".

Always travelling conspicuously well, though, was Pyledriver, who tussled for the lead early but was settled just off it after a quarter of a mile, leaving Broome to surge to the front with three furlongs to go. Two from home, McDonald could wait no longer for fear of disappointing his eager partner, and the pair quickly put a safe distance of ground between themselves and the game German raider.

It seems safe to say the final yards must have seemed like miles to his connections, and as Pyledriver began to wander around in front – perhaps wondering what all the Group 1 fuss was about – there were brief flickers of concern; but McDonald quickly reminded him of the shortest distance between two points and he saw out the rest of the race like a hardened professional.

It was the culmination of all the hopes and dreams of his owners, the faith they showed in both horse and trainer, and if the jockey will undoubtedly have put a consoling arm around the shoulder of his wounded colleague, Dwyer in turn was chuffed for them all. "I'd be lying if I didn't say I was gutted because I know it should have been me," he admitted, "but what a performance. It was brilliant for the whole team and I really think the horse deserves so much more credit than he gets."

A Racing Post Rating of 125 made this a clear personal-best from Pyledriver. The issue that ruled him out of a bid for the Arc was just a soft-tissue injury that kept him off the track for an untimely and infuriating spell, but Muir soon had his eyes on other targets, not least the prospect of Pyledriver racing on as a six-year-old.

Goliaths everywhere are still quaking in their sandals.

BEHIND EVERY RACEHORSE IS A GREAT TEAM.
BE PART OF IT.

- APPRENTICESHIP & TRAINING INFORMATION
- CASE STUDIES & JOB PROFILES
- CAREER MAP
- FREE JOB BOARD

EXPLORE THE ROLES AND PROGRESS ROUTES WITH OUR INTERACTIVE MAP • EXPLORE **YOUR** OPTIONS

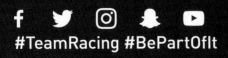

FREQUENT FLYER

Joseph O'Brien's ultra-tough State Of Rest capped a remarkable globetrotting journey with Royal Ascot victory in the Prince of Wales's Stakes

STATE OF REST is his name but it was a far from apt description of his racing career. He was always busy, always on the move, always working hard. This was not a restful existence but it was a highly successful one.

By the middle of his three-year-old season, the Joseph O'Brien-trained colt had won only a Fairyhouse maiden from seven starts, but then the fun started. Over the next 12 months he won top-level races in four countries across three continents, travelling more than 30,000 miles and rarely visiting the same place twice.

The pinnacle was his victory in the Prince of Wales's Stakes at Royal Ascot 2022, and fittingly it was against an international cast. The Irish raider's four rivals came from Britain, France and Japan, but he was the master of them all, just as he had been against American and Australian opponents the year before.

After an MRI scan highlighted an issue that brought a halt to State Of Rest's racing career a few weeks later, O'Brien paid a glowing tribute to his frequent flyer. "He had the most incredible constitution and will to win," he said. "He won Group/Grade 1 races on three different continents on a wide variety of tracks, ground conditions and race tempos. It all came alike to him. We asked a huge amount of him throughout his career and he delivered every time."

Even then, State Of Rest's travelling was far from over. His exploits on the racetrack had earned him a place at stud and of course it could only be as a dual-hemisphere stallion, shuttling between Ireland and Australia.

★★★★

IN THE summer of 2021 State Of Rest travelled to the United States for the one and only time and came back from Saratoga a Grade 1 winner.

On paper he didn't have the same credentials for the Saratoga Derby as the warm favourite Bolshoi Ballet (trained by O'Brien's father Aidan), who had also headed the market for the Epsom Derby two months earlier before winning the Grade 1 Belmont Derby. State Of Rest's third place in a Curragh Listed race didn't seem to measure up but O'Brien jnr's 21-1 shot rose to the challenge with a one-length victory, leaving Bolshoi Ballet only fourth.

O'Brien's next move was much bolder. The Cox Plate, famously won four times in a row by Australia's mighty mare Winx, had only once gone to a raider from the northern hemisphere – O'Brien snr's Adelaide in 2014 – and was always strongly defended by the home team around the tricky Moonee Valley track.

Having employed John Valezquez for his local knowledge at Saratoga, O'Brien did the same here with the booking of Johnny Allen, a Cork native with 12 Australian Group 1 wins to his name, and the result bore out his strategic skill. Allen burst through a gap two furlongs out and fended off Godolphin's locally trained Anamoe by a short head, exactly the kind of marginal gain O'Brien wanted. "Johnny gave the horse the most fantastic ride," the trainer said.

The first prize for the Cox Plate was a highly lucrative £1.7m but greater riches lay in store for State Of Rest's owners Teme Valley Racing. As a son of the brilliant Australian-bred sprinter-miler Starspangledbanner, State Of Rest was highly attractive to the Australian bloodstock industry, even more so given that he had won their biggest weight-for-age race as a three-year-old. It was not long before top Australian stud Newgate Farm, China Horse Club and a powerful consortium of Australian owners and breeders joined forces with Ireland's Rathbarry Stud to buy into State Of Rest.

Explaining the rationale, Newgate's managing director Henry Field said: "History often tells the future and what we have seen is that these Cox Plate winners, especially three-year-olds, have an elite record at stud. If we look at horses who were Cox Plate winners as three-year-olds and multiple Group 1 winners since the turn of the century there's only been three – So You Think,

Shamus Award and Savabeel – and they're excellent stallions, so State Of Rest profiles very well."

★★★★

SO YOU THINK, one of the Cox Plate winners highlighted by Field, had left Australia to further his reputation on the global stage, winning five Group 1s in Europe for Aidan O'Brien and ending his career with Royal Ascot glory in the Prince of Wales's Stakes. It was a story O'Brien jnr knew well, having put the Prince of Wales's on his CV for the only time with So You Think while riding for his father, and it was one he was about to repeat as a trainer.

In his new China Horse Club colours and with Shane Crosse taking over in the saddle for only the second time, State Of Rest started his European campaign as a four-year-old by taking the Prix Ganay at Longchamp. It was a third top-level win in a row, spread over a nine-month period across three continents. The ultimate target was another long-haul trip to the Cox Plate but for now State Of Rest's air miles would be more limited.

He stayed at home in Ireland for the Tattersalls Gold Cup, twice won by So You Think, but fell just short despite a strong finish, beaten about half a length in third behind Alenquer. Next came a short hop to Royal Ascot, which would bring the best performance

▸ *Continues page 136*

of State Of Rest's career. A key element was a change of tactics: instead of launching a powerful run from about a furlong and a half out, this time Crosse seized the initiative from the off.

The plan worked to perfection. Unchallenged by his four opponents, Crosse had it easy in front and was able to wind up State Of Rest down the straight to hold off Bay Bridge (later the Champion Stakes winner) by a length.

"I was quite relaxed watching the race because it was going how I hoped it would. It's not very often that happens in racing," said O'Brien after welcoming back his first Royal Ascot winner as a trainer. "We really wanted the lead today and we thought if he got it we had a great chance to win. Shane executed it perfectly."

It was an impressively cool ride by the 20-year-old. The average age of the four jockeys who lined up alongside him in the stalls was 37 and three of them were Derby winners, while the other was a dual winner of the French Derby. O'Brien had been just 19 and just as composed when he won the race on So You Think ten years earlier, but it was different as a trainer. "I certainly felt more pressure today," he admitted. "Maybe it's because I'm getting older."

State Of Rest was only eighth when dropped to a mile in the Prix Jacques le Marois at Deauville in August and it proved to be his final run. An MRI scan conducted by Racing Victoria later that month found an issue, meaning he would not pass the necessary protocols to travel to Melbourne for the Cox Plate.

"Everyone here is so disappointed that State Of Rest's racing career has come to a sudden end. He was without question a remarkably talented, durable and consistent performer," O'Brien said, while also looking forward to the stallion career that had long been set up. "We'll miss him greatly, but we look forward to training his progeny in the years ahead."

In mid-September, State Of Rest left O'Brien's yard in County Kilkenny for the hour-and-a-half transfer to Rathbarry Stud. For him it was a short journey but an important and well-earned one.

▼ Front man: Shane Crosse takes the Prince of Wales's on State Of Rest for Joseph O'Brien (right)

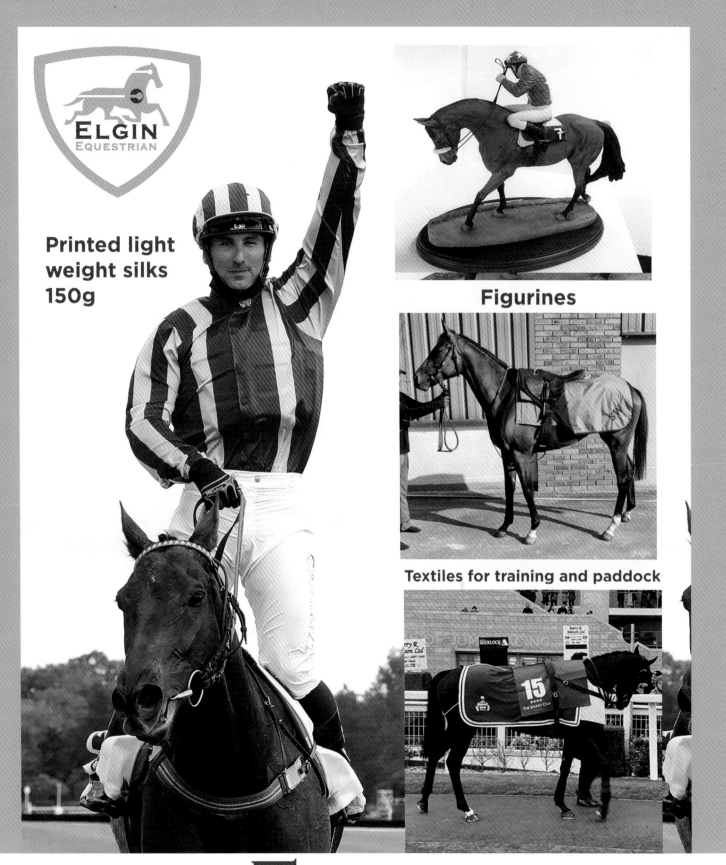

Printed light weight silks 150g

Figurines

Textiles for training and paddock

ELGIN
We deliver all over Europe
WWW.ELGINEQUESTRIAN.COM

GREEN ENERGY

By Scott Burton

THE sight of the famous emerald green silks of the Aga Khan being carried into the winner's enclosure after a British Group 1 is something many grew up with in racing. But Vadeni was bridging a six-year gap back to Harzand's Derby in 2016 when he arrowed up the Sandown hill to capture the Eclipse in July.

The arrival of this homebred son of Churchill on the European middle-distance scene could not have been better timed. The 2022 season marked the centenary of the Aga Khan's family involvement in European racing and Vadeni was a standard bearer who combined a potent turn of foot with the long-established stamina of their pedigrees.

He was prepared to the minute by Jean-Claude Rouget, the modern master of his own country's Derby who has shrugged off an undeserved reputation as a homebird in recent seasons and is now prepared to send his finest wherever the fixture list suits them best.

The final part of the equation was the mercurial talent of Christophe Soumillon, accompanied to Sandown by two of his three children and at that stage in the middle of a purple patch on the international stage. The relationship between the Aga Khan Studs and Soumillon did not make it unscathed to the end of the year but his role in Vadeni's rise to the top cannot be underestimated.

★★★★

VADENI began the season on plenty of longlists for potential Classic success after being given a typically easy time at two by Rouget. As a son of a 2,000 Guineas-winning sire, it was only

fair to give him a trial over a mile but Vadeni was not put under maximum pressure by Soumillon in the Prix de Fontainebleau, coming home two and a half lengths behind stablemate Welwal.

He was then sent to Chantilly to assess his suitability for the Prix du Jockey Club and won the 1m1f Prix de Guiche, one of Rouget's favourite trials. It was not the last time the trainer would subject him to a speed test that would sharpen him up for future projects.

The trouble for turfistes was that the stable had four legitimate contenders for the Jockey Club, with Al Hakeem in particular having drawn favourable comparisons from Rouget with the mighty Almanzor after brushing

away the opposition in his trial.

Appearing on the Radio Balances show two days before the Classic, I asked Soumillon if he felt Vadeni's stamina for a mile and two and a half furlongs was assured, a query he swatted away summarily: "If he's good enough he won't be beaten for lack of stamina."

From stall two Vadeni was given the perfect ground-saving ride before being launched two furlongs out. In a matter of strides it was all over and at the line there was an eased-down five lengths back to El Bodegon and Modern Games, both Group 1 winners.

"He did it in great style and now he'll need to really show us because he didn't just win today, he walked

away with it," said Rouget on the way out to the presentation in front of the stands. "I don't remember a horse winning this race that easily in a long while."

Rouget was right. The modern Jockey Club is almost designed to produce blanket finishes and the winner nearly always gets punished by the international handicappers in comparison to the Derby hero from 24 hours earlier. The fact that Vadeni was given the same 123 rating as the hugely exciting Desert Crown was an accolade in itself.

Vadeni would now attempt the same double achieved by St Mark's Basilica and Mishriff in the Eclipse and the last-named would also be among his starry opposition, along with Irish 2,000 Guineas winner

Vadeni carried the Aga Khan's famous colours to Eclipse victory before falling just short in the Arc

▲ Blanket finish: Vadeni (green) takes the Eclipse from Mishriff (near side), Native Trail (blue) and Lord North

Native Trail and the improving Bay Bridge.

Rouget had said on Jockey Club day that he was in possession of one of the best three-year-olds in Europe and that his job was to "confirm him as a true champion" by the end of the season. For all that the Eclipse offers the Classic generation a 10lb pull in the weights, this was a bold move and one that could have deflated Vadeni's rising stock just a month after he had shot up in value.

If anything the race went too well for Soumillon. He was forced to commit a shade earlier than ideal by the combined forces of how well his partner was travelling and a keen awareness that Mishriff was going nowhere under a powerless David Egan, barred from progress up the rail.

It was a brilliant piece of improvisation on a horse who had hitherto shown himself best when played late. Mishriff finally got clean air on the outside but the little green bird had flown.

Television and social media audiences were treated to Soumillon's young sons, Mika and Robin, roaring Papa home, images that were quickly followed by Rouget's assistant Marie Rohaut and Vadeni's groom Dominika Kleczynska overcome with emotion.

Even a 12-day ban for careless riding after the line failed to dampen the air of celebration – Soumillon subsequently got that reduced on appeal to eight days having represented himself in front of the independent disciplinary panel – and Princess Zahra Aga Khan summed up just what an important colt Vadeni was becoming, as well as sharing a sense of her vindication at rolling the dice instead of taking the easy option at Deauville.

"You get one shot at a career," she said. "You should take on the big boys. So there!"

★★★★

THE autumn is when Europe crowns its champions and Rouget has become increasingly attached to the Irish Champion Stakes following Almanzor's triumph there. Perhaps mirroring Princess Zahra's philosophy, it has become his target of choice rather than the Prix Niel or the Prix Foy on Longchamp's Arc trials card the same weekend. Sottsass had his blade sharpened at Leopardstown before winning the Arc in 2020, finishing what at the time looked an unpromising fourth.

Vadeni went into the race as clear favourite against compatriot Onesto and Coolmore's one-time Derby favourite Luxembourg and looked unlucky in the run. For almost the only time in a major race all season, Soumillon got caught in the wrong spot. Having planned to come down the middle to outer of the short Leopardstown straight in search of the best ground,

▶ Continues page 140

he found daylight in short supply and ended up diving for the rail.

Vadeni briefly picked up before the effort of changing tack began to tell and he flattened out in the final 100 yards. Almost the only person not disappointed was Rouget, who was adamant that he hadn't had Vadeni completely screwed to the floor for the race and had left him a little light of work.

This was partly to compensate for the travelling. But it also emerged that Vadeni doesn't like to be left lying around for too long. The gap from Sandown to Leopardstown had been longer than ideal and, while he undoubtedly had a tough race, the fact that it had turned into a sprint had spared him the worst. Three weeks would be a much more suitable space to his next race.

Three weeks, you say? The next target was the Prix de l'Arc de Triomphe, with connections hoping Vadeni could buck a 32-year trend and win Europe's greatest race on his first try at a mile and a half. By the time the race came around, Soumillon was riding not just to redeem any perceived error in Ireland but a far graver mistake, one that would cost him his retainer with the Aga Khan just two days after the Arc.

As seems to have been the case at every turn, there were plenty of questions stacked up against Vadeni's character, not least the ever deepening ground over which he would be asked to stretch his stamina. An epic cloudburst turned His Highness's green silks almost black but once again that trademark surge was there for all to see, enough to see off 18 of his 19 rivals. Only Alpinista was able to resist and she kept Vadeni at bay by half a length.

It was at that point that the stresses of walking the high wire with a colt of huge potential and enormous value in the breeding sheds broke over Rouget in waves of emotion, mixed in with wonder at the success enjoyed by his old friend Sir Mark Prescott.

Vadeni surprised at every turn in 2022 and his team had one final twist for us. On the day they announced the termination of Soumillon's retainer, the pill was sweetened immeasurably with the news that their wondrous horse would be back again at four. Europe watch out!

Shockwaves reverberate from Soumillon's elbow

Was there a more shocking sight on a racecourse anywhere in 2022?

Watching from the stands at Saint-Cloud there is a stretch of the back straight where binoculars are frustrated and the big screen comes into its own. It is also the point at which the camera angle is head-on to the runners and in the Prix Thomas Bryon – two days before the Prix de l'Arc de Triomphe – that meant Christophe Soumillon's errant elbow was there for all to see.

So too was the sickening sight of Rossa Ryan being shot out of the side door and cartwheeling across the turf.

The first replay gave the mind a chance to catch up with the eye. Had Soumillon's mount, Syros, taken a false step or shifted out? That would be the obvious explanation because the alternative was that one of the world's best jockeys had attempted to shift a rival from the ground he wished to occupy and had carelessly knocked him out of the saddle.

Yet that is exactly what subsequent replays showed and by the time Soumillon returned to weigh in, he knew his world had just changed in as yet unimaginable ways.

What followed threatened to divert attention away from the Arc itself. Officials and owners publicly tried to distance themselves from Soumillon and attempted to have him removed from taking any part at Longchamp.

Princess Zahra Aga Khan spoke to the Racing Post at Longchamp the next day and her description of his act as "unconscionable" effectively made his sacking a case of when, not if.

All weekend the man himself remained a model of composure and concentration, determined to show his worth to the Aga Khan Studs team in the arena that mattered most. On Erevann he was quite brilliant in the Prix Daniel Wildenstein and he almost pulled off the Arc itself aboard Vadeni.

Would it have saved his retainer? Almost certainly not. They parted on good terms and he will almost certainly ride in the emerald green silks again should one or more of the trainers request it for a specific horse.

The price to Soumillon was steep but for the unscathed Ryan it could have been so much worse.

When you return to those few seconds at Saint-Cloud, the images do not become more rational, the reasoning no clearer. It was quite simply a moment of madness.

▲ Under pressure: Christophe Soumillon on Arc weekend

Equine & Rural
Equestrian & Rural Mortgages & Finance

We believe in the personal touch…

Specialists in Mortgages and Finance for the Equine, Rural and Agricultural Sectors
Saving you time and Money...

Funding is one of those necessities that you sometimes must deal with and finding the right finance for your enterprise can be difficult and time consuming.

Our team of rural finance specialists have years of experience of working with equestrian, agricultural and rural businesses.

With strong relationships with a wide choice of specialist banks and lenders, we can find the best loan and terms for you – many of which aren't available on the high street.

We are with you every step of the way from application to completion and will work with your land agents and solicitors on your behalf too.

Projects We Can Help
- Buying property or land-based business, including equestrian tied properties.
- Buying bare land for new ventures.
- Re-mortgaging or consolidating existing debt to allow the business to develop
- Buying out business partners, matrimonial or partnerships splits
- Expanding or improving existing stabling or equine facilities
- Building a house on site
- Bridging loan

Typical Equestrian Business Mortgage Term:
- Terms up to 25 years
- Combined employment and business income considered

- Lump sum reductions with no or minimal early repayment penalty
- No Introductory interest rates: just competitive rate for the whole term
- Up to 70% loan to value (30% deposit) 100% mortgage considered with additional security (equity in existing property)

We've helped create, develop and grow many equestrian enterprises including:
- Training/competition yards
- Riding schools
- Racing yards
- Livery yards
- Polo yards
- Studs

Horsebox and equine equipment finance
Flexible finance for the equine industry

As horse owners ourselves, we have a rare insight into this specialist world and can advise you with the benefit of first hand experience. you'll need unbiased, straightforward advice.

We'll find an affordable loan to suit your needs.

Borrow £5,000 upwards 2–8 year loan term quick process to pay out

We'd love to talk to you about your project and see how we can help...

Call us now on: 07823 447752 or Email: linda@equineandrural.co.uk

www.equineandrural.co.uk

CLASSIC COMBINATION

Hollie Doyle made history when she won the Prix de Diane
on Nashwa – and there was more big-race success to come

By Nick Pulford

IMAD AL SAGAR, the prominent owner-breeder who employs Hollie Doyle as his retained jockey, made his point strongly and straightforwardly. "Gender should have nothing to do with it. Either you have it or you don't," he said. Doyle has it.

Al Sagar was speaking in the winner's enclosure at Glorious Goodwood after the Nassau Stakes, having just watched a cool and confident Doyle deliver his homebred filly Nashwa to another Group 1 victory. The previous month, Doyle's "horse of a lifetime" had carried her into the history books as the first female jockey to win a Group 1 European

Classic when they took the Prix de Diane. Not only does Doyle have it, she is making the most of it.

As much as gender shouldn't come into it, we know it does in all walks of life, and Doyle's feats are mould-breaking. They will remain that way for some time to come, simply because the barriers have long existed and still have to be broken. Three days after she landed

the Nassau, England's Lionesses won the European Women's Football Championship. It represented another seismic shift in attitudes towards women in sport. It was a momentous week.

A big difference in racing is that there is virtually no separation between men and women; they compete on the same playing field, compete for the same rides,

compete for the same prizes. Understandably, Doyle does not want to be defined simply by her gender. "I want to be seen as just a jockey. From my point of view I do the same as the lads," she said in a Racing Post interview in June. Yet she is also aware that her success has a different aspect and is having an impact.

"It can be quite hard, because when I get all the fuss I'm probably a bit ignorant towards it," she said in that interview. "But I do appreciate that hopefully I'm paving a path to inspire others and prove that they can do it too. It's really cool to see young girls come up to me and I recently went to see all the pupils at the racing school and there was only one boy on the course. They're all girls. Whereas when I went I was one of the only girls. It's changing."

★★★★

THAT interview came in Epsom week as Doyle looked forward to riding Nashwa in the Oaks with a big chance. Her filly ran well but could not go with the duelling Tuesday and Emily Upjohn and Doyle had to settle for third, just over three lengths back. If that was deflating, Doyle did not have to wait long for the pumped-up elation of Classic celebration.

Just over a fortnight later John and Thady Gosden sent Nashwa to Chantilly for the Prix de Diane. On this occasion France's version of the Oaks was of lesser quality than the Epsom original and, just as significantly, the distance of a mile and two and a half furlongs was more to Nashwa's liking. Having been second favourite at Epsom behind stablemate Emily Upjohn, she was the 3-1 market leader this time.

Whatever the pre-race pressure, it only increased for Doyle when things didn't go to plan once the stalls opened. Nashwa jumped well from her good draw in stall two but when Doyle looked around for

▶ Continues page 144

◀ Chantilly cream: Nashwa scores a narrow win over La Parisienne in the Prix de Diane; below, the Racing Post front page the next day

a good tow into the race, the expected pace wasn't there. Plan A scrubbed, she instead made sure she stayed in the front rank from her good position near the rail. Nashwa was there to be shot at turning into the straight, but Doyle fought hard to repel all challengers and take victory by a short neck from La Parisienne, the mount of wily veteran Gerald Mosse.

"I felt vulnerable at the two pole, I'm not going to lie," Doyle said. "It was a muddling race and I expected some of the others to be a bit more excited pace-wise than they were. I didn't want to be where I was but she was happy to be one off the rail with a bit of company. When the second horse came to my girth she dug deep."

A firm handshake from Mosse soon after crossing the line was a mark of respect for a battle well fought and there was high praise from John Gosden. "Nashwa is a very classy filly and was beautifully ridden by a hugely talented rider. You could ask for no more," he said. "Imad asked me a few years ago about having a jockey, and when he showed me the list I said, 'Hollie Doyle'. I told him horses run for her, she's very meticulous, a fabulous rider and a very serious person with a great sense of humour. She's got a bundle of talent and Imad has been rewarded. This win should get on the front pages."

The Racing Post front page certainly, as well as the ITV evening news bulletin, and Doyle was showered with congratulations. "It's really humbling to see how many people are behind me and are happy to see me have success like this," the 25-year-old said.

"If it wasn't for my job with Imad Al Sagar I'm not sure I'd have ever come across an opportunity like this in my career. To be associated with the top trainers has given me an opportunity to showcase my riding. If you'd told me two or three years ago I'd have been riding in a Classic for John Gosden, I'd have said you were mad. And it was mad!"

★★★★

GLORIOUS GOODWOOD was the next showcase for the ability of Doyle and Nashwa. The Classic-winning filly was hot favourite at 6-5 for the Nassau and this time it turned

out as easy as the betting suggested. Advised by John Gosden to "ride her like the best horse in the race", Doyle took a pull as soon as the stalls opened and made her run from the rear in the straight, scoring comfortably by a length and three-quarters.

"It was a change of tactics but I know she can win being ridden like that," Doyle said. "They steadied the pace up, which was a bit worrying for me from where I was, but she's got a high cruising speed and is push button. She gave me some feel, it's unreal. She's a horse of a lifetime."

Nashwa is an important flagbearer too for Al Sagar, who in partnership with Saleh Al Homaizi won the Derby with Authorized and has been developing Blue Diamond Stud near Newmarket over the past decade. "I must admit I'm very emotional when it comes to her. She's my first Classic homebred and I'm very proud of her," he said at Goodwood.

➤ *Continues page 146*

▲ Winning team: Hollie Doyle and Imad Al Sagar (right) with Nashwa; below, Doyle with the Nassau trophy

'It's incredible how far she's come'

Caroline Doyle was a proud but stressed mum watching her daughter Hollie's victory on Nashwa in the Nassau Stakes.

"I'm still shaking. I'm so excited," she said shortly after the race. "I don't know how Hollie stays so cool. I'd be an absolute wreck but she does so well. We're over the moon. I was really nervous today. I always get like that with short-priced favourites when they're expected to win. It can be nerve-racking."

Such has been the 25-year-old jockey's rapid ascent that even her mum can't quite believe it.

"She's always been competitive in everything she's done," she added. "She played rugby, football, all sports, and is so competitive. It's incredible how far she's come and we're all so proud – it still feels a little bit surreal. It's sunk in a little bit but she keeps managing to find a bit more."

▶ Glorious success: Nashwa stretches to victory in the Nassau

Al Sagar is also proud of the choice he made as his retained rider. "What I saw in Hollie is what she demonstrated today, but two years ago," he said. "Hollie is a gifted jockey, very intelligent and very dedicated. She has proved that again."

Unfortunately, a third Group 1 of the year with Nashwa proved just out of reach when they went back to France for the Prix de l'Opera on Arc day. Doyle made it to the front from a wide draw but the early efforts appeared to catch up with her mount as 66-1 outsider Place Du Carrousel swooped late to score by three-quarters of a length. "We were drawn in stall 13 and it costs you at the other end when you're beaten by a horse from a lower draw, but that's racing," said John Gosden. "She ran a blinder, a wonderful race."

That disappointment was followed quickly by more Group 1 honours for Doyle in the Prix de l'Abbaye on The Platinum Queen. This was a different filly for different connections but, even as the top-level wins continue to mount up in her burgeoning career, Doyle will remember how the doors were opened.

"It's incredible that Imad Al Sagar gave me the job really," Doyle reflected. "The whole point of it was hoping that I could come across a horse of the calibre of Nashwa and I'm just lucky to have come across one so early in my job. Imad cares so much about his breeding operation and the one thing we have in common is that we want to win. It's a good combination."

Nashwa and Doyle are a good combination too. A Classic combination in fact.

Longchamp queen

Hollie Doyle's other star filly of 2022 was The Platinum Queen, who gave her another French Group 1 win in the Prix de l'Abbaye on Arc day.

Just over half an hour after her defeat on Nashwa in the Prix de l'Opera, Doyle donned the Middleham Park Racing colours on Richard Fahey's flying two-year-old, who was in front before halfway and held on gamely in a driving finish (below).

The Platinum Queen had run a brave second to Highfield Princess in the Nunthorpe Stakes at York with Doyle in the saddle for the first time, but Group 1 victory was not long delayed. "We got one of the big ones, which is fantastic," Fahey said. "I've not had a two-year-old as physically and mentally mature as this girl."

Doyle's capability to ride at 8st 4lb was a factor in securing her the ride on The Platinum Queen – who received 21lb from most of the field as she became the first juvenile to win the Abbaye since Sigy in 1978 – but once again she packed a punch in a tough battle.

All challengers were repelled as The Platinum Queen won by a short neck from fellow Yorkshire raider White Lavender from Karl Burke's yard, with Coeur De Pierre a neck away in third.

At the other end of the scale for Doyle – both in terms of weight and distance – was her beloved veteran Trueshan's incredible staying performance under 10st 8lb in the Northumberland Plate in June.

From the Newcastle all-weather to the turf of Chantilly and Longchamp, Doyle was busting trends all year.

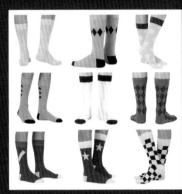

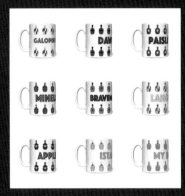

IN THE PICTURE

'Queen of racing' Enable produces striking first foal

SPECIAL moments are worth the wait. That was the message from Juddmonte Farms after the brilliant Enable gave birth to her first foal, a colt by Kingman, on February 11.

The 11-time Group/Grade 1 winner, who had been covered by Kingman on Valentine's Day 2021, had passed her due date but the late Prince Khalid Abdullah's breeding operation announced all had gone smoothly with mare and foal.

A statement said: "Juddmonte are delighted to announce that Enable gave birth to a strikingly marked colt foal by Kingman at 3.54pm, the day before her own birthday. Enable has taken to her maternal duties extremely well. Special moments are worth the wait!"

A few weeks later Edward Whitaker, the Racing Post's multiple award-winning photographer, was kindly granted the chance to visit the eight-year-old mare and her foal, and he took this lovely picture in the paddocks at Banstead Manor Stud near Newmarket.

Bred by Juddmonte and carrying Abdullah's famous green, pink and white colours, Enable was dubbed the queen of racing during a stellar career for John Gosden. The daughter of Nathaniel collected a record-equalling two Prix de l'Arc de Triomphes, a record-breaking three King George VI and Queen Elizabeth Stakes, a Breeders' Cup Turf, the Oaks and Irish Oaks. She bowed out after attempting a third Arc win when finishing sixth behind Sottsass in 2020, having won 15 of her 19 starts and more than £10.7 million in prize-money.

Her first mating was with Banstead Manor Stud supersire Kingman and she produced her colt foal on not just the day before her own birthday but on the actual birthday of another Juddmonte giant in Frankel. She was booked to Darley's top sire Dubawi for her second covering.

Like Enable, Kingman was a homebred champion for Abdullah who was trained by Gosden. The son of Invincible Spirit was the champion three-year-old miler of 2014 after Group 1 victories in the Irish 2,000 Guineas, St James's Palace Stakes, Sussex Stakes and Prix Jacques le Marois. His only defeat in an eight-race career was a close second to Night Of Thunder in the 2,000 Guineas and he earned £970,834.

The now 11-year-old stallion, who stands for a fee of £150,000, was the second-fastest sire to 50 northern hemisphere-bred stakes winners behind only Frankel. He has produced six individual Group 1 winners including world champion miler Palace Pier and French 2,000 Guineas hero Persian King, and his notable performers in 2022 included Fillies' Mile winner Commissioning and Kinross, who took the Prix de la Foret and British Champions Sprint.

Picture: EDWARD WHITAKER (RACINGPOST.COM/PHOTOS)

PARTY TIME

Flooring Porter dominated the Stayers' Hurdle for the second year in a row, sparking wild celebrations at the reopened Cheltenham Festival

By Nick Pulford

ST PATRICK'S DAY at lockdown Cheltenham was a quiet affair but it was a different story when the doors reopened at the 2022 festival. The partying was raucous and long, in the old tradition, and at the centre of it all was Stayers' Hurdle hero Flooring Porter. His achievement in becoming the first repeat winner since Big Buck's was well worth celebrating.

Flooring Porter has the right profile to be a folk hero. He has risen from humble origins, bought cheaply and emerging from the handicap ranks, and represents four owners who are living the dream and loving every moment. Above all, not only does their horse deliver on jump racing's biggest stage, he does it the hard way.

In a sense Flooring Porter had to prove himself all over again in his second Stayers' Hurdle. Having had a reputation as something of a hothead, he was aided by the absence of a heaving crowd in 2021 and nobody knew then how well his front-running style was going to work in his first test around Cheltenham. When he returned 12 months on, his form in the interim was questionable, the atmosphere was red-hot and his opponents knew what to expect.

The forces ranged against Gavin Cromwell's stable star were formidable. The 11-4 favourite was Klassical Dream, who had won the Champion Stayers Hurdle at Punchestown the previous April and added another Grade 1 victory in the Christmas Hurdle at Leopardstown. On the first occasion Flooring Porter had been pulled up and on the second he was the two-length runner-up, although it was arguably an unsatisfactory guide given that Klassical Dream had anticipated the start and stolen six lengths from the off.

The other fancied Irish contender was Royal Kahala, who had upset the odds-on Klassical Dream in the Galmoy Hurdle at Gowran Park in January, while the British challenge revolved around old rivals Champ, Thyme Hill and Paisley Park. They had been the first three in that order in the Long Walk Hurdle at Ascot before Christmas, while Paisley Park had reversed the form to beat Champ with an incredible run up the Cheltenham hill in the Cleeve Hurdle in January, with Thyme Hill absent then to keep him fresh for the festival.

★★★★

ON THE big day, however, there was no stopping Flooring Porter. Danny Mullins, now his regular jockey having picked up the ride by chance the previous year, simply pressed repeat on the tactics button and challenged the rest to catch him if they could. The task was beyond them again.

Even on ground turned soft by the previous day's rain, Flooring Porter was in his element. This time he had no problems at the start and was in front from flagfall, while in a role reversal Klassical Dream proved somewhat reluctant to line up and jumped off a little detached in last of the ten runners. Quickly opening a four-length lead, Flooring Porter jumped superbly as Mullins clocked the fractions in his head. That effortless hurdling allowed Mullins to give him a breather before the run down the hill on the final circuit, reducing his advantage as the chasers fanned out in close pursuit.

If it looked like the race was on, Mullins and Flooring Porter were soon to finish it. They powered away from the second-last after another smooth jump and it was clear there was plenty left in the tank. Champ tried to challenge up the inside but was going backwards before the final flight and Klassical Dream, having made his move, was also starting to look one-paced by then.

A slight jink at the last could not halt Flooring Porter's momentum and he never looked in any danger of being caught up the hill, coming

▸ *Continues page 152*

home a decisive winner by two and three-quarter lengths. Thyme Hill and Paisley Park made gallant late runs into second and third, separated by a nose, with Champ fourth and Klassical Dream fifth.

Having walked back to a near-empty winner's enclosure the previous year, Mullins was greeted with wildly different scenes this time. The syndicate members and their supporters – decked out in black and white scarves and said to number more than 100 – had roared Flooring Porter home and the bedlam continued as their St Patrick's Day hero returned to thunderous acclaim.

"It's a dream come true," said Ned Hogarty, one of the four owners from the County Galway town of Ballinasloe. "To be here and have a dual Stayers' Hurdle winner is fantastic – it will never be forgotten. The horse was due it, we were due it, the parish was due it and the country was due it. Hopefully we'll all celebrate in comfort now and drink a few pints on Paddy's Day."

A few days later, Hogarty had an update on the celebrations. "We went back to the Holiday Inn in the town on Thursday night and took a big gang there. They hadn't seen anything like it before and won't again until we come back next March. It was a night we'll never forget. We came back to Joe's in Ballinasloe on Friday and the publican there told us he hadn't seen scenes like it since Italia '90!"

★★★★

HOGARTY owns a flooring business in Galway, which explains the first part of the horse's name, and his partners are Kerril Creaven and father and son Tommy and Alan Sweeney. Creaven and Sweeney snr previously owned the Countryman pub in Creagh and the second part of the name comes from the original name for Guinness. Their black and white colours also pay homage to Ireland's famous stout.

They teamed up to buy Flooring Porter for a reported €5,000 in response to an advert on Cromwell's Facebook page and have seen the then unraced three-year-old become a dual Stayers' Hurdle winner with earnings in excess of £500,000. "It's amazing what Flooring Porter has done for the four of us," Hogarty said. "He's shown that syndicates can have success on the biggest stage of all and you don't need to be a multi-millionaire to own a racehorse. And, you know what, the craic is mighty too."

These once-in-a-lifetime experiences have been delivered by Cromwell and Mullins, although spare a thought for Jonathan Moore, who partnered Flooring Porter in 11 of his first 14 races but was unfit for Cheltenham 2021 and passed the ride to his friend Mullins. The new partnership continued throughout last season, culminating in another demonstration of pace-setting brilliance by Mullins.

▲ Cheerleader: Flooring Porter leaves his rivals trailing again to land his second Stayers' Hurdle; below, celebrations for jockey Danny Mullins (top), trainer Gavin Cromwell (bottom, right) and the whole entourage

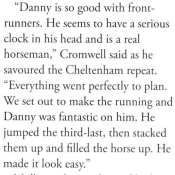

"Danny is so good with front-runners. He seems to have a serious clock in his head and is a real horseman," Cromwell said as he savoured the Cheltenham repeat. "Everything went perfectly to plan. We set out to make the running and Danny was fantastic on him. He jumped the third-last, then stacked them up and filled the horse up. He made it look easy."

Mullins, who was hoisted high into the air by the winner's huge entourage, returned the compliments to the trainer. "Gavin planned the whole season around this and brought the horse over a few days early just to allow the gas to get out of his system. He's a top-class horse and credit to him for doing the job."

The meticulous preparation showed at the start, where Flooring Porter was relaxed and ready, although Cromwell said he had never been worried. "He has really matured. He's just an older and wiser horse," he said.

Still young enough, however, for more dreams to be harboured. Like Big Buck's, Flooring Porter has racked up two Stayers' Hurdles by the age of seven, which raises hope of more to come. "He's the new Big Buck's! That's what I'm telling everyone and I think he can do what Big Buck's did," the bullish Hogarty said.

Flooring Porter may be only halfway to his tally of four, but that in itself was cause for celebration.

SUPER BOWL

Another Grade 1 triumph for Clan Des Obeaux at Aintree was the highlight of Paul Nicholls' latest title-winning campaign

By Nick Pulford

SOME important numbers in Paul Nicholls' life ticked around during the 2021-22 season. Just before Christmas he reached the 30th anniversary of his first winner and towards the end of the season he turned 60, which brought into focus that he has spent just over half of his life as a trainer.

And once again the numbers that guide his professional ambitions underlined the extraordinary level of success of those past 30 years and counting. With prize-money earnings of £2,964,486, he was champion trainer for the 13th time in his career and is now just two behind record-holder Martin Pipe. Being number one is what matters most to Nicholls.

In typical fashion, he finished the season strongly with a five-timer on the final day at Sandown, headed by Grade 1 Celebration Chase winner Greaneteen, but was already looking ahead. "We focus again now and get a good team for next season," he said. "If you win the Premier League in football you want to win it the year after and we'll do our best as always."

Greaneteen was a major player in the 2021-22 season, having landed another Grade 1 in the Tingle Creek Chase, but the stable star was Clan Des Obeaux, who came good in the spring again to take the Betway Bowl Chase at Aintree for the second year in a row.

Having failed to regain the King George VI Chase crown on his seasonal reappearance and then disappointed at Newbury second time out, Clan Des Obeaux looked vulnerable again in the Bowl,

▼ Bowled over: Harry Cobden celebrates a repeat win in the Bowl at Aintree with Clan Des Obeaux
◀ Paul Nicholls lifts the trainers' championship trophy for the 13th time, flanked by images of Clan Des Obeaux at Aintree

going off fifth favourite in a field containing Irish Gold Cup winner Conflated, the best of the British from the Cheltenham Gold Cup in Protektorat and Royale Pagaille, the Newbury winner Eldorado Allen and the battle-hardened Kemboy. Yet Nicholls, as always, had a plan.

In the previous year's Bowl he had fitted Clan Des Obeaux with cheekpieces and the result was a runaway 26-length win. This time

Nicholls dispensed with those and switched the headgear to blinkers, another new experience for the ten-year-old on the 30th start of his career. It did the trick again, although this time Clan Des Obeaux had to work much harder for victory.

On a rainy, grey day, with the ground good to soft, the 3m1f contest turned into a slog but Clan Des Obeaux showed he still had the heart for a battle. Up the home

straight his only remaining challengers were Conflated and Kemboy and Harry Cobden seized control at the second-last, with Clan Des Obeaux responding by opening up a five-length lead. That was enough to see off Kemboy but Conflated fought back on the long run-in, making late ground on the rapidly tiring Clan Des Obeaux. Fleetingly it looked as if the Irish challenger might get there but the line came in time for the

courageous Clan Des Obeaux to hang on by a length.

★★★★

A COUPLE of weeks later, when Nicholls reflected on the highlights of his season, he put the Bowl top of the list for him and Clifford Baker, the head lad who has been by his side all along. "Clan winning at Aintree was fantastic," he said. "Me and Clifford had that

▶ Continues page 156

◄ Greaneteen wins the Celebration Chase at Sandown
▲ Clockwise from top left: Stage Star in the Challow, Gelino Bello at Aintree, Complete Unknown and McFabulous

as his sole target all season to have him at his best then, so to pull that off was good, especially as he'd been written off a little bit. People know how much I love it when Clan does it."

The winning prize-money from the Bowl was something of a nerve-settler with around a fortnight left in the title race, putting £140,000 in the coffers after a lengthy period in which the Nicholls team had not been quite firing and Nicky Henderson had closed the gap to around £150,000.

"Some haven't run as well as I'd have liked and I've been pulling my hair out since Christmas," Nicholls admitted at Aintree, although his willingness to keep thinking had its reward after his decision to fit the blinkers.

Sir Alex Ferguson, the former Manchester United manager who co-owns Clan Des Obeaux, might have recognised something of himself in Nicholls' search for a winning formula. "The blinkers were a big help and that's what good trainers do, they try things and it worked," Ferguson said

in the Aintree winner's enclosure.

Earlier in the season, Nicholls had talked about his constant drive for improvement. "I love every minute of training," he said. "I still wake up at 4am, wondering what we're going to do to get the best out of a particular horse, and I'm still as positive and ambitious as I ever was."

A Racing Post Rating of 176 at Aintree ranked Clan Des Obeaux second in Britain for the season behind Shishkin, although he also suffered resounding defeats against top Irish-trained rivals – something of a recurring theme for the Nicholls string in recent years – when he had to settle for the runner-up spot behind Tornado Flyer in the King George and Allaho in the Punchestown Gold Cup.

Nicholls will never shy away from competition, however tough, and his first big winner of last season came in Ireland when the redoubtable Frodon downed Galvin and Minella Indo in the Down Royal Champion Chase. Further Grade 1 victories were provided by Bravemansgame, Stage

Star and Gelino Bello, but there was nothing at the Cheltenham Festival.

★★★★

THE rich French-bred seam that produced Clan Des Obeaux – as well as Kauto Star, Master Minded and Big Buck's in the Nicholls golden age – is harder to mine now prices have shot up and it is a similar story in the Irish market, making it increasingly difficult for Nicholls and other British trainers to find the top-level horses.

Nicholls keeps putting together a highly competitive string somehow, though, and what has never changed is his ability to place his horses where they can win. In the latest season his strike-rate was 23 per cent, a mark no other British trainer with more than 100 runners could beat, and that was his 27th consecutive year at 20 per cent or above.

Nor has the positivity ever waned. Nicholls relishes every challenge and is always looking forward to the next crop of potential stars. At his owners' day in the autumn, he said: "We're

really strong with our novice chasers. Potentially, we've got a lot of real nice horses, so it's quite exciting times." Among the standouts in that novice chase cohort are Gelino Bello, Monmiral, McFabulous, Complete Unknown and Stage Star.

He ended his 13th title-winning campaign on 3,420 winners over jumps in Britain and with more numbers in mind. "If equalling Martin Pipe's title wins happens, it happens, but what I'd love to do is train 4,000 jumps winners in Britain, as no-one has done that before. That really would be a nice aim. We'll keep doing what we're doing and as long as that keeps going it'll be fine," he said.

A bout of Covid in the middle of last season only served to sharpen his appetite for the job. "I had ten days in the house for the first time ever and they were the longest ten days of my life," he said. "I hated every minute of it and it made me realise I could never retire."

The obsession that has driven Nicholls for half of his life is far from over.

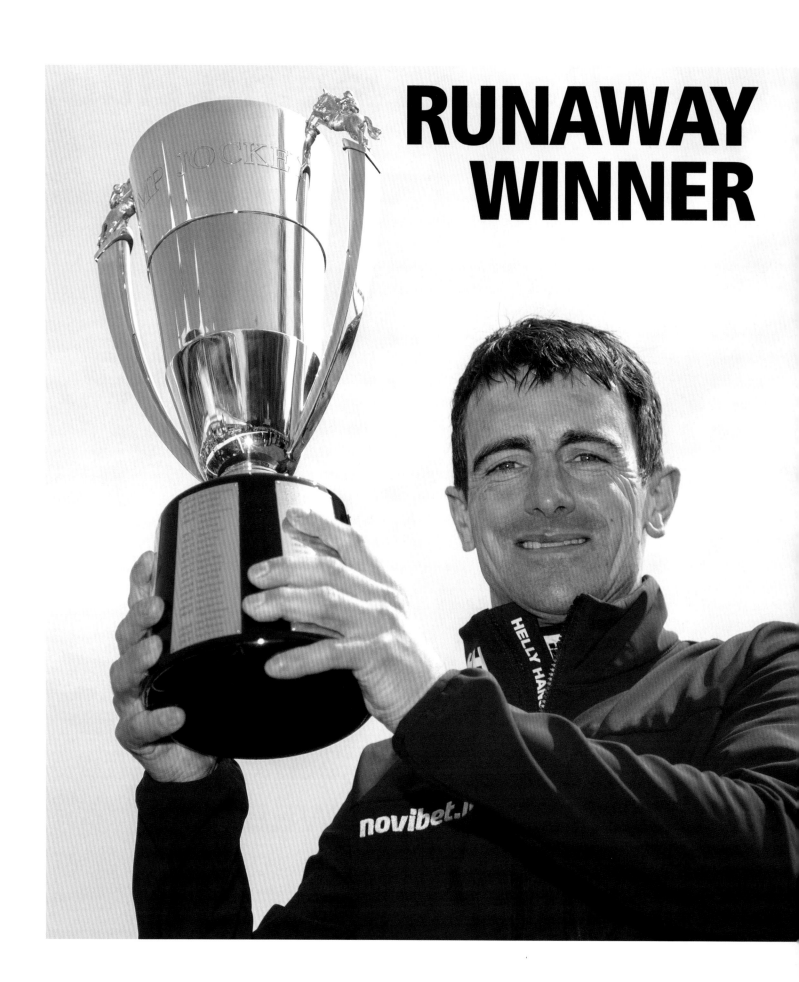

RUNAWAY WINNER

Brian Hughes took his second British jump jockeys' title with the authority of a true champion

By Nick Pulford

IF THERE is one mantra that rules Brian Hughes's professional life, it was summed up in a Racing Post interview in February. "Yesterday is gone, it's history," he said.

He was setting out his insatiable drive for winners and how his focus is on looking forward, not dwelling on things that can't be changed, but it could equally be applied to his desire to bounce back from disappointment and prove himself a true champion. As he powered to his second title in the 2021-22 season, achieved with a personal-best double century, it was an outlook that served Hughes well.

The trophy was handed over on April 23, the final day of the season, but it had been heading Hughes's way for many months before that. The North Yorkshire-based jockey set a relentless pace through the summer months and by the start of October, with the nights drawing in and thoughts turning to the winter jumps season, he already had 59 winners on the board and was 19 in front. With the tireless support of agent Richard Hale, Hughes hit 100 on November 22 and 150 with a Carlisle four-timer on February 7, shortly before that Racing Post interview.

After five solid seasons in a row that had brought final tallies in the 140s, with a best of 146 in 2018-19, Hughes knew then that a double century lay within reach over the two and a half months

that remained of the season. "Every day I ride with the same hunger," he said. "My agent would love to get us to 200 winners. I suppose it's possible, but I would need a lot of luck and for the horses to be in similar form as they have been."

The only luck Hughes needed was to stay injury-free; the hunger, hard graft and horses – principally supplied by Donald McCain's powerful yard – took care of the rest and propelled him to even greater heights.

Having eclipsed the 149 winners ridden by Jonjo O'Neill in 1977-78, the long-standing record by a northern jump jockey, Hughes moved that mark significantly upwards when he made it to the double century three days before the end of the campaign. He was only the fourth jump jockey to reach the landmark in a British season, joining Sir Anthony McCoy, Richard Johnson and Peter Scudamore.

Like those great champions, Hughes had made himself the dominant figure. Nobody could get anywhere near him. In the final standings Sam Twiston-Davies and Harry Skelton, close together in second and third, barely mustered more than the champion's total of 204 winners between them. In theory, Hughes could have stopped before Christmas and still finished top.

★★★★

WHEN the 36-year-old lifted the trophy at Sandown's season finale, there was a sense of occasion that had been entirely absent for his

first title two years earlier. Back then there was no Sandown, with British racing in lockdown during the first big wave of the Covid pandemic, and Hughes did not receive the trophy until a low-key presentation by Mick Fitzgerald at the new champion's home four months after the season had been abruptly halted.

This time it was a day to remember for Hughes. Along with his wife Lucy and young children Rory and Olivia, he got to celebrate with his wider family from Yorkshire and Northern Ireland, including his five sisters – one of whom lives in Canada and another in Australia. "I've had to sacrifice a lot to get to this position and I've missed weddings, but they sucked that up and accepted it, so this is a bit of payback," he said.

It was payback for Hughes too after all the years working the northern circuit, making contacts and a reputation for himself. He was champion conditional as far back as the 2007-08 season, just a few years after moving from his native County Armagh as he exited his teens, but the path to the senior title was far from easy. Even when he got there for the first time in 2020, becoming the first northern-based champion in 40 years, he was left with more to prove.

Hughes had been 19 winners clear of Johnson when the 2019-20 season came to a premature end in March and, with his rival having spent time on the sidelines with a broken arm, that first title was marked with an asterisk by some.

▶ *Continues page 160*

BRIAN HUGHES

"A few people said I'd only won it because the season stopped early, so I was eager to prove them wrong," he admitted.

The following season brought an unsatisfactory outcome of a different kind when Hughes was overhauled by Skelton's storming late run and had to settle for second place. "I felt I'd failed as I led all year and got beat. It's no different to a football team getting beaten in the FA Cup final. I was gutted," he said.

In the latest campaign Hughes left no room for argument with a season-long display of quiet authority that drew admiration from many great riders of the recent past. Among them was Ruby Walsh, who said: "Brian does what you need to do in order to be a top jockey every day. He's just incredibly consistent. He's now the one setting the standard."

Scudamore, eight times champion between 1982 and 1992, sees Hughes on a regular basis on the northern circuit in his role alongside partner Lucinda Russell, the Grand National-winning trainer, and he was effusive in his praise for the champion's qualities. "He's very confident and makes the right decisions," he said. "You need to have a brain on a horse and to think and he does that. It's all about the position you get into in a race, to be able to present your horse over the last several fences with a chance, and he repeatedly does that on whichever track he's at."

★★★★

WHICH rather begs the question of why Hughes gets so few big-race opportunities. He has ridden only three Cheltenham Festival winners, for instance, and wasn't even there for jump racing's big week in March, instead spending three of the four days at Sedgefield, Hexham and Fakenham.

Asked to reflect on the situation, Hughes said: "I'd love to go down there for rides with good chances but all of those good yards have a lot of good jockeys to ride them. I have no divine right to any of that. But going down there for 100-1 shots doesn't make me tick. I'd love to be winning the Grand National and Gold Cup but you need a good horse."

In future seasons that sort of

opportunity might be provided by McCain, whose resurgent yard recorded a new high of 155 winners in 2021-22. The Cheshire trainer regularly hit centuries in the days when he had Grand National hero Ballabriggs and Cheltenham Festival stars like Peddlers Cross, but this was his first time into three figures since 2014. "Sooner rather than later hopefully we'll unearth one of those good horses," said Hughes, who rode 104 winners for the McCain yard last season, just over half of his title-winning total.

Hughes is hardly likely to dwell on the standard of winner he is riding, as long as the numbers keep stacking up. "I want to be champion jockey and ride more winners than anybody else. That's what makes me tick," he said in February, when realistically his second title was already in the bag. "I want winners no matter if they're in sellers

▲ Work-life balance: Brian Hughes at home with wife Lucy and children Olivia and Rory; left and previous page, sharing his trophy win with Lucy; below, on the gallops and in the yard at main supporter Donald McCain's powerful Cheshire stable

or Grade 1s. Every winner gives me a kick and I'm always thinking of the next one. I know people like riding big winners, as do I, but I just like riding winners every day."

He also likes the feeling of being at the top of his profession. "It's not been an easy place to get to but now I'm in it I'm going to do as much as I can to stay there," he said.

With his appetite for grafting and winning, Hughes is going to be hard to topple from top spot.

THE
BIGGER
PICTURE

The runners jump the second fence in the
Sussex National at Plumpton on January 2.
Victory went to the Chris Gordon-trained
Go Whatever, ridden by Tom Cannon
EDWARD WHITAKER (RACINGPOST.COM/PHOTOS)

LEGENDARY LESTER

Lester Piggott, known as The Long Fellow and a supreme big-race jockey who won a record 30 British Classics, died in May at the age of 86

LEGENDARY jockey Lester Piggott, who died peacefully in Switzerland at the age of 86, was known worldwide for a hugely successful riding career that lasted the best part of 50 years and remained Britain's most famous jockey long after he quit the saddle.

That was in part due to the longevity that allowed him to ride a phenomenal 4,493 domestic winners, the third-highest tally in British racing history behind only Sir Gordon Richards and Pat Eddery, and an amazing big-race haul. He won the Derby a record nine times, including on 1970 Triple Crown winner Nijinsky.

And it also owed something to the way a 5ft 8in man nicknamed 'The Long Fellow' fought to ride at 30lb below his natural bodyweight and had an uncanny knack of bouncing back from adversity, most famously when he returned from retirement and a spell in prison to win the Breeders' Cup Mile on Royal Academy at the age of 54 in 1990.

Piggott was as well bred for the job as the choice horses he rode. His grandfather Ernie rode three Grand National winners and father Keith won the Champion Hurdle as a jockey and the National as a trainer. He rode his first winner at the age of just 12, on The Chase at Haydock in 1948, and the triple champion apprentice won his first Derby at 18 on Never Say Die in 1954. Piggott was champion jockey 11 times between 1960 and 1982 and won a record 30 British Classics.

After initially retiring in 1985, his training career was cut short by the conviction for tax fraud which earned him a year in prison, and he rode on for another four seasons after his shock return to the saddle.

'It has been a wonderful life'
Lee Mottershead recalls a memorable interview

WHEN the Racing Post newspaper returned following the sport's Covid hibernation in 2020 there was a determination to secure for the rebirth edition the very best and biggest interviewee. That could mean only one man. "Get Lester," was the cry. Thankfully, we got him. Then, as so often in the past, he delivered in style.

Even two years ago Piggott was marvelling at his own longevity, perhaps understandably given the punishment he put his body through in the pursuit of sporting excellence.

"It's quite unbelievable for me to think how old I am," he said, genuine surprise in his voice. There was incredulity in the voice of his interviewer when we spoke of him having ridden for so long while barely eating. "I think it was all down to having a lot of willpower," he suggested. "I got hungry, sometimes very hungry, but I got used to it. I don't eat too much now. I suppose I just got out of the habit."

Piggott rose to fame in a totally different era. His was a career that began on Pathe newsreels. The first of his nine Derby triumphs came a month before the end of food rationing. He did things that belonged to a different time. He also did things on a horse nobody else could manage, which is why when three years ago he walked into a room at the Curragh's Race apprentice school, 32 youngsters shot to their feet and gave him a rousing ovation. They knew they were in the presence of greatness.

"Lester was over the moon," said Nick O'Toole, a friend of Piggott and avid collector of his memorabilia. Along with fellow devotee Sean Magee, O'Toole had that year organised a Long Fellow exhibition at the Curragh. On both days of the Guineas weekend, Piggott was mobbed. He therefore asked for a chance to enjoy the exhibition himself the following morning. Over an hour and 40 minutes he went around it twice, studying each and every picture, reading each and every caption, his life, a most remarkable life, laid out before the man who had lived it.

What became apparent when we spoke was Piggott's sense of humour, something that had been equally obvious when he once asked fellow jockey Jimmy Lindley to stop outside an ice cream shop in London. Piggott got out of the passenger seat, entered the shop and came out with two cones. To the driver's astonishment, he polished off both. "I thought one was for me," Lindley said to him. "You never said you wanted one," replied Piggott, probably licking his lips for good measure.

It was a mighty line, as was one he kindly gave during our interview, in doing so raising the subject of his imprisonment for tax evasion without saying a single word about it. He had just been talking about carrying home Royal Academy in that still scarcely believable Breeders' Cup Mile. "It was a fairy story, really, wasn't it?" he suggested, meeting no disagreement from me.

"Most people remember me for three things," he continued. "That Breeders' Cup win is one of them. You know what the others are." He agreed that his unparalleled Derby record was one of the two others. Pushing my luck, while already knowing the answer, I asked if he wanted to state the third? "I'll leave it to you," he said. Then he laughed.

Piggott even knew the sort of words needed to close that piece and this one. "It's marvellous, you know," he said, summing up a life that now sadly has come to an end. "I think it's wonderful that people still take an interest in me and what I did. It's nice to be popular. It's better than having stones thrown at me anyway.

"It has been a wonderful life really. You couldn't ask for any more."

This section on Lester Piggott features edited versions of articles that appeared in the Racing Post on May 30 and 31

LESTER PIGGOTT

By John Randall

'Thirty British Classics is his greatest record – and it may stand for all time'

LESTER PIGGOTT'S greatness transcended statistics, but he accumulated some of the most important records for a British jockey, notably the most global wins in a career, the most British Classics (30) and the most Derbys (nine).

Most wins in a career

Piggott won a career total of about 5,300 races throughout the world between 1948 and 1995, which is a record for a British jockey. It is impossible to give a precise figure because he rode winners in more than 30 countries and no-one, least of all the man himself, kept count.

Piggott gained 4,493 of those victories on the Flat in Britain, and another 20 over hurdles. That puts him third to Sir Gordon Richards (4,870), who rarely rode abroad, and Irishman Pat Eddery (4,633) on the all-time list of jockeys who have won the most races in Britain.

Most Classic wins

Piggott won 30 British Classics between 1954 (Never Say Die's Derby) and 1992 (Rodrigo De Triano's 2,000 Guineas). It is his greatest record, and one that may stand for all time.

Those 30 victories comprised nine in the Derby, eight in the St Leger, six in the Oaks, five in the 2,000 Guineas, and two in the 1,000 Guineas. His most productive Classic partnerships were with trainers Vincent O'Brien (nine wins) and Noel Murless (seven).

The previous Classic record was 27 by Frank Buckle between 1792 and 1827.

Although Piggott is not the oldest jockey to ride a Classic winner, he holds the record for the longest span of Classic victories, with 38 years between his first and last wins.

Most Derby wins

The master of Epsom won the Derby nine times between 1954 (Never Say Die) and 1983 (Teenoso). The previous record of six was held by Jem Robinson and Steve Donoghue.

Most wins in other races

Piggott won a record 116 races at Royal Ascot between 1952 and 1993, among them a record 11 Gold Cups.

He also won the King George VI and Queen Elizabeth Stakes a record seven times, though that score has been equalled by Frankie Dettori.

His records for the most victories in other top races include ten July Cups, nine Coronation Cups, seven Eclipse Stakes and seven Nunthorpe Stakes.

Greatest rides

It was almost inevitable that when we conducted a poll of Racing Post readers in 2007 to determine the 100 Greatest Rides of all time, Piggott was the jockey represented by the most rides – eight.

No.2 on the list was the 54-year-old's Breeders' Cup Mile win on Royal Academy in 1990, beaten only by Fred Winter's epic bitless victory on Mandarin in the Grand Steeple-Chase de Paris. His other entries in the top ten were The Minstrel (1977 Derby) and Roberto (1972 Derby).

▲ Supreme master: Lester Piggott at Goodwood in 1990; below, after his 28th British Classic win with Commanche Run and on Rodrigo De Triano, his 30th and last

Greatest jockey?

By common consent, Lester Keith Piggott ranks with Fred Archer and Sir Gordon Richards as one of Britain's top three Flat jockeys, though to argue that he was the greatest jockey of all time would betray absurd insularity as well as ignorance of history.

In a 2003 poll, Racing Post readers voted him the second-greatest racing figure of all time, behind only Vincent O'Brien. Whatever Piggott's exact rank in the jockeys' pantheon, he excelled at displays of both utmost finesse, as when nursing home Ribero in the St Leger, and brute force, as in Roberto's Derby.

The pre-eminent figure in the sport for a quarter of a century, he had a matchless big-race temperament and was a supreme master of his profession.

Six great jockeys on Lester Piggott's qualities and their encounters with him

'Ruthless, confident, unique'

Willie Carson
Five British champion jockey titles; four Derby wins

Lester was ruthless in the saddle – no other word for it. The one thing that set him apart from the other jockeys was that he always got on the best horses – and he always got away with it. Of course, he had the ability to allow him to do that – and let's face it, he usually delivered.

Boy, was he good. He had that fantastic instinct on a horse, and nobody else had that natural balance. Lester had that and so much more.

Steve Cauthen
Three British champion jockey titles; two Derby wins

He was amazingly good. Riding against him was fun because when you beat him you'd beaten the best. He had huge confidence in himself and, on top of that, he was the best at getting on the best horse. When he felt he was on the best horse he'd ride it with supreme confidence and 99.9 per cent of the time he'd get the job done.

He was a great natural rider and a winner; he had raw desire, the killer instinct. That was probably the most important part of it.

Frankie Dettori
Three British champion jockey titles; two Derby wins

I asked him for advice when I was young; we all asked Lester how to ride Epsom. Before I won the Derby on Authorized, he just told me: "Listen, ride the horse, don't ride the race. Keep focused on what you have to do." Those were good words to have in the back of my mind.

We all know what Lester achieved in racing, he was a great jockey, that's all in black and white. But as a personal friend, I felt we had a great relationship.

Kieren Fallon
Six British champion jockey titles; three Derby wins

My first memory of Lester was when I

▲ Greats together: Frankie Dettori with Lester Piggott at Doncaster in 2017; below, Piggott and Willie Carson

was at Newbury and he popped into the stalls next to me. He asked me what I was doing and I told him "I'm going to make the running, sir." You can imagine as a young kid I couldn't wait to tell him what I was going to do. He tracked me through the race and got up to beat me on the line by a short head. He really educated me there.

The numbers he recorded were incredible and won't be matched again. It's good they won't – Lester was simply unique.

Mick Kinane
Thirteen Irish champion jockey titles; three Derby wins

Lester was my idol as a young man growing up. I just thought he was fantastic. He was a master around Epsom, a track that's likely the hardest in the world for horse and jockey. There was a string of phenomenal rides that showed you how good a horseman he was on Sir Ivor, Nijinsky

and The Minstrel. I thought the way he produced Sir Ivor with just hands and heels was incredible – the horse never knew he had a race.

I was fortunate to ride with him and spend time with him. Anything you got from him on the track was earned, I can assure you. He was a great man.

Yves Saint-Martin
Fifteen French champion jockey titles; nine French Derby wins

He was the greatest jockey I ever encountered. We had some great battles and he came out on top more often than me. But I think there was a great mutual respect for each other's professionalism and style in the saddle.

We were great friends and when I went to Newmarket I always went to his house. We were linked together in many ways and our stories often ran together. On the track we each fought our corner, but that never stopped us being friends out of the saddle.

NATIONAL HORSE RACING MUSEUM

SO MUCH MORE THAN A MUSEUM!

NHRM occupies a 5-acre site in the heart of Newmarket and provides a wonderful day out for all ages.

Using the latest interactive and audio-visual displays you can find out about the history of horseracing, enjoy some of the country's best examples of sporting art, meet former racehorses, have a go on the racehorse simulator and watch the sparks fly as a farrier works in the forge.

National Horseracing Museum Palace Street, Newmarket, Suffolk, CB8 8EP

EXPLORE GREAT EXHIBITIONS, BROWSE OUR GIFT SHOP & BOOKSTORE.

DISCOVER THE RESTAURANT AND BAKERY AT NHRM

@NHRMuseum

Book Online: www.nhrm.co.uk

Master of the Turf

Full name Lester Keith Piggott

Born Wantage, Berkshire, November 5, 1935

Family parents Keith Piggott (1904-93) and Iris (1905-87), daughter of Fred Rickaby senior. Wife Susan (married 1960), daughter of Sam Armstrong. Daughters Maureen (born 1961, wife of William Haggas), Tracy (born 1965). Also son Jamie (born 1993) with Anna Ludlow

Apprenticed to Keith Piggott, Lambourn, 1948-53

First mount The Chase (unplaced) Salisbury, April 7, 1948

First winner The Chase, Haydock, August 18, 1948

First Group 1-class winner Mystery (1951 Eclipse Stakes)

First Classic mount Manhattan (unplaced, 1951 2,000 Guineas)

First Derby mount Zucchero (13th, 1951)

First Royal Ascot winner Malka's Boy (1952 Wokingham)

First Classic winner Never Say Die (1954 Derby)

First winner in France Patras, Prix Saint-Roman, Longchamp, October 9, 1955

First winner in Ireland Rise Above, Phoenix Park, August 9, 1958

Cheltenham Festival winner Mull Sack (1954 Birdlip Selling Hurdle)

Triple Crown winner Nijinsky (1970)

Derby winners Nine (record): Never Say Die (1954), Crepello (1957), St Paddy (1960), Sir Ivor (1968), Nijinsky (1970), Roberto (1972), Empery (1976), The Minstrel (1977), Teenoso (1983)

King George VI and Queen Elizabeth Stakes winners Seven (record): Meadow Court (1965), Aunt Edith (1966), Park Top (1969), Nijinsky (1970), Dahlia (1974), The Minstrel (1977), Teenoso (1984)

Prix de l'Arc de Triomphe winners Rheingold (1973), Alleged (1977, 1978)

Washington DC International winners Sir Ivor (1968), Karabas (1969), Argument (1980)

Breeders' Cup winner/richest win Royal Academy (1990 Mile) £279,503

Prix du Jockey-Club winner Hard To Beat (1972)

Irish Derby winners Meadow Court (1965), Ribocco (1967), Ribero (1968), The Minstrel (1977), Shergar (1981)

2,000 Guineas winners Crepello (1957), Sir Ivor (1968), Nijinsky (1970), Shadeed (1985), Rodrigo De Triano (1992)

1,000 Guineas winners Humble Duty (1970), Fairy Footsteps (1981)

Oaks winners Carrozza (1957), Petite Etoile (1959), Valoris (1966), Juliette Marny (1975), Blue Wind (1981), Circus Plume (1984)

St Leger winners St Paddy (1960), Aurelius (1961), Ribocco (1967), Ribero (1968), Nijinsky (1970), Athens Wood (1971), Boucher (1972), Commanche Run (1984)

Ascot Gold Cup wins 11 (record): Zarathustra (1957), Gladness (1958), Pandofell (1961), Twilight Alley (1963), Fighting Charlie (1965), Sagaro (1975, 1976, 1977), Le Moss (1979), Ardross (1981, 1982)

Champion sprinters Right Boy (1958, 1959), Matatina (1963), Caterina (1966), Green God (1971), Thatch (1973), Saritamer (1974), Solinus (1978), Thatching (1979), Moorestyle (1980)

Last winner before first retirement Full Choke, Nottingham, October 29, 1985

First winner after comeback Nicholas, Chepstow, October 16, 1990

Last winner in Britain Palacegate Jack, Haydock, October 5, 1994

Champion apprentice 3 times (1950, 1951, 1952)

Champion jockey 11 times (1960, 1964-71, 1981-82); also runner-up six times, 3rd six times

British Classic wins 30 (record) from 166 rides, including nine Derbys (record) from 36 rides

Royal Ascot wins 116 (record) 1952-93, including eight in 1965 and 1975

Number of British centuries 25

Most wins in a British season 191 in 1966

Total wins in Britain 4,493 on Flat in 43 seasons, plus 20 over hurdles

Total wins worldwide about 5,300

Compiled by John Randall

▲ Tracy Piggott unveiling a statue in honour of her father at the Curragh in May

'He gave me so much in my life'

TRACY PIGGOTT paid a heartfelt and touching tribute to her late father, describing him as an inspiring figure who lived and breathed the sport throughout his life.

Piggott, who spent more than three decades as a broadcaster with RTE Racing, made special mention of her gratitude for being able to carve out a career in television with the help of her father. "When I came to Ireland back in the early 1980s, it was really because of the Irish people's love for him that I was taken in so well and made to feel so welcome. Without him, my opportunity to have a career with RTE would never have happened. He gave me so much in my life and I'm so appreciative of it."

On his horsemanship at the top level, she said: "Growing up, I was very aware he had a great talent and ability, but apart from anything else was his affinity with the horse. It was poetry in motion. Sometimes you'd watch him on a horse and they'd almost become one.

"It was his timing, the way he'd find a gap, the way he'd never panic. It was just unbelievable. Another thing that amazed me was his ability to know everything about the opposition. He was fascinating."

The outpouring of messages and tributes from around the globe had been warmly received by her family at a difficult time, she said. "I was delighted to hear some of the funny stories. I think it's wonderful that people know he did have this really dry sense of humour. He was often up to mischief and it's a side we always knew."

Asked how she believed her father would like to be remembered, Piggott replied: "He'd probably say, 'As the greatest', or something like that – it would be a one-liner. I heard him say a few times that people might have forgotten about him, or that nobody remembered him. Maybe being in Switzerland made him feel like that, but I know when he came to meetings in England and Ireland he was never forgotten."

IN THE PICTURE

Coroebus a Classic hero for Doyle – but tragedy strikes later

TEARS of joy and tears of sadness. A year that started with Classic triumph for Coroebus in the 2,000 Guineas at Newmarket, followed by Royal Ascot success in the St James's Palace Stakes, ended in utter devastation when he suffered a fatal injury in the Prix du Moulin at Longchamp in September.

The Godolphin colt stumbled and fell as he mounted his challenge a furlong and a half from home. Trainer Charlie Appleby said: "It is very sad to see a great horse, who gave so much to racing, lose his life in this way. Everyone took a lot of joy from his victories in the 2,000 Guineas and at Royal Ascot."

In those better times, the happy tears were shed by James Doyle after he broke his British Classic duck on Coroebus in the 2,000 Guineas, erasing the heartache of past defeats in the race and sparking an unforgettable weekend at Newmarket. Twenty-four hours later Doyle completed a rare double with victory in the 1,000 Guineas aboard Cachet.

Doyle has won two St James's Palace Stakes on champion milers Kingman and Barney Roy, yet both were beaten under him in the Guineas and he admitted those defeats had haunted him.

After Coroebus quickened away to defeat favourite and stablemate Native Trail by three-quarters of a length, the 34-year-old rider said: "For once I'm actually emotional about riding a big winner. This race has been something that has always annoyed me, looking at replays over and over again of Kingman's Guineas and Barney Roy's Guineas."

As usual, Doyle had to wait for William Buick to make his pick of the Appleby runners before he knew which ride would be his, and the trainer paid tribute to his professionalism.

"I'm delighted for James, and for him to have his first Classic for us is special," Appleby said. "What I love about the guy is that he sits there while William picks the rides and, while they're lovely second rides to be getting, he's got the character to then go out there and give everything he has."

The Guineas was the only time Doyle rode Coroebus, as Buick was back on board for the St James's Palace victory and again on that fateful day at Longchamp.

A second British Classic was quick to follow for Doyle when he led all the way on the George Boughey-trained Cachet in the next day's 1,000 Guineas. He joined an illustrious list of riders including George Moore (1967), Lester Piggott (1970), Kieren Fallon (2005) and Ryan Moore (2015) to partner winners of both Guineas in the same year.

Picture: EDWARD WHITAKER (RACINGPOST.COM/PHOTOS)

By Tom Peacock

WHEN James Doyle slipped Cachet straight into the lead in the 1,000 Guineas, few would have been sure she would stay there. Punters had not rated the form of her peripatetic two-year-old season highly enough to send her off any shorter than 16-1 and pedigree judges had been entitled to question whether the abundance of speed in her background would find her out in Classic company on the Rowley Mile.

The doubts appeared to be shared by some of Doyle's rival jockeys, who allowed him to conduct the pace and leave them in his wake. Classic glory went to a filly who had already confounded most reasonable expectations and to a trainer in George Boughey who has managed just the same since sending out his first runner in the summer of 2019.

Perhaps even now, they all might wonder how Cachet got home after her stride seemed to shorten running into the Dip with a furlong left, especially with the retrospective knowledge of what those in behind her were to achieve. The field that was outfoxed, outpaced or outlasted was headed by the Falmouth winner Prosperous Voyage, with Oaks heroine Tuesday and Tenebrism, who swept up the Prix Jean Prat, further back.

Nonetheless, it's indelibly in the records that Cachet's blunt tenacity held out by a neck, giving Boughey, then 30, an incredible career-boosting Classic success. Welcoming her back to the number one spot, the emotional trainer said: "I dreamed of having a winner at Bath two years ago, never mind winning the Guineas. It's all come very quick. It's pretty surreal."

★★★★

LESS than a year earlier, Cachet had cruised home on her debut in a mid-May novice stakes on that same Rowley Mile course. A daughter of Aclaim, the seven-furlong specialist who was an unknown quantity as a stallion with his first crop just starting to race, she had been bought only recently at the Tattersalls breeze-up sale for a not insignificant nor particularly dazzling 60,000gns.

Being part of the breeze-up process is unquestionably an advantage in newcomers' events, with youngsters likely to have been in some form of training from the turn of the year and tuned up to a certain extent to catch the eye of buyers.

There was the added positive for Cachet that Boughey, then in his second full season, was showing particular flair with his two-year-olds. He collected nine winners during that month alone and this filly, carrying the prestigious light blue colours of the Highclere Racing syndicate, quickly became a flagbearer for his Saffron House Stables on Newmarket's Hamilton Road.

For all that breeze-up graduates included a couple of other 2022 Classic winners in Native Trail and Eldar Eldarov, they are in the main touted as ready-made Royal Ascot juvenile packages. Sadly for Cachet, her yard's warm spell was not reflected in the mid-June weather. In the drizzle of the Albany Stakes, she seemed to labour on the heavy ground, plugging on for fifth in a high-class event won by Andrew Balding's Sandrine.

Through the rest of the summer, there were further respectable efforts that still did not exactly suggest world-beating prowess. Then, just when it looked as if Listed status might be Cachet's summit, she strode heartily onwards up the mountain.

Following a career-best Racing Post Rating of 104 in the Rockfel, she threw everything she had at Inspiral, the winter favourite for the Guineas, to finish third in the Fillies' Mile. That secured her a passage to Del Mar, Bing Crosby's playground, in the Breeders' Cup Juvenile Fillies Turf. Taking the spring-loaded Americans on at their own game, she passed all but one marker post in front before being swamped by Pizza Bianca

▸ Continues page 176

DREAM RESULT

Cachet led all the way in the 1,000 Guineas to give trainer George Boughey and the Highclere syndicate a landmark Classic success

and the closers, beaten a length in fourth.

Quite remarkably, this was little more than two years since Boughey had taken out his licence with a quartet of rag-tag recruits. Brought up in Dorset, where jumpers were trained on a family farm that raised the Champion Hurdle winner Rooster Booster, he would order the Racing Post at school and became obsessed with carving out a career in the sport. Having studied agriculture and business management at Newcastle University, he gained experience on the shop floor with Hugo Palmer and gradually became a trusted lieutenant who ran one of the trainer's barns.

After deciding to go it alone, Boughey's ambition and skill was noticed by such shrewd judges as ownership syndicator Nick Bradley. In that summer of 2021 he had provided Boughey with a first Listed winner in Mystery Angel, who was ambitiously supplemented for the Oaks at a cost of £30,000 and finished second to Snowfall.

Boughey was just as ambitious with Cachet as went into his third full season. It is not unusual for a Guineas prospect to have been busy in their first year; connections could take modern inspiration from no less than Aidan O'Brien, who had landed the previous three runnings with the heavily campaigned Hermosa, Love and Mother Earth. The difference with Cachet, though, was that despite such adventures she had only one minor win to show for it.

★★★★

IT WAS a record to be quickly amended when spring returned and the hard yards were put in on the gallops. Starting off in the seven-furlong Nell Gwyn Stakes on her favourite home track, she was entitled to win on the form book but accomplished it with a degree of swagger.

"I kept saying at the back end of last year that she was slightly weak and she did incredibly well over the winter," Boughey said. "This is a massive result for our yard. Having a horse owned by Highclere winning a Classic trial is everything really."

For all that he had reckoned on Cachet making some further natural progress, the rising star of the training ranks would not have envisaged eating his words about the pre-eminence of the Nell Gwyn in their story within the space of three weeks.

The stiff mile remained the most pressing issue for Cachet but she had earned her crack at the Guineas for owners who live for the big occasion. Boughey and his bright young team in Newmarket had her ready for the gifted hands of Doyle to provide the most special of memories.

What was a first Classic for the trainer was Doyle's second, just 24 hours after opening his account with Coroebus in the 2,000 Guineas. "I promised I wouldn't get emotional today but that was incredible, wasn't it?" the rider said. "That last half a furlong took forever and I was praying for the line. She's all guts."

Their heroics were not quite repeated a fortnight later in the French Guineas, with a charging pack led by Gerald Mosse on Mangoustine a little more alive to any front-running mischief. A head defeat, however, confirmed the Guineas was no one-off and Cachet can be forgiven a placing of only fifth behind a resurgent Inspiral in the Coronation Stakes as Ascot does not seem to produce her optimal performances.

Hopes of further appearances in the autumn were derailed by the news that Cachet had been hindered by a sinus problem. It perhaps says everything about the esteem in which Harry Herbert and John Warren of Highclere already place in the youthful trainer that they are to allow him to keep her for 2023 instead of securing a lucrative return at the breeding stock auctions.

Boughey's assertion that "we'd certainly be coming back in trip rather than going up" tees up Cachet for next season's major sprinting prizes. Fewer, now, will dare be sceptical about her chances.

▶ Classic star: George Boughey with Cachet at Saffron House Stables shortly after her 1,000 Guineas triumph

'This is incredible. It's off the scale'

The 20-strong Highclere Thoroughbred-Wild Flower syndicate were in raptures after Cachet became a coveted first British Classic winner in their colours.

Members came from as far away as Texas for the 1,000 Guineas and syndicate organiser Harry Herbert was among those almost moved to tears. "It's a dream, the ultimate dream," he said. "I've dreamed of those blue silks winning a British Classic. We did it in the Irish Oaks with Petrushka and the Royal Ascot Racing Club did it with Motivator in the Derby, but to win the 1,000 Guineas is incredible. I can't take it on board.

"This shows that syndicates can do this and we've won it for 20 lovely people. To do this here in the blue silks, it's off the scale."

George Boughey, celebrating his own Classic breakthrough, later reflected on how warmly Cachet's success was received. "It was an amazing atmosphere and there was huge admiration for what she did," he said. "We were taking on the big boys and I think a lot of people were pleased to see a lesser light go and do it.

"I had emails, WhatsApp messages, letters, texts and everything you can imagine – it's hugely appreciated. I think people have seen the work that's gone into where we are and a lot of people are taking a lot of satisfaction out of it."

SUNDAY BEST

Eldar Eldarov won a St Leger put back 24 hours following the death of Queen Elizabeth II

By Lewis Porteous

EMOTIONS were running high on Town Moor when racing returned from a two-day cessation to stage the St Leger on the second Sunday of September. Racing in Britain had been paused over the previous 48 hours as a mark of respect for Queen Elizabeth II, who died on September 8, and that meant the world's oldest Classic was moved back a day from its scheduled slot.

The Queen had enjoyed one of her racing highlights in the St Leger when Dunfermline marked her Silver Jubilee year of 1977 by carrying the royal colours to victory, and it felt a fitting tribute that the action should return with a race not only entrenched in turf history but that had played a pivotal role in the Queen's enduring love of the sport.

After the action on Friday and Saturday had been postponed, Doncaster put on a bumper nine-race card featuring four Group 2s – including the salvaged Doncaster Cup from Friday – and the Portland and Mallard Handicaps. But the focal point was the St Leger, which was first run in 1776 and rarely comes up short in terms of drama and excitement.

For many, New London held the key to the race. Touted as a Derby candidate early in the season, the Godolphin colt did not go to Epsom after defeat at Chester in May but a decisive win in the Gordon Stakes – a key trial for the St Leger at Goodwood at the end

of July – had sent him to the head of the Leger betting.

Godolphin were going for a record eighth success in the staying Classic and there were other contenders who know what it takes to pass Doncaster's stiff test. Roger Varian, who won the Leger in 2014 with Kingston Hill, had lined up Queen's Vase winner Eldar Eldarov, while Ralph Beckett, who won, lost and then regained the race with Simple Verse in 2015, had added £50,000 supplementary entry Haskoy to the nine-runner field. Even with the delayed running, Haskoy was only 44 days into her racing career but had won both starts, including a Listed event at York last time.

Also in the mix was Hoo Ya Mal, runner-up in the Derby and bidding to give George Boughey his second taste of Classic success before heading to Australia for the Melbourne Cup, so there was no shortage of intrigue in the contest.

★★★★

DANNY TUDHOPE cut out the early running on French Claim and had an easy time of it until challengers ranged up on both sides at the three-furlong pole. Haskoy was the first to strike the front but her inexperience meant she was wayward in the lead, interfering with 28-1 shot Giavellotto as she hung to the far rail. She still led approaching the final furlong but New London and Eldar Eldarov were in her shadow and it was all to play for.

New London's effort ran out of steam but the further Eldar Eldarov went, the more purposeful his stride became, carrying him into a decisive lead. Haskoy clung on for second and New London was third as the peloton finished in a tired heap.

There was no disguising what victory meant to David Egan, who punched the air in delight as he crossed the line. The son of veteran rider John Egan had endured a rollercoaster season to that point but winning a first Classic was the ultimate peak. "I'm gobsmacked," he admitted after the race. "To win a Classic at 23 . . . I never thought I'd do it. When you see Her Majesty has won this race and to think that I've done something similar – I'm just in awe really, it's all a bit of a blur."

The Queen was in everyone's thoughts but Egan also paid a poignant tribute to Jack de Bromhead, the 13-year-old son of trainer Henry de Bromhead who had died in a pony racing accident

▸▸ Continues page 180

▶ Special greeting: David Egan shakes hands with Roger Varian; inset, their victory celebrations; previous page, Eldar Eldarov passes the post in front of Haskoy (right) and New London (blue)

the previous weekend. "It's been a sad week with everything that's happened, Her Majesty and Jack de Bromhead. We live on, but we don't forget them," Egan said.

It was a first Group 1 triumph for the winning rider since landing the Juddmonte International and Dubai Sheema Classic the previous year on Mishriff, whose owner Prince Faisal had dispensed with his services during the summer. Egan largely kept his own counsel on the split and it was clear to see after the Leger that he is not a man to burn bridges that may yet prove integral to his future.

"When one door closes, another opens," he said. "My connection with Prince Faisal ended on good terms and we went our separate ways. Mishriff has had some great runs since. I always watch him and I'm a big fan."

★★★★

IT WAS an important win for Varian too. Not many trainers have a bigger string under their watch than he does in Newmarket and a second domestic Classic, eight years after the first, was not before time. Having helped nurture Egan since he arrived at his yard as an inexperienced 15-year-old, the trainer had reason to be deeply satisfied.

"Sometimes the longer you do something the harder things get and the more you crave the big successes," he said. "We'd only trained for three years when Kingston Hill won, so this is a very sweet success."

He also paid tribute to the winning jockey, describing Egan as someone who is gracious in defeat but never obnoxious in victory.

"I'm delighted for David, you won't meet a nicer guy," the trainer added. "He's genuine, hard working and thoroughly professional. You forget how young he is and his best days are still ahead of him. Hopefully we'll be a part of that as well."

Like most on a day when racing was preceded by a two-minute silence and a singing of God Save the King, Varian was also mindful of the period of national mourning.

"The whole nation is saddened by the loss of the Queen and everyone in racing is hit hard because we've lost our patron really," he said. "We're very grateful for racing to go ahead today, I think that's what she would have wanted. But it's a family grieving and our thoughts are with them."

Not for the first time, St Leger day ended in drama and

frustration for Beckett, who saw his runner-up Haskoy demoted to fourth for the interference she had caused to Giavellotto. Considering connections had paid £50,000 to run, it was a costly reverse in more ways than one, with £169,000 in prize-money for second compared to £42,000 for fourth.

Having seen Simple Verse pass the post first in 2015 before she lost the race in the stewards' room, only to be reinstated at a later date after an appeal in London, Beckett was no doubt cursing history repeating in South Yorkshire.

There was no such drama for Egan and Varian, who look to have a credible contender for the top staying races in 2023. On a day tinged with sadness, Eldar Eldarov's St Leger proved a fine tribute to racing's greatest supporter.

RACING
FOUNDATION

CREATING LASTING LEGACIES FOR THE SPORT OF HORSERACING

The Racing Foundation helps British racing prosper by supporting charitable work that creates positive change in the industry.

In 2012 the Racing Foundation was established to oversee the distribution of funds to charitable causes within the racing and thoroughbred industry following the sale of the Tote.

Since inception it has awarded over £30million in grants.

The Racing Foundation supports projects linked to people, equine welfare, community engagement and environmental sustainability.

We exist to make a difference in racing by acting as a catalyst and a funder of improvement.

To hear more about Racing Foundation funded projects visit
www.racingfoundation.co.uk **or follow** @RacingGrants

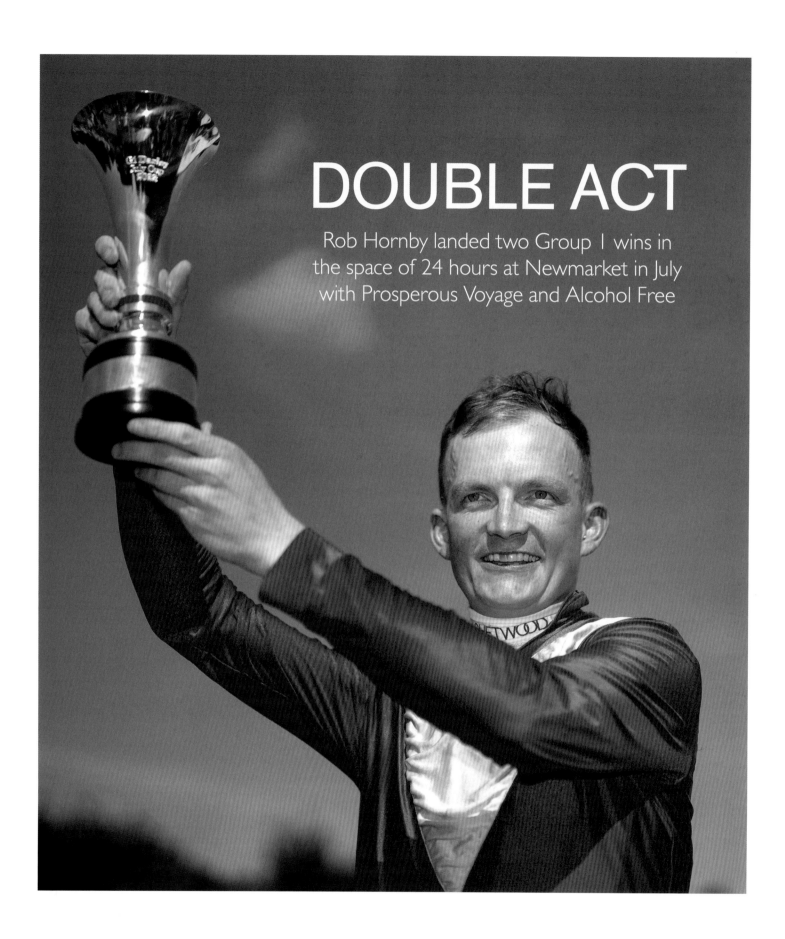

DOUBLE ACT

Rob Hornby landed two Group 1 wins in the space of 24 hours at Newmarket in July with Prosperous Voyage and Alcohol Free

ROB HORNBY didn't panic. A big opportunity was in danger of slipping out of his grasp but he refused to let the pressure get to him. Instead he got his head down and worked hard. Slowly but surely, he clawed his way back into contention. This one wasn't going to get away.

The Falmouth Stakes at Newmarket's July meeting wasn't supposed to be Hornby's race, but he made it his. He threw down the gauntlet from the off with a determined front-running effort on 16-1 shot Prosperous Voyage and refused to give up the fight when challenged and briefly headed at the furlong pole by 1-7 favourite Inspiral and Sandrine. Stoking up his filly for a final push on the rising ground, Hornby built up such a head of steam that they won going away.

"You've got to keep kicking and when the opportunity is given to you try your best and get it done," said Hornby, celebrating a breakthrough first Group 1 win in Britain.

His words were given added meaning by what had happened the month before. After finishing third in the Derby on Westover, trained like Prosperous Voyage by Ralph Beckett, Hornby would have gone to the Irish Derby with high hopes of Classic victory. Except he didn't go. The ride was taken off him and given to Irish champion Colin Keane, who duly had the glory on the Juddmonte-owned colt at the Curragh. That was the one that got away from Hornby.

There was also an altogether different loss in June. Scope, who had given Hornby his first Group 1 win in the Prix Royal-Oak the previous autumn, suffered a fatal injury on the gallops at Beckett's Kimpton Down Stables. It was the most bitter blow.

If fate owed Hornby a break,

perhaps Prosperous Voyage did too, having lost by a neck to Cachet in the 1,000 Guineas in May. He felt the 33-1 shot had done her best that day but admitted it was "very numbing" to get so close to winning a Classic. When opportunity knocked again in the Falmouth, he was ready to answer the call.

"It's crazy how things can change," he said in the winner's enclosure. "It's bonkers, isn't it? I'm in a very privileged position thanks to Ralph and the owners. To be riding in these Group 1s is where all jockeys want to be and days like this make everything worthwhile."

Reflecting on his hard-won elevation to the top level, the 27-year-old rider added: "Nothing's ever happened for me straight away. I plugged away through my apprenticeship under the guidance of Mr [Andrew] Balding and the academy there probably stood me in good stead for the highs and lows of what was to come."

Hornby, whose star has been on the rise since a difficult first season without his claim in 2017, does not have a contract with Beckett but has built a strong relationship with the stable over the past four years. The bond held tight despite the disappointment of losing the Irish Derby ride, and at the end of the season Juddmonte put Hornby back on Westover for the Arc.

"He's become an integral part of our operation," the trainer said after the Falmouth. "Whether he rides all the horses or not is not the be-all and end-all. He's a very laid-back character and nothing bothers him."

Beckett also noted how Hornby had kept a cool head on Prosperous Voyage when the heat was turned up. "He gave her a lovely ride," he said. "When he was challenged he sat still, which suits this filly, and she came good underneath him. He never panics."

★★★★

IF HORNBY thought things had been slow to happen for him in the past, another special moment came along quickly this time. Twenty-fours after Prosperous Voyage's Falmouth, he lined up in the July Cup on the Balding-trained Alcohol Free, another filly at double-figure odds in a Group 1, and once again he seized the opportunity with both hands.

Riding in the famous Jeff Smith silks for the trainer he joined as a 16-year-old "because I wasn't very good at school", Hornby produced another driving run to turn the dual Group 1-winning miler into a top-level sprinter in one of the hottest contests of the summer. He had the race wrapped up well before the line, allowing him to stand up in his irons and punch the air in the last three or four strides.

Earlier that week, Hornby had excitedly told his mother that he had two Group 1 rides. Now, coolly, he had turned them into two Group 1 winners.

"It's crazy really. I'm speechless," he said. "Yesterday was amazing

but to have two Group 1 rides in two days is fantastic, let alone two winners. These rides are huge to get and I'm very thankful to Mr Balding and Mr Smith."

In this case Alcohol Free was an opportunity that had been passed to Hornby. Oisin Murphy had ridden the four-year-old to her previous Group 1 successes but his 14-month ban for Covid-19 and alcohol breaches left the position vacant and Balding turned to Hornby, who had partnered her once in her juvenile days.

Like any jockey, Murphy was feeling the hurt of missing big days but he was delighted for Hornby. "He's been riding brilliantly for a couple of years, but getting on these better horses is what you need for your career to take off. Winning two Group 1s in 24 hours is the stuff of dreams," he said on Sky Racing.

Hornby had the best line to round off the most memorable week of his career. Asked how he would celebrate after the July Cup, he quipped: "It won't be an alcohol-free weekend."

A double toast to his two Group 1-winning fillies was in order.

Rollercoaster month

June 4 Hornby finishes an unlucky third in the Derby on Westover, being short of room at a key point of the race

June 21 He loses the ride on Westover in the Irish Derby as connections opt for local jockey Colin Keane

June 25 Westover wins the Irish Derby by seven lengths under Keane

June 28 Scope, Hornby's first Group 1 winner, suffers a fatal injury on the gallops

July 8 A breakthrough first British Group 1 for Hornby as Prosperous Voyage beats 1-7 shot Inspiral in the Falmouth Stakes

July 9 His second top-level winner in 24 hours as Alcohol Free causes an upset in the July Cup

◀ Double first: Rob Hornby lifts the July Cup after his victory on Alcohol Free; right, celebratory moments in his quick-fire Group 1 wins on Prosperous Voyage (pink and green) and Alcohol Free

FROM DOWNSIZING TO
MASSIVE DAYS

A year of change brought Owen Burrows his first Group 1 wins with Hukum and Minzaal

BY HIS own admission Owen Burrows needed 2022 to be a good year. In terms of racecourse success it turned out to be a great one for the Lambourn trainer. In June he celebrated a first Group 1 winner when Hukum took the Coronation Cup and within three months he had a second on the board with Minzaal in the Haydock Sprint Cup.

It was a welcome upturn in fortunes after Burrows started the year with 38 horses, down from the 90 he once had as private trainer for Sheikh Hamdan Al Maktoum. The sheikh's death in March 2021 led to downsizing and a move across Lambourn from Kingwood House to the smaller Farncombe Down Stables, but importantly Hukum and Minzaal remained in his team in the famous blue and white colours of the late Sheikh's Shadwell Estate.

Farncombe had been a rehabilitation yard for the Shadwell string in the south and now it was to be the base for Burrows' most invigorating year since he took out a licence in 2016. He achieved by far the best strike-rate of his career as well as his biggest wins, with the first coming in an emphatic display by Hukum at Epsom.

Baaeed's year-older brother always looked a different type to his superstar sibling, possessing stamina and grit rather than electrifying speed and dazzling brilliance, and at the start of 2022 he seemed rather stuck as a multiple Group 3 winner. A trip to Dubai yielded a first Group 2,

however, and on his return he made it to the top level in the Coronation Cup, beating the 2021 winner Pyledriver by four and a quarter lengths.

"It's massive," said Burrows, savouring the moment. "We have reduced numbers now but we still have a good team and it means a lot to do it for Shadwell and Sheikh Hamdan's family. It's been well documented that it's been a tough 12 months but I'm thrilled for everyone."

Within hours, however, the high was followed by a gut-wrenching low. Hukum was lame on arrival back at Farncombe and had surgery on his hind leg the following morning. "I was floating home from Epsom and then bang," Burrows said. While it was not a career-ending injury, it was a season-ending one and there was Hukum's value as a stallion to consider as well.

★★★★

THE stable's Group 1 hopes were pinned on Minzaal now. The four-year-old sprinter had threatened to make his mark at the top level ever since his Gimcrack win as a juvenile but had not quite delivered. He got the closest yet when runner-up to Highfield Princess in the Prix Maurice de Gheest at Deauville in August and Burrows was in confident mood going into the Sprint Cup the following month.

"I never like to be too bullish but he's got a favourite's chance," he said. Minzaal actually went off 7-2 second favourite behind

Platinum Jubilee winner Naval Crown but justified every ounce of his trainer's confidence, blasting home three and three-quarter lengths in front of the 2021 winner Emaraaty Ana.

"It was a big performance and he deserved it," Burrows said. "He'd been knocking on the door at two and had an interrupted season last year, through no fault of his own as he injured himself in the box. This has been a massively important year. We don't have a lot of horses to run and big winners on a Saturday in Group 1s are certainly hard to come by."

Once again, however, misfortune followed a big moment. Like Hukum, Minzaal returned home from his Group 1 breakthrough with an injury. "He was pretty sore the next morning, we ran a few tests and x-rays and unfortunately he's got a fracture of his left knee. He's had to have a pin in but that's him retired," Burrows reported a few days later.

Minzaal had been pencilled in for a final run on British Champions Day but instead went out on a high in the Sprint Cup. "At Haydock he proved to everybody what we'd been seeing at home for the last couple of years," Burrows said. "We knew he was certainly a Group 1 horse. He didn't just get his head in front either, he went out in a blaze of glory."

Even the loss of his two Group 1 stars did not stop Burrows' momentum. On Longchamp's Arc weekend he achieved another notable success when Anmaat, also

racing in the Shadwell colours, took the Group 2 Prix Dollar. Having delivered the trainer's most valuable handicap victory in the John Smith's Cup at York in July, the four-year-old was now his most important overseas winner.

★★★★

IN A Racing Post interview shortly before Minzaal's Haydock triumph, Burrows made no bones about the importance of 2022. "I needed to have a good season because if I'd had a bad one I'd have been dead and buried," he admitted, before laying out the graft that had gone into making a success of his downsized operation.

"I had the luxury of a lot of staff at Kingwood, but that's been reined back and my assistant, head lad and I are mucking out before first lot," he said. "I don't think anyone enjoys it, but if guys come in and see me mucking out, they can't moan, especially if I've been up an hour and a half beforehand feeding."

The hard work will be redoubled in 2023 when Burrows goes from being a salaried trainer for Shadwell to renting his yard. "It will be difficult, but I have 40 boxes and we had 38 on the books this year, so we've nearly filled it. I'd love to get to 60 again and accommodating them won't be a problem," he said.

"We've got a bit of momentum now, so I don't want to be glass-half-empty worrying about doing this. I think I've got one chance and I've got to go for it."

Another big year lies ahead.

▲ Top scorers: Hukum lands a first Group 1 win for Owen Burrows (right) at Epsom; below, Minzaal strikes at Haydock

OH LORD!

DERMOT McLOUGHLIN'S first triumph in the Irish Grand National was a massive shock. By comparison, his repeat success 12 months later was merely a surprise, but it shouldn't have been. Having dreamed for so long of winning the storied showpiece at his local track, McLoughlin has hit upon the magic formula that has turned him into something of a race specialist.

In 2021 McLoughlin, who trains just a few miles from Fairyhouse, made history with Freewheelin Dylan's front-running victory at record odds of 150-1. Few outside his Ratoath yard believed he could do it again and Lord Lariat, his new challenger, was sent off at 40-1, yet there were more barriers to be broken.

When Lord Lariat galloped home in front by four and three-quarter lengths, McLoughlin became the first trainer in almost half a century to saddle back-to-back Irish National winners – and with different horses to boot. For a relatively small-scale operation of just 40 horses, it was a mighty feat to come out on top again when faced by the massed ranks of Willie Mullins – who was third with 11-2 favourite Gaillard Du Mesnil – and Gordon Elliott, who saddled runner-up Frontal Assault among a team of ten.

"To do it again is unbelievable," McLoughlin said. "To have a runner in these big races, it's massive for us. To win is great for me and all the lads in the yard. I've been coming here from a young age with my father, so it's very special."

The family bond with the Irish National is even stronger after Lord Lariat's victory. The record books now show two wins for the 48-year-old trainer, whose late father Liam took the race as a jockey on Kerforo in 1962. The other claim to fame for McLoughlin snr was that he was the first rider to win on the Tom Dreaper-trained Arkle, the greatest chaser of all time and winner of the Irish National in 1964.

McLoughlin jnr later learned his trade with Dreaper's son Jim and it was fitting that with Lord Lariat's success he became the first trainer to saddle back-to-back Irish National winners since his old boss did it with Brown Lad in 1975 and 1976. Dreaper jnr had also been the last to win the race in successive years with different horses, having scored with Colebridge in 1974.

★★★★

ALL the years of watching and waiting for his own Irish National moment had given McLoughlin a clear appreciation of the qualities needed for success and he saw them in Lord Lariat early enough to lay out the seven-year-old for the race and try to sneak in at the bottom of the weights. Ireland's richest jumps race was almost five months away when Lord Lariat won at Fairyhouse under Joanna Walton in late November 2021, over a mile less than the National distance, but that was the moment his wily trainer spotted his opportunity.

"We've laid him out for this since before Christmas," McLoughlin said after his plan had come to glorious fruition. "When Joanna Walton won the ladies' race on him, he nearly ran away with her and she said he'd get further, so we said we'd have a go if we could get in. We only snuck in right at the bottom, so we had a bit of luck there."

The booking of 7lb claimer Paddy O'Hanlon took Lord Lariat's weight down to 9st 12lb in the 27-runner field and McLoughlin had the same attacking outlook that had worked with Freewheelin Dylan 12 months earlier. "I was concerned he wouldn't get the trip, but I said to Paddy to do like we did last year and let him pop out, because I wanted to utilise his jumping. He enjoyed himself and jumped and travelled. Paddy gave him breathers at the right time and it all worked out. It doesn't usually happen like that."

It has happened twice now for McLoughlin on the big stage and none of his peers are surprised, given his well-earned reputation as a target trainer. After Lord Lariat's victory, eight-time champion jumps trainer Noel Meade said: "That's an incredible stroke to win two Irish Nationals one after the other, just incredible. To have the horses right on the day and get them to peak is some going. He's a lovely man to go along with it. The same as his father. I'm sure Liam would be very proud if he was still alive."

The big difference between McLoughlin's two triumphs was the scenes afterwards. Freewheelin Dylan's jaw-dropping victory played out to a near-empty arena in the behind-closed-doors Covid era but this time there was a full crowd, whose joy at being there was evident in a chorus of "ole, ole" as the race got under way. "There was no-one here last year, but now all my family and staff are here, which is great," McLoughlin said. "To have my wife and kids here this time makes up for last year."

O'Hanlon, for whom Lord Lariat was a tenth winner of the campaign, had experienced nothing like it, crowd or no crowd. "It's unbelievable – I'm lost for words," the 24-year-old said. "I was only saying to my father coming here this morning, I was

The 40-1 shot Lord Lariat gave trainer Dermot McLoughlin a second successive win in the Irish Grand National

delighted to have a ride in the race. I said I'd enjoy it and soak it all up, so to ride the winner, I don't know what to say."

Lord Lariat's starring role seemed less of a surprise for owners PJ Casey, who bought him for just €5,500 as a three-year-old, and Pat Blake. "PJ always said there was a big pot in this horse," Blake said. "Lord Lariat was very good looking as a youngster. He had a great walk and would catch your eye. We're just so proud of him. I wouldn't be a big gambling man but I had a couple of pounds on him."

Lord Lariat might not have attracted much money from the punters but McLoughlin's next runner in the Irish National will not be ignored so easily. After a second successive win in the €500,000 race, he's the man with the Midas touch.

▲ Lord and master: Paddy O'Hanlon celebrates his Irish Grand National win on Lord Lariat and (inset) embraces trainer Dermot McLoughlin

THE BIGGER PICTURE

Third Wind, a 25-1 shot trained by Hughie Morrison and ridden by Tom O'Brien, leads home the strung-out field in the Pertemps Handicap Hurdle in front of a full house at the Cheltenham Festival in March
EDWARD WHITAKER (RACINGPOST.COM/PHOTOS)

Our selection of the horses and people likely to be hitting the headlines in 2023

CALLUM HUTCHINSON

A FIRST winner at Royal Ascot as a 5lb apprentice is a great feeling; to do it by fending off Ryan Moore in a close finish at the end of a gruelling two and a half miles is extra special.

That achievement was a notable feather in the cap of Callum Hutchinson in June when he landed the Ascot Stakes on Coltrane, trained by his boss Andrew Balding, by three-quarters of a length from the Moore-ridden favourite Bring On The Night.

The 20-year-old took the lead over a furlong out but was quickly challenged by Moore and their mounts went head to head until Hutchinson finally gained the upper hand in the final 50 yards.

"I saw Ryan coming upsides me and I thought it could be game over, but he's a tough horse and he galloped strongly all the way to the line," Hutchinson said after returning to the hallowed winner's enclosure on the 14-1 shot.

Balding was impressed. "Callum gave him a beautiful ride," he said. "He was always in the right spot and made his space like a seasoned pro in the straight. I thought, 'oh, Ryan's going to come and do us here', but Callum is strong in a finish as well. I'm very proud of the jockey and very proud of the horse."

Royal Ascot success came only 20 months after Hutchinson's first winner, which in turn was just over a year after his father Wayne had retired from his long and successful career as a jump jockey. Having decided at 15 he wanted to follow in his dad's footsteps, Hutchinson spent time with Brendan Powell's Lambourn yard before joining the famed apprentice academy at Balding's Kingsclere base.

He rode 19 winners in 2021, his first full season, and exceeded that in the latest campaign. Among his other notable winners was Balding's Spirit Mixer, who went close to giving him another big victory when second to Trueshan in the Northumberland Plate.

With his valuable claim, and having shown his cool head and strength in a finish at Royal Ascot, Hutchinson will continue to be in demand and looks set for a big push in the apprentice championship.

LITTLE BIG BEAR

EVERY high-class two-year-old has questions to answer about their ultimate distance preference and whether they will train on, but the early end to Little Big Bear's season meant even more was left unanswered with him.

Aidan O'Brien was unable to test the son of No Nay Never over seven furlongs, as he had intended to do at Group 1 level in the National Stakes and possibly the Dewhurst Stakes, and that left plenty of room for argument over whether the top two-year-old of 2022 would turn out to be a sprinter or a miler.

What we knew for sure by August 6, when Little Big Bear ran away with the Group 1 Phoenix Stakes by seven lengths, was that he was a top-notch juvenile. A Racing Post Rating of 122 ranked that as the joint-seventh-best winning performance on O'Brien's long roll of honour with star two-year-olds.

The Phoenix win was all the more meritorious given that O'Brien later revealed Little Big Bear had kicked a wall after arriving after the track, causing the clip of his shoe to go into his hind foot – "for humans it might be the equivalent of pulling off a fingernail," he said.

With O'Brien mindful of giving him enough recovery time, Little Big Bear was stood down for the season in mid-September. "He's perfect, there's not a bother on him, we just didn't want to be rushing him back," he reported.

While Little Big Bear never got the chance to race beyond six and a half furlongs, his form stacked up well. His second win at five furlongs came in the Windsor Castle Stakes at Royal Ascot and six of the next ten home were successful afterwards, four of them in Group or Listed company. In the six-furlong Phoenix he left three Group 2 winners trailing in his wake and two of them went on to finish much closer in Group 1s.

What we never found out was whether Little Big Bear could carry his power and speed to a longer distance and it was perhaps telling that O'Brien gave some consideration to taking on the older sprinters in the Nunthorpe.

Yet there is also the example of George Washington. He produced a similarly explosive performance for O'Brien in the Phoenix in 2005, winning by eight lengths, and was a top-class miler the following season with victories in the 2,000 Guineas and Queen Elizabeth II Stakes.

Will Little Big Bear be like that? Or something different? The questions are waiting to be answered.

COMMISSIONING

FOR Robert Havlin, Commissioning's victory in the Fillies' Mile at Newmarket had a special significance – his first Group 1 win after more than 30 years in the saddle. It is a performance that might also have wider importance when it comes to the 2023 Classics.

The ride on the John and Thady Gosden-trained daughter of Kingman became vacant when Frankie Dettori was suspended and Havlin, for so long a key member of the Clarehaven team, grabbed the opportunity to land a one-length victory. It wasn't straightforward on the 8-13 favourite, who became unbalanced in the Dip, but ultimately it was comfortable enough.

"Frankie doesn't get banned nearly enough," Havlin quipped in the winner's enclosure, having been welcomed back by a group of fellow riders who came out of the weighing room to mark his achievement.

The Fillies' Mile was only Commissioning's third start following victories over seven furlongs in a novice on the July course and the Group 2 Rockfel Stakes on the Rowley Mile. A lack of experience seemed a reasonable explanation for her little difficulty in the Dip and her runs at Newmarket are likely to stand her in good stead next season.

"She's still some way from being the finished article mentally," Havlin said after the Fillies' Mile. "She was quick to correct herself and she was really strong at the end. I put my stick down for the last half a furlong and she was really going on."

Valued for his input as a work-rider, Havlin is well placed to assess Commissioning's likely capabilities, having ridden her dam Sovereign Parade to a maiden victory over a mile and a quarter and a decent seventh place in the Group 2 Ribblesdale Stakes at a mile and a half.

"Commissioning has got the tactical speed for a Guineas and also stays very well," Havlin said. "Her mother only had two starts and the second was the Ribblesdale when she was green but stayed on well. This filly has the right mind to get a bit of a trip. She relaxes and then she's push-button to ride. With a winter on her back she'll be a special filly next year."

MARK McDONAGH

AT THE age of 21 Mark McDonagh has a wise head on young shoulders. Having combined race-riding with studying for a business degree at the University of Limerick, he has a bright future.

The grandson of County Clare trainer Michael McDonagh certainly looked the business at the Cheltenham Festival in March when he won the Martin Pipe Conditional Jockeys' Handicap Hurdle on Banbridge for his boss Joseph O'Brien. Not only was it his debut at the festival, it was his first ride in Britain.

"It was unreal when I crossed the line," he said. "I've never witnessed anything like it before. Walking back in was class."

Praised by O'Brien for "a great ride", McDonagh kept out of trouble in the 23-runner field, although he admitted afterwards: "There were loose horses coming past me every few seconds and I thought, Jesus, what's going on behind me?"

That win came against fellow conditionals but he had notable success in Ireland against the senior riders last season. In December he won a Grade 3 novice hurdle at Cork without his claim, scoring by eight lengths on the Sean O'Brien-trained Nell's Well. His 7lb came in handy for Enda Bolger at the Dublin Racing Festival when he took a valuable handicap chase on Birchdale, his first ride in the JP McManus colours, and again when he won the Ulster National on the Gavin Cromwell-trained Spades Are Trumps.

Even with a reduction in his claim thanks to his early successes, McDonagh is a conditional rider to watch.

THE NICE GUY

WITH just one hurdles run before the Cheltenham Festival, the Willie Mullins-trained seven-year-old became the least experienced horse to win the Albert Bartlett Novices' Hurdle and did it impressively, beating his stablemate Minella Cocooner by five lengths. It was the same one-two in the Grade 1 novice three-miler at the Punchestown festival, albeit with the margin reduced to three-quarters of a length.

In the previous 15 years only two horses had won the Albert Bartlett after fewer than six outings (in points, bumpers or over hurdles) and they were Bobs Worth and Minella Indo, who both went on to win the Cheltenham Gold Cup.

The Nice Guy was late getting started because the Mullins team didn't really know what to make of him. "We didn't have much respect at all for him on his homework," the trainer said. "We said we'd better run him in a bumper as he'd been in training an awful long time and he literally shows us nothing at home."

He won his two bumpers at the end of 2021 and then took a 22-runner maiden hurdle easily at Naas in January to earn his festival chance. By the end of the season he was a dual Grade 1 winner after just five runs.

"He just keeps producing more, and it's great to have a horse like that, one who does it in the afternoon," Mullins said. "I don't think anyone in our yard would have backed him or fancied him at any stage of his career and he keeps on surprising us."

There may be more surprises to come in his novice chasing campaign.

TAHIYRA

THE Aga Khan celebrated the centenary of his family's racehorse ownership in 2022 and in Tahiyra there is every hope he has found a new torchbearer in the famous silks.

The Dermot Weld-trained filly produced an electrifying display in the Group 1 Moyglare Stud Stakes in September, whetting the appetite for even better to come next season. When the previously unbeaten favourite Meditate went clear over a furlong out, she traded at 1-5 in running but Tahiyra unleashed a dazzling turn of foot to pass her with ease and go two and a quarter lengths clear.

The only thing that surprised Weld was that Tahiyra was so ready for the top level on only her second start, albeit she had shown heaps of promise in running away with a hot Galway maiden on her debut.

"It was an excellent renewal of the race. I was afraid it might just come a little soon in her career, at Group 1 level, and I've always said what a beautiful filly she would be next spring," the trainer said.

Tahiyra was a beautiful two-year-old too – "a little sweetheart" was jockey Chris Hayes's description – but it is the future that is so exciting. The daughter of Siyouni is a half-sister to Tarnawa, who was a slow burner by comparison but lit up the world stage at the ages of four and five. She won three times at the top level, including the 2020 Breeders' Cup Turf, and was second in the 2021 Prix de l'Arc de Triomphe.

That record will take some matching but Tahiyra is already well on her way. She was given a Racing Post Rating of 116 after the Moyglare, which far outstrips Tarnawa's 96 as a two-year-old and is just 6lb shy of her illustrious half-sister's top mark.

Tarnawa did not contest a Guineas and was only 11th in the Oaks at Epsom but a Classics campaign will be the aim for Tahiyra. Alongside the quality of the dam's side, Siyouni has sired French Classic winners at a mile and 1m2½f (including St Mark's Basilica, who did the French Guineas-Derby double) as well as Arc hero Sottsass (who also won the French Derby).

"We have a lot to look forward to," Weld said, with some degree of understatement. "There is tremendous stamina in the pedigree, brilliance and speed."

It's an intoxicating blend.

IMPERIAL EMPEROR

THE Godolphin homebred made a highly impressive debut, winning a mile maiden at Newmarket by three and a half lengths to stamp himself as a Derby prospect. A big run was clearly expected from the well-backed 13-8 favourite and he didn't disappoint, lengthening powerfully for William Buick.

Trainer Charlie Appleby has high regard for the son of Dubawi from the family of Ghaiyyath. "He has a lovely pedigree and had been doing the right things at home," he said. "We came here with the confidence that he was going to run a nice race. He's a proper mile-and-a-half horse for next year."

THREE STRIPE LIFE

FOURTH in the Champion Bumper to Sir Gerhard in 2021, the Gordon Elliott-trained six-year-old was never out of the first three in six hurdles starts last season and the last five were all Grade 1s. He chased home Sir Gerhard at Leopardstown and in the Ballymore at Cheltenham and finally cracked it at the top level with a comfortable success in the Mersey Novices' Hurdle at Aintree.

Staying trips over fences are likely to bring out the best in him and his battle-hardened spirit will stand him in good stead for the next phase of his career. As Elliott put it succinctly: "He's bred to be a chaser and looks like a chaser."

TAYLOR FISHER

STAR apprentices Benoit de la Sayette and Harry Davies cut their teeth in pony racing and Fisher, 18, could be another success story on that path. He regularly vied with Davies for leading rider honours on the pony racing circuit and, having started a few months behind him as an apprentice, was quick to make an impression on the Flat.

Having been snapped up by Archie Watson's powerful stable in July, the Devon-born jockey had his first winner shortly afterwards and continued to impress over the rest of the season. He had winners for more than a dozen stables and is set to be in big demand in 2023.

FACILE VEGA

THE son of six-time Cheltenham Festival winner Quevega attracted plenty of interest from the start and did not disappoint in his first season for Willie Mullins, going off favourite in all four bumpers and winning every time. He went from Leopardstown's Christmas meeting to a Grade 2 at the Dublin Racing Festival and then Grade 1 victories in the champion bumpers at Cheltenham and Punchestown.

Having retained Quevega for breeding, the Hammer and Trowel Syndicate have been rewarded with a highly exciting novice hurdling prospect in the red and blue colours made famous by their celebrated mare.

CHALDEAN

ANDREW BALDING was added to the roster of Juddmonte Farms trainers in 2022 and the very first horse to arrive at his Kingsclere yard was Chaldean. The Frankel colt proved to be a most exciting addition to his squad.

On his final outing of five as a two-year-old, Chaldean stamped himself as a serious 2,000 Guineas contender with a first Group 1 victory in the Dewhurst Stakes at Newmarket. Having made the majority of the running, he showed an impressive burst of speed over two furlongs out before holding on gamely to defeat Royal Scotsman by a head.

Frankie Dettori, riding Chaldean for the second time, said: "He's a proper horse for the Guineas and they can dream now for next year."

Royal Scotsman, trained by Paul and Oliver Cole, ran a stormer and arguably should have won, but Dettori felt Chaldean might have scored more decisively in different circumstances. "When we shot clear I thought we had it in the bag, and I think Chaldean lost his concentration a bit as he was all on his own. I probably kicked a bit too early," the jockey said.

Dettori advised a shot at the Dewhurst after being impressed on his first ride on Chaldean in the Group 2 Champagne Stakes at Doncaster. On soft ground, which had been a concern for Balding, he made all to win the three-runner contest by three and a half lengths.

The trainer stressed after the Dewhurst that pacesetting or a long run for home is not an essential tactic for Chaldean. "He doesn't have to make it and the bigger the field, probably the better off he'll be," he said. "He should go on next year and certainly stay a mile, so we've got lots to look forward to. He's all speed on his dam's side, so I'd be surprised if he gets further than a mile."

Juddmonte's colours were also carried in the Dewhurst by third-placed Nostrum, who shared joint-favouritism with Chaldean. The Sir Michael Stoute-trained son of Kingman was less experienced and his promising performance added depth to the form.

Discussing the pair, Juddmonte racing manager Barry Mahon said: "Chaldean won't have any problem staying a mile and neither will Nostrum. We've got two lovely horses who will keep us dreaming through the winter."

Whereas Nostrum is a homebred, Chaldean was a relatively rare sales purchase for Juddmonte, having cost 550,000gns as a foal. It was a shrewd move.

LOSE YOURSELF

RALPH BECKETT was highly competitive in the 2022 Classics, winning the Irish Derby with Westover and going close in several others, and Lose Yourself is a likely contender from his next crop.

The daughter of Lope De Vega beat several future winners when scoring first time out on the July course and looked all set to follow up in the Group 3 Oh So Sharp Stakes on the Rowley Mile until she seemed to be let down by her lack of experience when she found herself alone in front.

The 260,000gns buy will have learned a lot from those two runs over seven furlongs and is bred to improve in her second season.

THOMASINA EYSTON

NEIL MULHOLLAND'S conditional jockey had a couple of great results in the space of 24 hours in mid-July. First she rode her first winner for her boss, Agent Saonois in a two-mile handicap hurdle at Uttoxeter, and 24 hours later she got a first in her chemistry degree at Bristol University.

Eyston, 22, from Devon, is a late starter in the professional ranks after her studies but has plenty of experience from pony racing and the point-to-point circuit. Having ridden out for Colin and Joe Tizzard while at university, she has made an impressive start with Mulholland and looks set to prove good value for her claim.

BETWEEN WATERS

A BIG run was expected from this four-year-old daughter of Walk In The Park when she made her point-to-point debut at Lisronagh in February. She had impressed in a schooling hurdle at Fairyhouse and trainer Sean Doyle couldn't see her being beaten as she tackled three miles over fences. His confidence was fully justified as she made most of the running and quickened off the home bend to score by eight lengths.

Now with Nicky Henderson, she has continued to catch the eye. "You won't see a better-looking filly," the Seven Barrows trainer said at his autumn open day. "She might just be something."

UNEXPECTED PARTY

LAST season ended disappointingly for Dan Skelton's seven-year-old when he was pulled up in the Coral Cup at the Cheltenham Festival, but before that he had made impressive progress in handicap hurdles as a novice, notably when winning over 2m3½f at Ascot in January.

Skelton rated him as Graded class over hurdles and further progress is expected as a novice chaser. Most of his hurdles runs were at around two and a half miles but he has the pace to drop back in trip. With form on good and soft, and with a solid second at Cheltenham on his record, he has plenty of positive attributes.

HARNESS YOUR POTENTIAL

THE BRITISH RACING SCHOOL

Assistant Trainers

The 3-day Assistant Trainers course illustrates the impotrtance of an Assistant Trainer both in the yard and on the racecourse. The course covers subjects including, staff Management, handicapping, media training, Health and Safety, Racing Welfare, BHA's Licensing and Security functions and Weatherbys Operations and the Rules. The costs for this course are fully funded for anyone already working within the industry.

Racing Secretaries

This course is for Secretaries new to Racing and anyone considering working in this role but is also suitable for those looking to progress to administrative roles within the industry. The course, run over three days, provides knowledge of the role of a racing secretary, and introduces you to key organisations such as the International Racing Bureau, the National Trainers Federation, and the British Horseracing Authority that you will deal with as a racing secretary. You will also hear from experienced and well-established racing secretaries who will give a practical insight into fulfilling this demanding role.

Intro to Riding Work

This course is designed to give competent stable staff the opportunity to learn about riding work, covering the basic theory and aims behind riding work. This is transferred to the simulators for body position training and then to the gallops with two ridden sessions, which are filmed and reviewed.

Yard Managers

The yard Managers course is suitable for anyone who currently supervises staff in a racing yard or stud farm. This course is run over two days and covers aspects of communication, handling conflict, employment law, motivation, team building and styles of leadership. Delegates are encouraged to get involved in discussion and practical tasks. The costs for this course are fully funded for anyone already working within the industry.

Level 3 Diploma in Work Based Racehorse Care and Management

This Diploma has been designed specifically for the racing industry and is a nationally recognised, skill-based qualification. This qualification is the ideal way to increase your knowledge about racehorse care and management and, with experience, prepare you for a position of responsibility. A Level 3 Diploma is a mandatory requirement for all prospective permit holders and licensed racehorse trainers, and it is linked to the Grade A racing wage.

Interested?

Email courses@brs.org.uk to register your interest or phone Beth on 01638 675907

JAMES HORTON

ASSISTANT to Sir Michael Stoute for seven years until branching out on his own, Horton has an exciting future as private trainer for John and Jess Dance after a solid first year.

This winter Horton, 36, will move into Manor House Farm, a new state-of-the-art training complex in Middleham built on the site where the last northern-trained Derby winner, Dante, was born and raised.

As well as investing "north of £10 million" in the facilities, John Dance, the stockbroking CEO who hit the big time with multiple Group 1 winner Laurens, was also active at the autumn sales. With stables for more than 70 horses at the new yard, Horton will have a strong team in the Dances' new gold and black silks.

In his first year, while the building work was going on, Horton operated from former trainer Sally Hall's Brecongill Stables. It was a stiff challenge given that he had moved from Newmarket with no prior knowledge of Middleham or its gallops, but he took it in his stride.

He had his first runner in March, recorded a Redcar treble in April and by August had a Listed winner when Sam Maximus took the Hopeful Stakes at Newmarket.

Explaining how he got involved, Horton said: "I didn't know a huge amount about John and Jess but I came up to see them at the start of last year. I spoke to some confidants in Newmarket and all my peers said I'd be mad not to go. So I said yes. They're lovely, down-to-earth people. We share the same ideas."

Dance is excited about working with Horton. "We talked racing philosophies and everything James said was more and more attuned to what we were thinking. Some of his own ideas really struck a chord with us and it evolved from there. We wanted someone with a fresh perspective who wanted a foot on the ladder and it felt like the perfect fit."

The next phase of their partnership will be fascinating to watch.

HI ROYAL

THE Kevin Ryan-trained juvenile started at 50-1 for his debut in the Convivial Maiden at York, but don't expect the bookmakers ever to be so generous again.

He ran a huge race there to be beaten little more than half a length behind two horses with previous experience, finishing strongly after a slow start left him with an awful lot to do.

Jaber Abdullah's son of Kodiac showed that was no fluke with a comfortable win at Ayr a month later and he's a big colt who will improve plenty in his second season. He promises to stay a mile and a quarter and looks sure to win more races.

L'HOMME PRESSE

PART-OWNER Andy Edwards was sure about Venetia Williams' Cheltenham Gold Cup contender after watching him storm to victory in the Brown Advisory Novices' Chase in March.

"Back him now for the Gold Cup. Why wouldn't you? He was still going away up the hill in this ground and he'll be stronger next year," he declared.

Many would agree. L'Homme Presse is an immaculate jumper with a huge engine and clearly relishes Cheltenham. He improved 36lb once he was sent chasing and won't need to find much more to be a serious threat even in a strong Gold Cup division.

LOOKAWAY

THIS Neil King-trained five-year-old might be the best British graduate from last season's bumper scene. On his final start he was an impressive two-length winner of the Grade 2 Aintree contest landed by subsequent Grade 1 scorers The New One, Barters Hill, Bacardys and Lalor in the past decade. That kept the £170,000 purchase unbeaten after one point-to-point and two bumpers.

King rates him higher than his popular Graded hurdler Lil Rockerfeller, saying: "We're a small stable but he's going to be a serious horse. He won a point-to-point, in which he jumped great. I think he has everything, I really do."

SAKHEER

AFTER finishing second on his debut at Windsor in August, the Roger Varian-trained juvenile developed quickly to land a Haydock novice by six lengths and the Group 2 Mill Reef Stakes at Newbury by three and a half lengths. Connections paid £35,000 to supplement him for the Group 1 Dewhurst Stakes but he was unable to run after scoping dirty.

Sakheer's elevation to the top level looks to be merely delayed, with Varian saying: "He's got size and scope, so he looks like a horse who'll train on. He's very exciting and he's won over six furlongs, but I think he'll stay seven furlongs and maybe a mile."

Shares from as little as £49

Give a gift that provides anticipation, excitement, days out and the thrill of a day at the races as an owner.

theracingemporium.com
call us on 01377 267114

THE RACING EMPORIUM
EST. 2019

Scan to
buy now

As an owner you will receive

OWNERS CERTIFICATE

All shares include Owners Certificate & Gift Pack.

RACE-DAY REWARDS

You are able to opt in to receive Owners Badges drawn every race.

BE PART OF THE COMMUNITY

Vote on the naming of horses, what you would like to see as an owner such as apparel and merchandise.

STABLE VISITS

You can visit your horse at Cottam Grange and enjoy hospitality at our visitors centre, taking in the breath-taking views of the Yorkshire Wolds.

EXCLUSIVE CONTENT

We send out pre-race reports, post-race reports, exclusive photo shoots, race day photoshoots and a monthly newsletter.

A SHARE OF THE WINNINGS

Any winnings your horse takes will be paid out in line with the percentage of your share.

THE
BIGGER
PICTURE

Vital Island (no.13), the winner for trainer
Richard O'Keeffe and rider Benny Walsh, is
on the far side as the leaders tackle the Laurel
Bank in the Ladies' Perpetual Cup at the
Punchestown festival in April
PATRICK McCANN (RACINGPOST.COM/PHOTOS)

A-Z of 2022

The year digested into 26 bite-size chunks

A is for awesome. Baaeed fitted the description perfectly as he joined the Flat racing greats with another electrifying season that had his signature performance in the International at York as its centrepiece.

B is for back from the brink. Josh Moore came perilously close to losing his life when complications from a Haydock fall in April left him suffering from fat embolism syndrome. At one point doctors feared there was nothing more that could be done to help one of jumping's most popular jockeys but he miraculously emerged from an induced coma and much more besides to return home in one piece and with the promise of a future training career.

C is for corinthian. Having announced he would retire after the Grand National, amateur rider Sam Waley-Cohen proceeded to go out in the best possible style with a brilliant victory on 50-1 shot Noble Yeats, owned by his father Robert and trained by Emmet Mullins.

D is for double figures. Willie Mullins won ten of the 28 races at the Cheltenham Festival, beating the trainers' record of eight that he himself set in 2015 and was equalled by Gordon Elliott in 2018.

E is for European record. Stradivarius exited the stage in 2022 but not before he had given one last crowd-pleasing performance in the Yorkshire Cup to claim the outright record for the most Group wins by a horse trained in Europe. Eighteen was his final number.

F is for fightback. The British were nearly wiped out at the 2021 Cheltenham Festival, losing 23-5, but doubled their score a year later including Grade 1s with Constitution Hill, Edwardstone and L'Homme Presse. Even so, Willie Mullins matched the home team's total of ten on his own.

G is for gamble. Or in this case the one that didn't quite come off on a dramatic evening at Tramore in August. Four horses trained or ridden by members of the Mullins family were combined in a number of multiple bets, including one whose odds were cut from 100-1 into 5-4. A huge payout was averted when only two of them won, although another was beaten in a photo.

H is for humanitarian effort. Many in racing responded to the war in Ukraine with aid donations and selfless acts of assistance on the ground for people and horses displaced by the conflict. Newmarket trainer Gay Kelleway, who has made multiple trips to the Poland-Ukraine border, said: "Racing has been different class. It would break your heart the things we've seen over there. It has been a life-changing experience."

I is for inflation busting. Amid the cost of living crisis, stable staff secured an average 14.5 per cent increase in their minimum pay in October. The deal between the National Association of Racing Staff and National Trainers Federation brought a 30 per cent increase (to £250.12 per week) for level one school leavers entering the sport, while minimum rates for level six employees in a supervisory role rose by 25 per cent to £475 per week.

J is for jumping. That's the name of the game and it let Galopin Des Champs down spectacularly at Cheltenham in March. He had three hooves on the Turners Novices' Chase trophy as he cleared the final fence with a 12-length lead. But he failed to get his landing gear out, slithered to the turf and handed the race to the fortunate Bob Olinger.

K is for king of the Classics. Aidan O'Brien claimed the outright trainers' record of British Classic wins with Tuesday's thrilling Oaks, which took him to 41. The Ballydoyle maestro has accumulated his total over a 24-year period since his first with King Of Kings in the 1998 2,000 Guineas, which means on average he has won one in every three British Classics in that period.

L is for load bearing. Trueshan had to carry 10st 8lb over 2m½f in the Northumberland Plate, conceding at least 19lb to his 19 rivals, but made light of the enormous burden to record a half-length victory under Hollie Doyle. "That is unreal," his rider said in awe and admiration.

M is for mourning. It was a sad year for racing with the deaths of Queen Elizabeth II and Lester Piggott, two of the greatest figures in the sport who had combined for Classic success back in 1957 with Oaks winner Carrozza. Most tragic of all was the death of Jack de Bromhead, aged just 13, in a pony racing fall. "Our hearts are broken," said Henry and Heather, his grief-stricken parents, and everyone's hearts went out to them.

N is for Newmarket. Flat racing's major training centre had a great year, headlined by Baaeed, Alpinista's Arc and victories in four of the five British Classics, all for different yards.

O is for offers rejected. The small-scale owner-breeders of Highfield Princess and Pyledriver turned down big money to retain their once-in-a-lifetime horses and were

rewarded with memorable triumphs in some of the biggest Group 1s of the year.

P is for party pooper. Delta Work might well have been the most unpopular winner of the year, even for his connections, when he denied stablemate Tiger Roll a perfect end to his career in the cross-country chase at Cheltenham. "I'd say a lot of people will hate me now," said winning jockey Jack Kennedy.

Q is for quick double. Ten years after his first ride in a British Classic, James Doyle finally tasted success with Coroebus in the 2,000 Guineas and a second victory took only 24 hours to come along when he teamed up with Cachet to land the 1,000 Guineas.

R is for royal first. Just Fine made history in a minor handicap at Leicester on October 4 when he became the first winner in the name of King Charles III. The Sir Michael Stoute-trained four-year-old was the King's sixth runner following the transfer of the royal colours and horses on the death of Queen Elizabeth II.

S is for sabbatical. That was the word used by Frankie Dettori and John Gosden to describe a break in their seven-year relationship after a far from happy Royal Ascot. Nobody knew if it was a split or a trial separation but it turned out to be a brief parting and they were back together within a couple of weeks. "The only reason it ever happened was I couldn't get his attention," Gosden later explained. "I couldn't get him to concentrate, that's all. In the end, it required a bit of a public warning. What would you call it if you were

a football manager? Leaving him on the bench?"

T is for telephone numbers. Juddmonte supersire Frankel was the highest-grossing stallion at Book 1 of the Tattersalls October Yearling Sale in Newmarket, with his 25 lots returning receipts totalling 18,745,000gns. The 2,800,000gns top lot *(above)* was his colt out of So Mi Dar, consigned by Watership Down Stud and bought by Godolphin. Day two of the sale became the highest-grossing session of selling in European auction history as 49,545,000gns was traded.

U is for unconscionable and unthinkable. That is how Princess Zahra Aga Khan described Christophe Soumillon's elbowing of Rossa Ryan out of the saddle in a race at Saint-Cloud on September 30. The highest-profile jockey in France was given a 60-day ban and had his contract terminated as first rider for the Aga Khan.

V is for virtuoso. Having just missed out on the big Cheltenham double in 2021, Rachael Blackmore kept faith with A Plus Tard and produced a superb ride to go one better in the Gold Cup. With the ever-reliable Honeysuckle having set up the double chance again with her second Champion Hurdle, the brilliance of Blackmore and A Plus Tard did the rest.

W is for wait, wait, wait. Those were the words in Sir Mark Prescott's head as he watched Luke Morris's serene progress through the Prix de l'Arc de Triomphe on Alpinista. Morris waited, waited, waited – and won.

X is for x-ray. The picture was bad for Minzaal a few days after his Haydock Sprint Cup victory when he was found to have a fractured left knee and had to be retired. It was a second piece of rotten news for trainer Owen Burrows, who lost Hukum, his other Group 1 winner, to season-ending injury after the Coronation Cup.

Y is for Yeats the second? Kyprios became the dominant stayer in the mould of Ballydoyle legend Yeats and is already ahead of him on Racing Post Ratings, although he is only a quarter of the way to matching his illustrious predecessor's record four Gold Cups at Royal Ascot.

Z is for Zoom call. A full six hours was spent in online argument at an appeal hearing into the hugely controversial Norfolk Stakes. The Ridler had been allowed to keep the race despite causing so much interference that jockey Paul Hanagan was banned for ten days. After that appeal, plus another week of deliberation, the BHA's independent panel upheld the original verdict.

RACING POST ANNUAL AWARDS

Our pick of the best of 2022

HORSE OF THE YEAR (FLAT) *Alpinista*

The head says Baaeed but the Arc winner captured the heart

HORSE OF THE YEAR (JUMPS) *A Plus Tard*

Stamped his class on the Cheltenham Gold Cup with a record margin of victory

RACE OF THE YEAR (FLAT) *Eclipse Stakes*

Vadeni was an exciting winner, Mishriff an unlucky runner-up and just a length covered the first four

RACE OF THE YEAR (JUMPS) *Clarence House Chase*

Exceeded great expectations as the heavyweights Shishkin and Energumene went toe to toe

RIDE OF THE YEAR (FLAT) *Luke Morris, Alpinista, Prix de l'Arc de Triomphe*

The biggest pressure ride of his career by miles and he executed it with perfect positioning and timing

RIDE OF THE YEAR (JUMPS) *Derek Fox, Corach Rambler, Ultima H'cap Chase*

Short of racing room and with ten ahead of him going into the final bend, Fox slalomed through and came with a strong run to thread his way between the two leaders up the hill

RISING STAR *Harry Davies*

The 17-year-old looks set for big things after just missing out on the British apprentice title

SURPRISE OF THE YEAR *Highfield Princess*

Three all-weather defeats in the spring didn't give any hint that she was a sprint sensation waiting to happen

UNLUCKIEST HORSE *Maljoom*

Flew home from an impossible position when fourth in the St James's Palace Stakes and kept out for the rest of the season by illness and injury

MOST IMPROVED HORSE *L'Homme Presse*

From chasing debutant to Grade 1 winner in two months and festival hero just six weeks later

COMEBACK OF THE YEAR *Aidan Macdonald*

The 23-year-old conditional made a happy return at Sedgefield in September, 18 months after suffering a stroke

DISAPPOINTMENT OF THE YEAR *Desert Crown*

Simply because we didn't get to see him again after a Derby packed with promise

BEST 'I WAS THERE' MOMENT *The start of the Cheltenham Festival*

The Roar was back with the return to full capacity after the emptiness of the previous year

▲ Leading players: clockwise from top left, A Plus Tard, Luke Morris in the winner's enclosure at Longchamp, Derek Fox on Corach Rambler, Harry Davies, Maljoom, L'Homme Presse after winning at the Cheltenham Festival, Aidan Macdonald, and Desert Crown heading for home in the Derby

WorldHorseWelfare

World Horse Welfare strives to support and improve the horse-human partnership in all of its guises

We are the only equine welfare charity that promotes the responsible involvement of horses in sport

Working for a world where every horse is treated with respect, compassion, and understanding

Find out more at worldhorsewelfare.org/sport-and-leisure-horses

Registered charity no. 206658 and SC038384

THE
BIGGER
PICTURE

Cross-country runners race through the
trees at Pardubice in the Czech Republic
on Velka Pardubicka day in October
PATRICK McCANN (RACINGPOST.COM/PHOTOS)

ENDPIECE

The war in Ukraine prompted an inspirational aid effort
from volunteers in the racing community seeking to play
their part in relieving the humanitarian and equine crisis

▲ From left: Sharon Ingram, Neil Carson, son of Willie Carson and one of the drivers, Gay Kelleway, Jonathan Harding, Julia Bennet and Charlie Thornycroft with the horsebox travelling to Poland; next page, Thornycroft, who chose to drop everything to help rescue the thousands of horses running loose throughout Ukraine

HOPE AMID THE HORROR

In late June, the Racing Post's Jonathan Harding joined a 1,000-mile aid trip from the UK to the Poland-Ukraine border, just over four months after Russia's invasion of Ukraine. He set off in a horsebox driven by Newmarket trainer Gay Kelleway and met a growing band of volunteers including Julia Bennet, who has worked in racing for most of her life; David Dormer, who was head lad to leading trainers including Geoff Lewis; and Sharon Ingram, wife of trainer Roger. This is the story of that journey.

By Jonathan Harding

Monday, June 27
Glogow Malopolski

We arrive at the Polish equine hub in Glogow Malopolski, just 100 miles from Lviv. Here we meet Charlie Thornycroft, who arrived on a fact-finding mission for the British Equestrian Federation in March and lives at the hub.

A former PA to Khalid Abdullah and Juddmonte chief executive Douglas Erskine-Crum, Thornycroft worked in events and was planning Platinum Jubilee celebrations at Royal Windsor when she chose to drop everything to help rescue the thousands of horses running loose throughout Ukraine.

She survives on next to no sleep and has been back to Britain only once since March. Using the hub as a base, and with five drivers, she has orchestrated the rescue of close to 500 horses and sent veterinary supplies in the other direction.

Getting horses over the border from Ukraine is a logistical nightmare. It requires mountains of paperwork and it can take up to 48 hours to get them into Poland after they are collected from hubs in Lviv and near Chernobyl. These are horses of all types, including a few racehorses. They often arrive in terrible condition.

The hub consists of around 60 boxes in four basic, temporary tents on the site of a stylish equestrian centre. It currently houses 17 horses belonging to a showjumping team led by a man called Greg, who moved to Ukraine from France. Surnames and details of old lives are mostly left at the door.

He travelled to Poland with three grooms and three riders, and they have formed a makeshift family as Greg has had to take on the role of father and mentor alongside coach. One of the riders, Natalia, won a competition in Krakow the week before we arrived.

The riders are young girls living away from their families. Their mothers crossed the border shortly before May 9, Russian Victory Day, as they feared the Russians would launch an extreme offensive to mark the day. They were worried they might not be able to see their daughters again. Thornycroft says she will never forget seeing the young girls shaking, watching the Russian military parade with tears pouring down their faces.

"Originally, horses were in fairly good nick as they'd only been without food for a couple of weeks," Thornycroft says. "They were dehydrated, tired and hungry but they were okay. It's progressively got worse and the ones I'm getting now are covered in ticks, cuts and are often emaciated.

"They have minor injuries caused by being on a lorry for a few days, and several lorries have been shot at. The first two horses who arrived a few weeks ago were dead. Then in the next lot, one was cast and got stuck underneath another. He was battered and broken but we patched him up. I get a lot of colic when they arrive, which is why I don't sleep for days."

Behind every animal is a person, and it did not take long for Thornycroft's role to evolve beyond rescuing hundreds of pets. She is the linchpin of the hub and has become a key contact in the area. In addition to mucking out up to 65 horses a day, she has stood at train stations to direct people away from traffickers, set up a nursing home and orphanage, helped with visa processes and driven traumatised refugees to abortion clinics.

She does all of this completely unpaid while she rents out her London flat and, while she is not in the market for praise as for her this is an ongoing responsibility, she is an inspiration. If only people like her ran the world.

"I thought we'd go out, round up the horses and bring them back but that was never going to happen," Thornycroft adds. "As soon as the first horse arrived we had to sort out visas for their owners and look after the horse.

"The animals come with people and you're the only one there to sort it. If I walk away, then it will all stop, but I can't leave as every time the phone rings it's somebody else who is desperate. You become involved in their story and have to find them the next place to go to. You have to look after each human, dog, horse, cat, rabbit and anything else that comes over here as you are the only person there to support them. I feel 100 per cent responsible for every breathing thing that arrives here."

Thornycroft encounters tragedy on an almost daily basis. The stories she has heard must have left a mark but she feels such a strong sense of duty to the people and their animals that she is determined to carry on.

"I had to take an 11-year-old for an abortion," she says. "She said she'd rather die than have a Russian baby. We found her hidden in a lorry; even the driver didn't know she was there. The girl's mother had used Instagram, so the Russians came and beat her up and raped her. They killed her brother, who was eight, and made her dig her family's graves while she was assaulted. She was left for dead. She climbed aboard the lorry and arrived here four days later."

How does Thornycroft handle dealing with these situations?

"There's an element of keeping busy but it's more you can't show weakness around the people who have fled Ukraine. You have to be strong and remain positive for them," she says. "You can't show you're horrified by hearing difficult situations – you can't react that way. I've cried every single time a person has left. Once they've gone, I'll take a horse out to graze and sob into their mane."

Monday, June 27
Przemysl

We head to the town of Debica, roughly 40 minutes west from the equine hub, to drop off the first batch of supplies at a makeshift refugee centre. Feed and electric fencing is carried in excruciating heat into a spacious wood-floored gymnasium. The electric fencing will be taken into Ukraine to enable horses to be kept safely outdoors during the summer – the first batch will go to Irpin, where there are many unexploded mines.

Our next stop is the main refugee centre in Przemysl, where we drop off humanitarian supplies including shoes, suitcases and a wheelchair, which was donated to Julia Bennet by a family who had suffered a loss of their own.

We often witness scenes from refugee centres on TV but nothing can ever prepare you for seeing displaced people with your own eyes. Inside, the walls are lined with desks, above which there are the flags of most major countries. The British one is run by a Christian group called Love Bristol. After arriving at the centre, life-altering decisions have to be made quickly by desperate, tired people.

There are various stations in the middle of the room with corresponding flags and these are filled with cabin beds. Here, families are able to sleep in four-hour stints, as there are not enough beds to go around even though many refugees have been placed with host families in the town.

It is difficult to see but what is most striking are the children's play area made out of wooden slats and an old woman clutching her bag

➡️ *Continues page 208*

on a cabin bed. She should be living in peace and quiet at home, not here. The play area has a desk next to it with two chairs where children can speak to a trained counsellor. The war has cost an entire generation their childhood and it will take them years to recover.

"Today has probably been the toughest day I've spent out here and the full range of human emotions are put through their paces at top speed," Bennet says. "There were times when I thought I would burst into tears due to the enormity of it all but the fear that if I started crying I would never stop meant I kept myself from pressing that self-pity button."

Our next stop is a small storage facility in Medyka, a village so close to the Ukrainian border that our phones jump forward an hour to the new timezone. We are delivering humanitarian supplies and we pass a queue of lorries and cars trying to get back into Ukraine. It extends for miles.

Tuesday, June 28
Dabrowa Gornicza

Every displaced person has the date they left home etched in their mind and the Ukrainian couple we collect from the refugee centre in Przemysl are no different. Anatoliy and Nataliia left Odessa in March and thanks to Bennet, Thornycroft and Love Bristol, they will have a new life in the UK.

Bennet, who is part of the National Association of Racing Staff executive and, even more impressively, has fostered 16 children in Lambourn, was the first point of contact for the couple when we met them at the centre. Both in their sixties, the couple have had to leave behind their children – their son was called up to fight – and their grandchildren, whose passports are being arranged. There is the relief of moving towards a more settled existence near Bristol, without uncertainty, but there is the realisation that the further they travel, the further they are from home.

It takes a huge leap of faith for

them to place their life in the hands of complete strangers and it is a privilege to meet them. There are lots of hugs and tears as they leave their host family but the volunteers are on hand to put them at ease. "We're going to help you," says Sharon Ingram. It becomes clear that empathy is as natural to her as breathing and they are soon sharing pictures of their families.

Language is not a major barrier. The team is able to demonstrate compassion without words but with hugs and smiles. Anatoliy and Nataliia did not need to be told. They knew they were surrounded by good people, and even contacted their host to say so.

After dropping off the last of our supplies of dog and cat food at a hub near Przemysl, it is time to start the long journey home, but not without an important detour. I join Bennet in a smaller horsebox and travel to the city of Dabrowa Gornicza to pick up a Ukrainian grandmother, Alla, and her granddaughter, Anna, as well as their cats Leah and Simba.

We had hoped to have horses too, but there was a hold-up on the border, which is common. We do, however, have a Great Dane called Bella. She weighs in at 60kg and was something of a mascot for the equine hub.

Our satnav takes us on a brief tour of the city but we eventually find their temporary home and we spot a teenage girl waving from the window. Her English is impeccable and we are soon loading their suitcases into the van. They then share a brief goodbye with their host before we set off.

They are from Kharkiv, where Alla had been studying at university, and left the city on March 9. The historic city has been relentlessly bombed and was described as being "like Chernobyl" by residents in a BBC story.

It is a grey afternoon as we pull out of the city but there are still glimmers of hope, with Alla and Anna set for a second chance in Leeds.

Wednesday, June 29
Hook of Holland

Anatoliy, who has been through a rollercoaster of emotions since joining our merry band, smiles deeply as he steps off the lorry and gives me a big bear hug before taking Bella for a walk. The dog actually suits him.

He has struck up an amazing friendship with David Dormer, who took his duty to make him feel at ease incredibly seriously. The 69-year-old asked if the team would be interested in recruiting a "retired pensioner with terminal cancer". I was so glad they were. He stayed behind at the hotel one morning to ensure our new

passengers did not think we had left without them and exchanged stories using Google Translate throughout the trip.

His outlook on life is refreshing. He was retired due to his illness and, after undergoing chemotherapy, spent much of the last two years indoors during the pandemic as he was classed as clinically vulnerable. After a life spent in racing, including as a box driver and as head lad to a number of trainers, Dormer said he felt a bit useless, but not any more.

"I'm proud of what we've achieved," he says, sipping a cup of tea in the McDonald's by the port. "We did what we set out to do, which was to help the animals and people coming to the UK. It's been tough and some things broke my heart, but you need to see them to understand.

"I was sitting at home doing nothing and thought I could help on the trip. It gave me some sort of purpose and made me feel like I could make a difference to somebody else. I can't change having cancer. I'll never be able to. I might not die of it but I will die with it, and I can't change that. But I can make a difference to the lives of the people we brought back."

This is an edited version of an article that appeared in the Racing Post on July 10